# Scientific Evidence and
# Equal Protection of the Law

# Scientific Evidence and Equal Protection of the Law

WITHDRAWN
UTSA LIBRARIES

ANGELO N. ANCHETA

RUTGERS UNIVERSITY PRESS

NEW BRUNSWICK, NEW JERSEY, AND LONDON

Library of Congress Cataloging-in-Publication Data

Ancheta, Angelo N., 1960–
    Scientific evidence and equal protection of the law / Angelo N. Ancheta.
        p.  cm.
    Includes bbliographical references and index.
    ISBN-13: 978-0-8135-3734-4 (hardcover : alk. paper)
    ISBN-13: 978-0-8135-3735-1 (pbk. : alk. paper)
    1. Discrimination–Law and legislation–United States. 2. Equality before the
law–United States. 3. Discrimination–United States–Research. 4. Equality before
law–United States–Research. 5. Science and law.  I. Title.
    KF4755.A96  2006
    342.7308'7–dc22

                                                                                                2005011267


A British Cataloging-in-Publication record for this book is available from the British Library.

Manufactured in the United States of America

To my godchildren

# CONTENTS

# PREFACE AND ACKNOWLEDGMENTS

During a nearly twenty-year legal career in which I have straddled the worlds of advocacy and academia, I have been intrigued—and often frustrated—by the gulf that exists between lawyers and judges on the one hand and academic researchers steeped in the rigor of scientific method on the other. Of course, one should not be surprised that such a chasm exists. Although increasingly entwined because of the many advances in science and technology that affect our daily lives, science and law often appear to occupy entirely different worlds—with dissimilar cultures, norms, methods, and vocabularies. Indeed, many who enter the law as a profession do so because they have an aversion to science, and those who pursue knowledge through science are frequently perplexed by the contentiousness of legal advocacy and the often results-driven process of judicial decision making.

Yet the interrelationships and interdependencies are inescapable. Moral uncertainties that have accompanied scientific and technological advancement (human genetics, stem-cell research, and life-extending medical techniques are just a few recent examples) often find their resolution in the courts. Meanwhile, the courts are increasingly turning to scientific evidence such as statistical studies, DNA testing, and a wide variety of forensic analyses to assist them with their decision making and their development of legal rules. Scientists and legal professionals can ill afford to be ignorant of each other's worlds.

Still, the cultural gaps are powerful and persistent. Scientific research, with its emphasis on exacting empirical methodologies, moves at its own peculiar pace, as do the calendars of the judicial and legislative processes. Most scientists do not pursue their research with an underlying goal of resolving a pressing legal or political dilemma, and legal policymakers—whether they are judges, legislators, or regulatory agencies—may move forward with only the scarcest of empirical data to support their conclusions and policies.

Consider a personal example. One of my first professional encounters with social science research and the law came in the early 1990s, when I was a civil rights lawyer working on redistricting and voting rights affecting Asian American populations in California. At the time, empirical studies on Asian American voting behavior were rare and largely inconclusive, which did little to help advocates create legislative lines that concentrated the voting power of Asian Americans in key districts in both northern and southern California. Yet the lack of a solid empirical base did not stop us from asserting claims that Asian Americans could be harmed by districting plans that fragmented communities. Although a relatively small group, Asian Americans were a fast-growing population, and the formation of significant political blocs was possible over the next decade.

Nevertheless, in preparing to argue for the protection of Asian American voting rights before the California Supreme Court, which had been charged with producing the final districting plans for the state, I wondered whether advocates' arguments were based more on smoke and mirrors than on concrete evidence of cohesive voting among Asian Americans. We were arguing that Asian Americans voted together as a racial bloc to support Asian American candidates, just as black voters in the south and Latino voters in the southwest had voted in blocs, and that the Voting Rights Act compelled policymakers to maintain geographic concentrations of Asian Americans within key districts in California. There had been decades of past racial discrimination against Asian Americans, but what we did not know—and empirical research might have informed our advocacy—was whether bloc voting within this fast-growing, largely foreign-born population was a reality. We were ultimately successful in convincing the court to modify a few district lines in southern California, which eventually led to the election of an Asian American to the state assembly, but we were never pushed hard to justify our arguments, and we would have had a difficult time satisfying the requirements of the Voting Rights Act if we had been forced to litigate the claims that we were asserting. The supreme court had to issue its districting plans when it did, regardless of what data existed at the time.

But I am also convinced that when scientific research is available, it can have a significant influence on the outcome of legal controversies. As an advocate in the University of Michigan affirmative action cases, which involved constitutional challenges to race-conscious admissions policies in higher education, I saw firsthand how social science evidence can play a role in judicial decision making. I was the lead counsel for the American Educational Research Association and other major educational organizations that submitted amicus curiae (friend-of-the court) briefs to the U.S. Supreme Court summarizing research that demonstrated the educational benefits of student-body diversity, and I believe we played a role in influencing the Court's decision to uphold race-conscious admissions plans. To underscore its conclusion that promoting diversity is a compelling governmental interest that can justify race-conscious measures, the Court quoted one of our briefs and cited several recent social science studies supporting the diversity rationale. The Court relied on other sources and arguments as well, but the arguments favoring the University of Michigan were no doubt strengthened by the scientific research that had been introduced in the trial courts and through amicus curiae briefs.

At the same time, I take a guarded view of the role that scientific evidence should play in resolving some of the difficult moral and policy questions that are confronting our courts. Science can inform many of these questions, but it cannot tell us what is right or what is just, and we do ourselves a tremendous disservice if we rely unquestioningly on scientific research to develop interpretations of the meaning of *due process* or *equal protection of the law.* Indeed, as we have seen in the past, the science of the day can easily become an ideological mask for the creation of unjust laws and policies.

DURING MY TENURE as the legal director for The Civil Rights Project at Harvard University, a unique academic venture that links social scientists and advocates in the advancement of racial justice, I had the opportunity to work directly with some of the nation's leading researchers and to see more clearly the crucial links between scientific research and civil rights advocacy. The impetus for writing this book grew out of those experiences, as well as from my realization that in the federal appellate courts, where most of the nation's constitutional law is expounded, the law regarding the use of scientific evidence is strikingly underdeveloped.

There is no shortage of books or scholarly articles addressing the problems of science in the law, and I have very modest objectives in adding to the literature. My focus is on the development of civil rights law by the courts—in particular, the law governing rights under the equal protection clause of the Fourteenth Amendment to the U.S. Constitution, and the role of scientific evidence in the creation of that law. For much of American history, science has played a central role in reinforcing *inequalities*, and it is only in recent decades that scientific evidence has helped illuminate and redress problems of discrimination, though, even now, it may still involve controversy.

I am a lawyer by training, not a scientist. While I have become more fluent than I used to be in the basic language of statistics and survey research, primarily through graduate work in public policy and the osmosis that comes with working closely with social scientists, this is essentially a book about law, not about science. I do not attempt to provide a systematic treatment of scientific method or statistics. Nor is a background in these areas necessary to grapple with some of the fundamental legal questions covered in the book. I do mention some of the recent scientific findings that address discrimination and inequality, but my treatment is selective and is designed not as a literature review or a survey but as an illustration of some of the major issues that arise when using scientific evidence to promote equality under the law. I do not attempt to employ quantitative methods myself (there are already empirical studies on so-cial science evidence and Supreme Court decision making) but opt instead to rely largely on histories and case studies.

Science is a process, not a product. In examining court cases for their use, misuse, or nonuse of scientific evidence, I employ a broad definition of science that includes the physical and natural sciences; the medical sciences; the social sciences, including economics, psychology, sociology, and anthropology; and statistical analyses, which employ mathematical tools that are used across a number of disciplines. At the risk of being essentialist, I do not attempt to ad-dress the many distinctions between and within various disciplines, even though there can be major differences between the assumptions and method-ologies of, say, epidemiologists versus geneticists versus anthropologists versus economists. Moreover, scientific methods have evolved significantly since the late 1700s, when the Constitution was first drafted. Certain principles of empiri-cism and inductive reasoning have been commonly employed in research using scientific methods, such as generating hypotheses based on initial observations about a subject; testing hypotheses through measures that are replicable and are as objective and unbiased as possible; and drawing inferences and generat-ing theories from this testing. Yet methodological refinements and revisions are the stuff of scientific progress, and neither science nor law can be examined ahistorically. What counted as science in 1790 might not be considered scien-tific by contemporary standards, but if it was labeled "science" at the time, then for purposes of examining its influence on a court or other legal actor, that label should be taken into account, even with qualification.

As a disclaimer of sorts, I repeat my disclosure that I was an advocate in the University of Michigan affirmative action cases, *Grutter v. Bollinger* and *Gratz v. Bollinger*, representing the American Educational Research Association, the As-sociation of American Colleges and Universities, and the American Association of Higher Education as amici curiae in support of the University of Michigan. I discuss legal advocacy and the scientific evidence offered in the *Grutter* and *Gratz* cases in chapter 6, and some of the discussion is based on my personal experience and recollections. I certainly cannot claim to have been an unbiased observer, but I do try to present a balanced account of what led up to the Su-preme Court's decisions in the University of Michigan cases.

Many individuals have influenced my work in this area, all of whom deserve acknowledgment, but I will limit my naming to just two. Dean Christopher F. Edley, Jr., of the Boalt Hall School of Law at the University of California, Berkeley, and Professor Gary Orfield of the Graduate School of Education at Har-vard University were the founding co-directors of The Civil Rights Project at Harvard University and placed enormous trust in me as that office's legal director. They provided me with exceptional opportunities for growth and scholarship, and my second career as an academic lawyer sprouted during my tenure at that office.

I must certainly give credit to all of my colleagues and friends who have influenced my thinking and writing in the field of civil rights law, but any shortcomings or errors in this book are, of course, entirely my own.

# Scientific Evidence and
# Equal Protection of the Law

# 1

## Introduction

How to inform the judicial mind, as you know, is one of the most complicated problems.

—Justice Felix Frankfurter, oral arguments in *Briggs v. Elliott*
(companion case to *Brown v. Board of Education*)

The U.S. Supreme Court's 1954 ruling in *Brown v. Board of Education* is no doubt the most important legal decision of the twentieth century. By declaring that racially segregated schools were inherently unequal schools, the Supreme Court unanimously ruled that widespread educational segregation in the south was unconstitutional and initiated the chain reaction that toppled America's system of racial apartheid, not just in education but in all areas of public life.

Widely lauded for its cogency and moral clarity, the landmark *Brown* decision has also been a major source of controversy among social scientists and scholars of constitutional law. Much of the debate has revolved around Chief Justice Earl Warren's use of psychological and sociological research to undergird the Court's legal conclusions regarding the constitutionality of segregated schools. Footnote 11 of the *Brown* opinion, at once the most celebrated and infamous footnote in Supreme Court history, contains citations to seven social science studies addressing the harms of educational segregation. According to the Court, segregated schools created in black children "a feeling of inferiority as to their status in the community that may affect their hearts and minds in a way unlikely ever to be undone," and modern psychological authority trumped any prior presuppositions that justified separate-but-equal schools.[1]

Despite the obvious inequities that segregation had created in the south, critics attacked footnote 11 and the *Brown* reasoning on several fronts: proponents of segregation upbraided the Court for usurping state prerogatives and relying on pseudo-science rather than law to support its conclusions; many legal commentators, while agreeing with the ultimate outcome of *Brown*, found the Court's apparent reliance on psychological authority rather than constitutional theory to be troubling, especially if tethering the law to social science meant that the law could be destabilized by new findings that undermined prior findings; and numerous scholars criticized the underlying validity of the studies, proposing that the empirical basis for the Court's ruling was lacking. Nonetheless, the import of *Brown v. Board of Education* is undeniable, and it is widely cited as the case that ushered in the era of the judiciary's use of modern social science to address questions of constitutional law.

In the fifty-plus years that have passed since the *Brown* decision, scientific authority has come to enjoy a prominent but no less contentious place in constitutional interpretation and the development of civil rights law. Consider the Supreme Court's 2003 decisions in *Grutter v. Bollinger* and *Gratz v. Bollinger,* the constitutional challenges to race-conscious affirmative action policies at the University of Michigan. Revisiting its ruling of twenty-five years earlier in *Regents of the University of California v. Bakke,* the *Grutter* Court relied on multiple sources of scientific authority to support its holding that the interest in student-body diversity is a "compelling interest" that can justify race-conscious measures in university admissions. Citing evidence of the educational benefits of diversity that had been introduced in the trial courts as well as authorities contained in amicus curiae briefs filed by scientific research associations, Justice Sandra Day O'Connor's majority opinion in *Grutter* concluded that student-body diversity "promotes 'cross-racial understanding,' helps to break down racial stereotypes, and 'enables [students] to better understand persons of different races.'"[2] The Court further concluded that "student body diversity promotes learning outcomes, and 'better prepares students for an increasingly diverse workforce and society, and better prepares them as professionals.'"[3]

But the use of social science literature in *Grutter v. Bollinger,* a case decided by a five-to-four vote, did not enjoy a consensus among the members of the Supreme Court. Justice Clarence Thomas, dissenting in *Grutter,* chastised the majority's deference to the university and cited opposing research literature, which suggested that increased racial diversity on college campuses "hinders students' perception of academic quality." He further criticized the *Grutter* majority for ignoring research on students at historically black colleges and universities, which indicated that racial heterogeneity could impair learning among African American students. Moreover, Justice Thomas proposed that "no social science has disproved the notion that [affirmative action] engenders attitudes of superiority or, alternatively, provokes resentment among those who believe that they have been wronged by the government's use of race."[4]

Justice Antonin Scalia, also dissenting in *Grutter,* was more blunt and sarcastic in his denigration of the social science literature supporting the diversity rationale. Proposing that cross-racial understanding "is not, of course, an 'educational benefit' on which students will be graded on their Law School transcript (Works and Plays Well with Others: B+) or tested by the bar examiners (Q: Describe in 500 words or less your cross-racial understanding)," he argued that "if properly considered an 'educational benefit' at all, it is surely not one that is either uniquely relevant to law school or uniquely 'teachable' in a formal educational setting."[5]

The colloquy in *Grutter v. Bollinger* demonstrates some of the serious divisions that commonly occur within the Supreme Court, but it also illuminates the uncertain and controversial roles that scientific research can play in judicial decision making. Social science findings buttressed the majority's arguments upholding the diversity interest, just as the university, its attorneys, and its various amici curiae had sought. But the findings were not unassailable. Justice Thomas countered with a handful of contrary studies, and Justice Scalia belittled the majority's reliance on social science as trifling. Moreover, if one examines *Grutter* against a larger, more historical landscape, the actual necessity of a "science of affirmative action" becomes more cloudy: Justice Lewis F. Powell had reached the same legal conclusion twenty-five years earlier in the *Bakke* case, but not by relying on social science findings. Instead, he pointed to a single example of a diversity-based admissions policy, the undergraduate admissions policy at Harvard College, and deferred to the judgment of educators that student-body diversity was a vitally important interest for universities. At the time, there was only a small body of scientific literature on the educational benefits of diversity. Thus, scientific authorities, if they are at all available to inform a legal dispute, can be relied upon, declared irrelevant, ignored, or even discredited by judges in a given case.

## Science and Fact Finding

*Brown v. Board of Education* did not inaugurate the use of scientific evidence to inform judicial decision making. The use of contemporaneous science to support legal judgments can be traced back to the founding of the nation; and since the mid-nineteenth century, American legal educators and reformers have proposed one form or another of scientific jurisprudence that incorporates scientific findings and reasoning into judicial decision making. Still, *Brown* remains one of the U.S. Supreme Court's most prominent cases applying social science to constitutional interpretation, and it typifies the use of scientific research findings as extralegal sources of authority that can support and legitimate judicial rulings, particularly those that may be highly controversial.

Scientific evidence can serve many functions in litigation. As demonstrated by *Brown* and *Grutter v. Bollinger,* it can be a source of authoritative information, one that is wholly separate from a legal authority such as the text of the constitution, a statute, or a court precedent and that informs the creation of new case law or the revision of existing law. In *Brown,* the Supreme Court had been asked to resolve the controversies between black parents and their children on one side and public school officials seeking to maintain educational segregation on the other. The Court could have issued a ruling based on evidence addressing tangible inequalities in educational facilities and conditions and ordered that black schools be improved so that educational opportunities would be substantially equal. If it had ruled in this way, the Court could have left intact precedents tracing back to its 1896 ruling in *Plessy v. Ferguson*, in which the Court upheld separate-but-equal facilities in public transportation. Instead, the Court turned to social science findings that discredited one of *Plessy*'s central underpinnings—namely, that separate facilities inflicted no harms on blacks. The *Brown* Court cited psychological and sociological literature suggesting that segregated schools caused both immediate and long-term harms to black students. Consequently, the Court could rule that separate-but-equal had no place in public education and that new constitutional mandates were required.

In a similar way, the Supreme Court in *Grutter v. Bollinger* employed social science findings as a source of information showing that student-body diversity leads to concrete educational benefits for all students. Studies cited by the Court demonstrated that student-body diversity improves learning outcomes, helps break down stereotypes, and better prepares students for their entry into a diverse workforce. The Court could thus conclude that the diversity interest was sufficiently important to satisfy the constitutional requirement that race-conscious policies serve a compelling governmental interest. The Court's argument upholding the diversity rationale in *Grutter* could have been seriously undermined if the bulk of scientific authority had suggested that diversity does not produce significant educational benefits or that diversity actually causes educational harms.

A distinctly different use of scientific evidence is to establish the core facts of a case in order to resolve the immediate dispute between the parties. An example in contemporary civil rights litigation is the use of statistical evidence to demonstrate that a facially race-neutral policy leads to outcomes that have an adverse impact on members of racial minority groups. For instance, statistical evidence might demonstrate that minority employees at a private company score significantly lower on a standardized written test that is heavily weighted in promotion decisions; as a result, few minorities are ever promoted at the company. Although the statistical evidence would not be conclusive, it could provide an initial basis for a class of plaintiffs to challenge the legality of the test under Title VII of the Civil Rights Act of 1964, the major federal employment discrimination statute. After gathering the appropriate evidence from both parties, including the statistical evidence and the employer's evidence of a business necessity for the test, a court could then issue a ruling in favor of one side or the other without having to create any new laws in the process.

Kenneth Culp Davis has offered a dichotomy to distinguish these two uses of scientific evidence.[6] When evidence is used to resolve a dispute between the immediate parties, a court is engaging in *adjudicative* fact finding. In other words, the court (or a jury) is using evidence to help make specific factual findings that will lead to a decision that resolves—adjudicates—the basic disagreement between the parties. Adjudicative facts are limited to the immediate parties and their dispute, and no laws are being created or changed in the process. In contrast, when evidence is used as an authority to develop or revise the law, a court is engaging in *legislative* fact finding. Like a legislative body gathering information about social conditions in order to draft an effective statute, a court engaged in legislative fact finding is using evidence to help formulate new case law—law that is applicable not only to the immediate parties but to a broader set of individuals or institutions. Accordingly, legislative facts are more general in scope and can be drawn from a wider variety of sources.

In practice, adjudicative fact finding and legislative fact finding are not mutually exclusive processes; in a given case, a court may engage in both types of fact finding. For instance, the trial court in *Grutter v. Bollinger* heard statistical evidence from both the plaintiffs and the defendants on the specific workings of the admissions policy at the University of Michigan Law School and thus engaged in adjudicative fact finding to determine whether the law school employed quotas or separate admissions tracks for minority students. The trial court also accepted evidence from the university on the benefits of educational diversity to address the constitutional issue of whether promoting student-body diversity is a compelling interest, an example of legislative fact finding. But the lines can blur since a fact that may be very specific to a lawsuit could have significant implications for the constitutionality of not only that particular policy but also similar policies employed at other institutions. For instance, the mechanics of how a particular admissions policy operates would normally be classified as an adjudicative fact, but fact finding related to that policy might determine the legality of policies at other universities.

Understanding the theoretical distinction between adjudicative fact finding and legislative fact finding is critical, however, because there are well-established rules of evidence and court decisions that govern the introduction of scientific evidence used for adjudicative fact finding; and federal appellate courts usually take the results of adjudicative fact finding as given and only second-guess the facts if the findings in a trial court were "clearly erroneous."[7] But there are no explicit rules or guidelines governing the use of scientific evidence for legislative fact finding, and courts can obtain legislative facts from practically any source.

## Dismissing Scientific Evidence

The courts also frequently disregard or dismiss scientific evidence in civil rights litigation, despite the apparent relevance of the evidence. An example is the 1987 case of *McCleskey v. Kemp*, in which the petitioner Warren McCleskey, a black man who had been sentenced to death for the killing of a white police officer, challenged his sentence under Georgia's capital punishment law as a violation of both the equal protection clause and the Eighth Amendment's prohibition against cruel and unusual punishment. In support of McCleskey's constitutional challenges, an elaborate statistical study had been introduced on death penalty cases in Georgia, which found that "defendants charged with killing white victims were 4.3 times as likely to receive a death sentence as defendants charged with killing blacks."[8] The data thus showed that McCleskey had been placed at a much greater risk of being put to death because his victim was white rather than black.

The Supreme Court, by a five-to-four vote, did not challenge the legitimacy of the statistical study but nevertheless ruled against the petitioner's claims. Under the equal protection claim, McCleskey had to establish the government's intent to discriminate against him, and the Court ruled that the statistical evidence alone was insufficient to prove intentional discrimination in his case. Ruling on the Eighth Amendment claim, the Court held that McCleskey had failed to show that considerations of the victim's race in his specific case had tainted his trial. Despite its powerful conclusions, the statistical study was essentially ruled to be irrelevant to the petitioner's claim because the study had only identified system-wide problems of racial bias, not bias against him in particular. In so ruling, the Supreme Court revised prior case law holding that systemic defects that created the risk of "arbitrary and capricious" decision making in death penalty cases could violate the Eighth Amendment.

Critics of *McCleskey v. Kemp* have found the case troubling for several reasons. The Supreme Court accepted the validity of the scientific study, which documented evidence of extensive racial bias in the Georgia criminal justice system, but dismissed the biases as unavoidable. The Court stated that the "study indicates a discrepancy that appears to correlate with race. Apparent disparities in sentencing are an inevitable part of our criminal justice system."[9] It further admitted that "McCleskey's claim, taken to its logical conclusion, throws into serious question the principles that underlie our entire criminal justice system."[10] Yet the Court still rejected the constitutional claims. In addition, the Court not only found the statistical evidence to be of no consequence, but it also went out of its way to change the law so that statistical evidence of racial bias would be useless in a capital punishment case unless there was also proof of intentional discrimination or the evidence could prove that bias had tainted the individual defendant's trial. The burden on defendants who were challenging their death sentences on equal protection or Eighth Amendment grounds became almost insurmountable, notwithstanding the evidence of extensive bias in the justice system.

Recognizing how the *McCleskey* Court's treatment of empirical evidence influenced its judgment to reject the petitioner's constitutional challenges, David L. Faigman has offered another potential role for science in the law: to provide a restraining influence on judicial decision making. "In forcing the Court to recognize the racial bias in capital sentencing," he writes, "the data constricted the Court. Because the facts could not be manipulated or ignored, the Court became more accountable for its decision." He adds, "The data forced the Court to explicate an alternative basis for its judgment—a normative basis rather than an empirical one. This judgment is now subjected to the harsh light of public debate."[11] Although a restraining role presumes that science is "right" most of the time, in *McCleskey* the Court did not challenge the study itself, just whether it was sufficient to decide the constitutional questions. The fact that the Court had to confront the data did not make the *McCleskey* decision any less controversial, but it did require the members of the Court—and ultimately legislators and the public—to grapple with the realities of racial bias in the criminal justice system and to clarify their moral and policy judgments about the problem.

## Science As Rhetoric

In addition to fact-finding and restraining roles, scientific evidence often works as a rhetorical tool in judicial opinions. Independent of the Supreme Court's need to inform its own decision making in *Brown*, the Court's invocation of psychological studies on segregation can be seen as augmenting the opinion's rhetorical power and adding greater legitimacy to the Court's decision outlawing segregated schools. As Scott Brewer notes, "writing in the third century in which science enjoyed its ascendancy over religion as the dominant cultural authority, the Court might reasonably have sought to invoke social-scientific expertise to provide cultural authority for its profoundly controversial decision."[12] Scientific evidence can be especially resonant because, unlike a legal source, it carries an independent authoritativeness as well as an appearance of value-neutrality, free from the biases of lawyers and advocates seeking a particular outcome in the litigation. Of course, scientific research, like any human endeavor, is never entirely value-free; and the studies cited in footnote 11 of *Brown* still ignited significant criticism among social scientists and legal commentators for being value-laden and litigation-driven. But as Dean M. Hashimoto has suggested, scientific authority can possess a powerful mystique because it is largely inaccessible to nonscientists; and when the courts invoke scientific authority, they raise it to an almost mythological status that has a forceful rhetorical appeal: "By functioning as mythology, scientific facts in court opinions do not invite analysis. Instead, they ask us to accept the underlying premises of legal rules as truth."[13]

The use of scientific evidence as a rhetorical device does, however, raise the potential for the courts to employ science simply to serve ideological purposes, regardless of the legitimacy of the evidence or its bearing on the legal questions at hand. Historically, contemporaneous science has been used to justify severe deprivations of rights and to maintain harsh inequalities. For example, during the early 1920s the Supreme Court relied on ethnology, a scientific field that focused on racial and cultural categorization, when it concluded that Japanese immigrants were ineligible for American citizenship under a federal law limiting naturalized citizenship to "free white persons." In *Ozawa v. United States*, the Supreme Court ruled that Takao Ozawa, a twenty-year resident of the United States and an individual otherwise fully qualified for citizenship, was "clearly of a race which is not Caucasian and therefore . . . entirely outside the zone [of groups eligible for citizenship] on the negative side."[14] The Court added, "A large number of the federal and state courts have so decided and . . . [t]hese decisions are sustained by numerous scientific authorities, which we do not deem it necessary to review." Safely behind the shields of both case law and science, the Court declined to address the more fundamental question of whether a statute barring American citizenship on the basis of race violated the Constitution.

The Supreme Court's later opinions on race have been critiqued as well for their rhetorical uses of science. A frequent criticism of the *Brown* opinion is that a number of the social science studies in footnote 11 were either biased or methodologically suspect and were only included to bolster a legal argument that actually had little support in the law itself. The Court did not discuss the actual findings of the studies in any depth and simply relegated them to a string of citations in a single footnote; critics propose that a more thorough discussion of the scientific literature would have been included in the opinion if the Court had actually engaged in a methodical legislative fact-finding process to support its conclusions.[15] The actual motives of the Supreme Court justices are difficult to divine solely from the language of an opinion and a single footnote, but the potential for judicial legerdemain does spark important questions about how courts evaluate the legitimacy of scientific evidence and whether the use of scientific evidence is actually central to resolving a case or developing new law.

## Is Science Necessary?

Categorizing the various roles of scientific evidence provides a convenient typology to describe how scientific evidence may actually be used by courts, but it does not address the more difficult and complicated normative questions that arise when the courts rely on scientific evidence. One set of normative questions revolves around whether scientific evidence should be used by the courts at all. In many cases involving adjudicative fact finding, scientific evidence seems indispensable. For example, if proving a violation of the federal Voting Rights Act requires plaintiffs to show that members of a racial minority group vote cohesively—to demonstrate bloc voting and possible injury against the group arising from a particular electoral policy—evidence of past voting patterns gleaned from survey data or demographic data would seem essential to establish this element of the plaintiffs' case. There might be questions about the reliability of the data or the sufficiency of the evidence, but some form of statistical analysis or social science evidence would be crucial to demonstrate cohesive voting.

On the other hand, scientific authorities may not be necessary to settle every fundamental question of law. One could certainly argue that when cases such as *Brown v. Board of Education* involve basic claims about the meaning of equality under the law, the Supreme Court could—and should—decide cases without having to resort to scientific findings. For instance, by relying on a theory of equal protection that guarantees equal citizenship to all members of society and prohibits subordination on the basis of race or other group characteristics, a court would not need to rely on empirical evidence of the psychological harms caused by segregated schools. An anti-subordination theory recognizes that there are inherent harms in denying educational opportunities to black students by segregating them; the harm is that black students are treated as inferior and unequal citizens.[16] Scientific evidence of psychological harm would demonstrate a major symptom of inferior treatment, but it would not be necessary to show a violation of rights under the equal protection clause.

A theory of constitutional interpretation can thus prescribe a specific use, or nonuse, of scientific evidence in constitutional litigation. Yet a quandary remains because there is no single theory of constitutional interpretation that courts apply to all cases and no one theory with which all judges agree. Anti-subordination theory, for example, is a model of equal protection that many judges reject, turning instead to more conservative forms of constitutional interpretation, such as focusing on the text of the Constitution or relying on strict adherence to the Constitution's "original meaning" or the "original intent" of its framers. Science might actually play a very limited role under any of these theories. Reflecting a typical aversion to scientific authority as a substitute for constitutionalism, Justice Felix Frankfurter remarked during the oral arguments in *Briggs v. Elliott*, a companion case to *Brown v. Board of Education*, "if it is in the Constitution, then all the [scientific] testimony that you introduced is beside the point, in general. . . . I do not care what any associate or full professor in sociology tells me. If it is in the Constitution, I do not care about what they say."[17]

Yet some approaches to constitutional interpretation clearly raise the need for empirical information in order for courts to reach a decision. For instance, "balancing theory" has become a dominant model of constitutional interpretation that comes into play when a court analyzes a question by identifying the different interests implicated in the case and then reaches a decision by assigning values to those interests and weighing them accordingly. A common example is a due process case in which the court must weigh the state's interest in efficient governmental administration against the interests of the individual in receiving fair and adequate safeguards against a deprivation of life, liberty, or property. A court must balance the various interests, examine the relative effectiveness of the procedural safeguard (such as a written notice, hearing, or trial), and engage in a rough cost-benefit calculus to determine if due process rights have been preserved or violated. Employing social science findings could prove highly useful, if not vital, in determining the strengths of the interests and the effectiveness of different public policies.

Some scholars and judges have even gone so far as to suggest that empiricism itself should be a guiding principle for judicial decision making rather than an overarching theory of constitutional interpretation, a trend that Timothy Zick has labeled "constitutional empiricism."[18] Judge Richard A. Posner, for instance, has argued that "constitutional theory, while often rhetorically powerful, lacks the agreement-coercing power of the best natural and social science.... An even more serious problem is that constitutional theory is not responsive to, and indeed tends to occlude, the greatest need of constitutional adjudicators, which is the need for empirical knowledge."[19] Judge Posner has proposed that constitutional law making must be more thoroughly grounded in an understanding of social realities and that legal scholars should refocus their energies on empirical research rather than on theorizing. Of course, Judge Posner's approach presupposes a strong trust in empirical investigation as well as the development of consensus around scientific evidence, and many judges and legal scholars may be unwilling to embrace empiricism as a replacement for an overriding constitutional theory. As Deborah Jones Merritt notes in a rejoinder to Judge Posner, "human beings and the societies they form are too complex and changeable to generate precise social science answers to constitutional controversies.... Social science offers no answer key for constitutional questions."[20]

The Supreme Court's treatment of abortion rights, beginning with its landmark 1973 ruling in *Roe v. Wade*, illustrates the contestation of science's role in constitutional law. Justice Harry Blackmun's majority opinion in *Roe* relied heavily on contemporaneous medical science to align the trimesters of a typical pregnancy with a legal structure that balanced various individual and state interests.[21] Under *Roe*'s trimestral scheme, a woman's interest in being able to terminate a pregnancy became almost absolute during the first trimester, when the mortality rates for an abortion were less than the mortality rates for carrying a pregnancy to term. But the state's interests in protecting maternal health and fetal life gained increasing recognition and strength through the second and third trimesters, with fetal viability outside the womb linked to the start of the third trimester.

In later abortion rights cases, however, members of the Court questioned the appropriateness of the trimestral framework, arguing that the progress of science and technology could destabilize the links between constitutional rights and the stages of a pregnancy. Because scientific advances could decrease the medical risks of abortion beyond the first trimester and because fetal viability might move to a point earlier than the third trimester, Justice O'Connor suggested ten years after *Roe* that the trimestral framework was "clearly on a collision course with itself."[22] In 1992, less than twenty years after its ruling in *Roe v. Wade*, the Supreme Court reaffirmed the basic right to an abortion in *Planned Parenthood of Southeastern Pennsylvania v. Casey* but abandoned *Roe*'s medically rooted trimestral guidelines in favor of a less structured, and less science-based, standard focusing on whether a state regulation imposes an "undue burden" on a woman seeking an abortion prior to fetal viability.[23] Scientific evidence had thus guided the Court's original articulation of abortion rights, but the Court's more durable guidelines were strongly rooted in legal language and standards.

## Gatekeeping

Another set of normative questions revolves around the screening and filtering duties that courts must perform in admitting scientific evidence as part of the fact-finding process. The Federal Rules of Evidence and recent Supreme Court cases have placed a heavy burden on the federal trial courts to act as "gatekeepers" of expert testimony and scientific evidence, even though many judges may lack the technical expertise in science and mathematics that would enable them to become the types of "amateur scientists" who could be truly effective gatekeepers.[24] In *Daubert v. Merrell Dow Pharmaceuticals, Inc.*, the Supreme Court assigned federal trial judges the responsibility for making a preliminary assessment "of whether the reasoning or methodology underlying the testimony is scientifically valid and of whether that reasoning or methodology can properly be applied to the facts in issue."[25] In evaluating the validity of the expert testimony, courts can look at factors such as testability (whether a study can be falsified or refuted, which is a well-known tenet in the philosophy of science), peer review and publication, error rates and standards for particular scientific techniques, and general acceptance within the scientific community.

The judicial gatekeeping function engenders a host of questions involving the nature of scientific evidence. What counts as science? What is "good" science versus "bad" science? Should social science disciplines, such as economics, psychology, sociology, anthropology, or political science, be treated in the same way as natural or physical sciences? Should the results of experiments be preferred to results based on observational methods? Are quantitative studies that are dependent on statistical analyses any more valid than qualitative methodologies that focus on case studies? The general principles established by *Daubert* and later cases suggest that the courts should take a broad and flexible view in admitting expert testimony—screening out junk science but not insisting that any single type of evidence is necessarily beyond reproach.

Whether a court or a jury would actually find a particular piece of scientific evidence to be persuasive, however, is another matter. Compared with findings in the "hard" sciences, social science findings may not enjoy the same credibility or possess the same degree of persuasiveness. Experimental studies that conjure up visions of scientists in white lab coats may be more convincing than qualitative studies that seem more like journalism to a lay audience. Statistical evidence may trump individual case studies. On the other hand, a court or a jury might find scientific evidence that is too technical or sophisticated to be so impenetrable that it is assigned little weight and might opt instead for commonsense inferences and conclusions. Moreover, because litigation is an adversarial process, a court or a jury may have to reconcile competing bodies of expert testimony and scientific evidence and then dismiss one or more of the studies offered by one side, even if shown to be methodologically valid, because one side's evidence is more persuasive than the other's.

A major complication in constitutional litigation is caused by the fact that the Federal Rules of Evidence and the *Daubert* line of cases apply to adjudicative fact finding but not to legislative fact finding. There are no comparable gatekeeping responsibilities enumerated in the Federal Rules of Appellate Procedure or in the Rules of the U.S. Supreme Court, nor are there general guidelines that the courts have established for themselves through case law. Courts at all levels can draw on a wide variety of sources when engaged in legislative fact finding. What, then, are the best ways for courts to obtain legislative facts? Should scientific evidence used for legislative fact finding be subject to the same standards applied to adjudicative fact finding? Should courts play a gatekeeping role with scientific studies that are introduced through amicus curiae briefs? Should appellate courts turn to their own research or to outside experts, or should they create research bodies to assist them? Or should appellate courts simply stay out of the business of fact finding altogether and rely on whatever scientific evidence is screened and accepted by the trial courts below? The law is underdeveloped in this area; and as a result, the courts are free to rely on practically any source of empirical authority, valid or invalid, when they search for legislative facts.

Adding to these challenges is the gatekeepers' frequent lack of specialized knowledge of scientific methods. Some judges may be fluent in the language of science and quite comfortable with the evidence: Justice Harry Blackmun, for example, earned a bachelor's degree in mathematics, worked for several years as general counsel to the Mayo Clinic in Minnesota, and authored the *Daubert* opinion and several opinions in which scientific evidence played a central role, including *Roe v. Wade* and cases involving the use of statistics in civil rights litigation. On the other hand, some judges by their own admission are averse to scientific evidence or reasoning. For instance, Justice Lewis F. Powell authored the majority opinion in *McCleskey v. Kemp*, a case in which he disregarded scientific evidence of bias in capital sentencing; but a biography of Justice Powell reveals that he once confessed his personal ignorance of statistical methodologies, remarking, "My understanding of statistical analysis . . . ranges from limited to zero."[26]

## "Advocacy Science"

Litigation and its inherent adversarial processes also provoke serious questions about the value-neutrality of scientific evidence and of expert witnesses. How closely together should scientists and advocates work in developing legal strategies and evidence? Are expert witnesses testifying for one side inherently biased? Should scientific studies that are designed specifically for litigation be treated in the same way as studies that are developed through the normal course of academic investigation? From a scientist's perspective, some of these questions can be disconcerting because they are countercultural: scientists are engaged in the pursuit of knowledge, not advocacy, and intimations of bias, however minor, can be seen as discourteous and even threatening.

The salience of empirical authorities in many recent civil rights controversies raises important questions about how scientific research is generated and whether science and advocacy can be too closely linked. Consider the role of scientific evidence in the University of Michigan affirmative action cases. Much of the research on the educational benefits of diversity in higher education was developed after the mid-1990s, when the courts began entertaining claims that challenged the Supreme Court's 1978 ruling in *Regents of the University of California v. Bakke*. Recall that Justice Powell did not rely on social science evidence in *Bakke*; instead, he relied on statements and declarations from leading educators on the importance of diversity in higher education. But after 1996, when a federal appeals court struck down the race-conscious admissions policy at the University of Texas School of Law and concluded that *Bakke* was no longer good law (a conclusion ultimately overruled by the U.S. Supreme Court's decision in *Grutter v. Bollinger*), social scientists across the country began efforts to better document the benefits of diversity.[27] The research was not designed for any lawsuit in particular, but it was clearly generated in response to an extant legal controversy.

In the Michigan cases themselves, several research studies were offered in the trial courts to support the compelling interest in diversity. Although the plaintiffs did not initially challenge the scientific evidence (they instead argued that the studies were irrelevant to the basic constitutional questions), the litigation spawned outside critiques and amicus curiae briefs in support of the plaintiffs, as well as rebuttals. Some researchers developed studies to challenge the benefits-of-diversity literature, and one of the counterstudies was cited by Justice Thomas in his *Grutter* dissent. The Supreme Court eventually endorsed the studies introduced by the University of Michigan and its amici curiae, but the process by which the scientific evidence and the various critiques were generated and offered to the Court was hardly typical of most academic research efforts. Yet it was not unusual for a major civil rights controversy. *Brown v. Board of Education* and other major cases have engendered comparable relationships and conflicts among lawyers, social scientists, and judges. There will no doubt be similar exchanges in the future.

## Legal versus Scientific Standards

Additional normative questions involve the elements of proof employed by the courts and the effects of science on those legal standards. Assuming that scientific evidence satisfies the requisite tests of validity and relevancy, what standards should determine the sufficiency of the evidence? Should scientific standards dictate legal standards, or vice versa? Scientific definitions of proof and legal definitions of proof are not the same: legal proof (with standards such as proof "beyond a reasonable doubt" in criminal cases or proof by a "preponderance of the evidence" in civil cases) is quite different from a rigorous mathematical or logical proof, which is distinct from a statistical analysis that expresses proof in terms of likelihoods and probabilities rather than absolutes. Since courts set most of the ground rules in legal disputes, legal standards govern in the end, but scientific standards can still play a central role in defining and refining the legal standards.

For example, during the late 1970s, the Supreme Court began suggesting specific statistical analyses for two types of cases involving intentional discrimination against racial minority groups: cases known as "systemic disparate treatment" claims under Title VII of the Civil Rights Act of 1964 and equal protection cases dealing with racial and national discrimination in jury selection.[28] Although the Court did not require one statistical model in particular, it approved statistical tests that checked for significant disparities between actual outcomes (for example, the racial composition of an employer's current workforce) and expected outcomes that one would likely see if there had been no discrimination (such as the racial composition of the available labor pool). Large-enough disparities between the two outcomes could imply that an employer's practices intentionally discriminated against a minority group—in legal terms, "systemic disparate treatment." In *Castaneda v. Partida*, an equal protection case involving the exclusion of Latinos from grand jury selection in Texas, the Supreme Court even went so far as to discuss the mechanics of statistical models focusing on a "binomial distribution" and the calculation of "standard deviations" as a measure of disparities—terms that were drawn directly from statistics texts, not from the law.[29] The Supreme Court's specific endorsements on statistics have since become the basic metrics for evidence in these types of cases.

The inevitable progress of scientific research also raises important questions about the role of scientific advancements in the evolution of legal standards and doctrines. Neither law nor science is static. Advances in science may suggest that current legal tests are inadequate or even outmoded. New techniques in statistical analysis that are gaining broad acceptance among statisticians and social scientists may influence legal standards for proving discrimination. In fields such as cognitive psychology, where researchers have documented problems of subconscious bias, recent advances may inform new theories of discrimination and undermine existing models. New developments in science and technology in fields such as human genome research and DNA testing may engender entirely new forms of discrimination that are not yet defined or prohibited under federal antidiscrimination statutes or the Constitution.

## Judicial Misinterpretation

And judges are not infallible. Even with the best of intentions and training, they may still misinterpret the science. Consider, for example, the Supreme Court's 1976 ruling in *Ballew v. Georgia*, in which the Court ruled that a criminal defendant who had been tried and convicted by a five-person jury was deprived of his constitutional right to trial by jury guaranteed by the Sixth and Fourteenth Amendments.[30] Justice Blackmun's opinion drew heavily on social science studies that had been published during the eight years since the Supreme Court's earlier ruling in *Williams v. Florida*, where the Court had upheld the constitutionally of six-member juries in non–capital-punishment cases, to show that jury functions were seriously impaired by reducing the number of members from six to five. In an opinion that contained a lengthy analysis of social science literature, with more than seventy citations to nearly twenty references in the text and footnotes, Justice Blackmun found that jury-size reduction would lead to less effective jury deliberations, less accurate results, biases against defendants, and less minority representation on juries. Justice Blackmun concluded, therefore, that "the purpose and functioning of the jury in a criminal trial is seriously impaired, and to a constitutional degree, by a reduction in size to below six members."[31]

But a significant problem with Justice Blackmun's analysis was revealed on closer inspection of the studies themselves. Critics noted that none of the studies specifically compared six-member jury panels to five-member panels; instead, most of the research addressed comparisons between six-member panels and twelve-member panels, a question to which the Supreme Court had already reached a legal conclusion in upholding the constitutionality of six-member juries in non-capital cases. If anything, the studies that Justice Blackmun reviewed tended to contradict the Court's earlier ruling in *Williams v. Florida* (which found that reducing jury sizes from twelve to six would not infringe on constitutional rights) rather than reinforce the ruling in *Ballew*. One critic noted that "while *Ballew* presents a masterful analysis of empirical data, it also distorts and ignores the thrust of empirical materials in order to reaffirm an earlier decision."[32] Representing a less science-oriented perspective, Justice Powell concurred in the judgment in *Ballew* and agreed that "a line has to be drawn somewhere if the substance of jury trial is to be preserved"[33] He also, however, criticized Justice Blackmun's "heavy reliance on numerology derived from statistical studies" and questioned the process of accepting studies that had not been "subjected to the traditional testing mechanisms of the adversary process."[34]

## Science and Values

Neither science nor law exists in a vacuum. Science cannot be isolated from its social context; dominant ideologies can pervade not only scientific research but also cultural values, economic systems, social institutions, as well as law and the courts. Scientific knowledge, once deeply engrained in the popular understanding, can become common knowledge that is undisputed and often taken for granted as part of an overarching ideology. Yet changing values and new science can frequently upend old science and change what is perceived to be common knowledge or understood to be normatively correct or preferred because of the scientific implications. For instance, until it fell into disrepute during the twentieth century, biological determinism was the underlying scientific ideology that fueled American slavery and the ongoing subordination of blacks during the Jim Crow era of segregation. During the nineteenth century, physical differences between whites and blacks such as cranial dimensions and brain size were scientifically measured and chronicled, social theories of biological evolution were employed to justify laissez-faire economics and racial separation, and laws and court decisions enforced segregation as part of the natural order.

The Supreme Court's decision in *Plessy v. Ferguson* is not at all surprising if placed in the context of the social Darwinist ideology that dominated much of American social and scientific thought during the late nineteenth century. The Court treated racial segregation as a simple reflection of the normal and natural separation of the races. The state of Louisiana could enact a law that separated white from black in the railway system because it was "at liberty to act with reference to the established usages, customs, and traditions of the people."[35] And since racial separation was a custom rooted in "racial instincts" and innate distinctions based upon physical differences, segregation merely codified the natural order. Any attempt by the courts to upset this order would only make matters worse. The *Plessy* opinion does not cite scientific evidence in the way that the Supreme Court cited evidence in footnote 11 of *Brown v. Board of Educa-*

*tion*, but citing studies was unnecessary. Racial inequality based on biological differences was already engrained in the dominant ideology. With *Brown's* science of the day, however, the "nature versus nurture" balance had been tipped away from biological determinants toward environmental determinants, and segregation itself was identified as a source of injury. What is now taken as obvious—that racial segregation is inherently harmful and wrong—was not so obvious just over fifty years ago and was fundamentally incorrect according to the ideologies of more than one hundred years ago.

## Plan of the Book

The remaining chapters study the links between science, law, and equality through an examination of civil rights litigation and the law of equal protection. The focus on equal protection cases is central not only because of the importance of major constitutional cases such as *Brown, McCleskey,* and *Grutter* but also because many of the most intriguing questions of science and law involve the relationship between science and empiricism on the one hand and value-driven constitutional norms of equality and justice on the other. As both early court cases and contemporary civil rights litigation demonstrate, contemporaneous norms of equality have pervaded both science and the law, often driving scientific inquiry and legal outcomes to move in new directions. The central role of scientific evidence in equal protection law, as I show throughout the book, has not been merely to inform judicial decision making but to serve as a value-reinforcing mechanism—a tool by which courts can undergird normative judgments on the meaning of constitutional equality. In turn, core constitutional norms such as equality under law, as they have evolved over time, have helped drive the science of the day—to develop new hypotheses and fields of inquiry as well as to discourage and limit lines of investigation that run counter to prevailing societal values.

The book focuses on decisions of the federal courts, particularly the U.S. Supreme Court, and does not examine, notwithstanding their importance, the roles that scientific research can play in other arenas, such as state court litigation, legislative activity, government enforcement, and public debates about civil rights. The book is almost exclusively devoted to analyses of constitutional law and equal protection doctrine and only occasionally glances at the use of scientific evidence to prove violations of civil rights statutes such as the Voting Rights Act or Title VII of the Civil Rights Act of 1964. The focus on constitutional questions best illustrates the relationships and tensions between scientific findings and values of equality and is not intended to make light of the many important problems of proof and statutory interpretation that the courts also address. And while this is a book about science in the law, the approach is jurisprudential and historical, not scientific; there is no attempt to employ traditional empirical methodologies, and the discussion of laws and legal cases is selective and decidedly unscientific.

Chapter 2 provides a background history of the intersection of science and civil rights law through the mid-twentieth century, with an emphasis on how leading ideologies reinforced both the scientific and legal theories of the time. Chapter 3 continues the historical overview and focuses on the extensive uses of scientific evidence in the desegregation cases that culminated in the Supreme Court's decision in *Brown v. Board of Education.* Chapter 4 discusses the role of scientific authority in the development of constitutional law after *Brown* and specifically examines cases in which scientific evidence has been used to shape evolving constitutional standards to assess equality under the law. Chapter 5 addresses the role of scientific evidence in proving discrimination under the equal protection clause. Chapter 6 examines the gatekeeping process for considering scientific evidence as well as the relationship between legal advocacy and scientific research in the adversarial process. Chapter 7 concludes with a discussion of new directions and likely developments in the intersection of scientific research and constitutional equality.

# 2

# Science and Law,
# Ideology and Inequality

In his 1897 essay *The Path of the Law*, Oliver Wendell Holmes, Jr., offered an insight familiar to many lawyers and students of law: "For the rational study of the law the black letter man may be the man of the present, but the man of the future is the man of statistics and the master of economics."[1] Although Holmes's late nineteenth-century analysis was typically inattentive to the role of women in the legal profession, it was prophetic in its appreciation of extralegal influences on law and the importance of scientific knowledge in judicial decision making. More than sixty-five years later, Chief Justice Earl Warren sounded a similar but more cautionary tone in commenting on the law's need to keep up with the progress of twentieth-century science and technology: "Each year brings its wealth of scientific discovery and invention. And each year requires an equal wealth of legislative inventiveness and judicial insight . . . to make sure that human dignity is preserved and that throughout our broad land there will be 'liberty and justice for all.'"[2] But in direct and less sanguine terms, Chief Justice Warren also declared that "the law is slow to move" and "the simple fact is that law has not kept abreast of science."[3]

The interrelationships of science and law are just as manifest in the early twenty-first century. The law can still lag behind the progress of science and technology, and the role of science in the law remains tentative and often contentious. Pointing to differences between the cultures of science and law provides an apt set of explanations, so much so that the typical comparisons and dichotomies, although often oversimplified, have become almost clichés: Law is normative, while science is descriptive. Law is value-laden, while science is value-free. Legal reasoning is largely deductive, while scientific method is primarily inductive. Legal findings are based on certainties and standards such as proof beyond a reasonable doubt, while scientific findings are based on probabilities and contingencies. Litigation is adversarial, while scientific research is cooperative.

Without question, there are significant differences in the philosophies, methods, and basic vocabularies of contemporary science and the American legal system. But focusing on these differences elides some of the close relationships and interdependencies that have marked the progress of science and of law since the nation's founding. Science and American law have possessed both commonalities and disjunctions; and it is too facile to simply say that, when the two worlds intersect, there is a culture clash between scientists on the one hand and lawyers and judges on the other. Moreover, an analysis focusing just on the similarities and differences between science and law, without also considering societal values and ideologies, is fundamentally incomplete. Contemporaneous science has always had a powerful influence on judicial decision making, and the jurisprudence of equality and civil rights is just one of many normative sources that have touched science and scientific thinking.

This chapter explores some of the historical relationships between science and civil rights law. It begins by tracing the close ties between scientific thought and judicial reasoning in the nineteenth and early twentieth centuries and examines the growth of science as a source of extralegal authority through the mid-twentieth century. In the process, I discuss some of the leading cases in which the Supreme Court has incorporated or dismissed scientific evidence in its decision making. Chapter 3 continues the historical overview and focuses on the Supreme Court's desegregation cases, including *Brown v. Board of Education*.

## The Science of Racism

Integrating science into the law has been a challenge since the founding of the United States. As David L. Faigman writes, "the Constitution's framers were products of the Enlightenment. They expressly sought to bring the science of their time into the document that would govern the times to come."[4] Indeed, as products of the Enlightenment, many of the nation's founders were themselves among the leading scientists of the day; and an overarching naturalist philosophy pervaded science, social inquiry, and the law in the late eighteenth and early nineteenth centuries. The "universal truths" revealed through natural law and natural rights flowed from an understanding of human nature and the nature of the world, which were also the basic subjects of scientific inquiry.

Science, however advanced or not advanced it may have been at the time, provided at least some support for legal reasoning, if only because science could reinforce ideologies and commonsense notions of social reality. "Scientific racism," for example, has a centuries-old history and provided underlying support for the ideological foundations of American slavery. The systematic classification of racial stocks can be traced to the 1600s; comparative studies of the races, whether focused on physiology, intellectual ability, sexuality, or culture, were significant areas of inquiry. Biological theories on the inferiority of blacks were among the most prevalent.

For instance, Thomas Jefferson, considered one of the leading scientific minds of his time, described some of the differences between blacks and whites in his *Notes on the State of Virginia*: "Comparing them by their faculties of memory, reason, and imagination, it appears to me, that in memory they are equal to whites; in reason much inferior, as I think one could scarcely be found capable of tracing and comprehending the investigations of Euclid; that in imagination they are dull, tasteless, and anomalous."[5] According to Jefferson, whose sample of study included both free blacks and many of his own slaves, "their inferiority is not the effect merely of their condition of life." Basic human nature was the root of the distinction. A reliance on biological causes rather than on environmental causes such as the institution of slavery itself provided support for the defenders of slavery, who backhandedly argued that slavery could in fact be beneficial to members of an inferior race.

The American Constitution, as originally written, incorporated slavery into its text through its apportionment clause counting slaves as three-fifths of a person for representation and taxation purposes. And the institution of southern slavery flourished with the strong support of state and federal laws through the mid-nineteenth century. But the deep moral and political contradictions caused by slavery would ultimately lead to the Civil War; and one of the precursors to the war, the infamous *Dred Scott* case, illustrates how scientific racism played a central role in Supreme Court decision making. Language from the 1857 *Scott v. Sandford* decision, in which the Supreme Court invalidated the Missouri Compromise and ruled that blacks were not citizens of the United States, drew freely from widely held biological theories of racial inequality.

Dred Scott's lawsuit revolved around the basic question of whether, by traveling to a free territory north of the free-state/slave-state line established by the Missouri Compromise of 1820, he could claim that he had become emancipated from slave status. Writing for the Court, Chief Justice Roger Taney focused on the original intent of the framers of the Constitution and concluded that, since the founding of the nation, blacks had been "considered as a subordinate and inferior class of beings, who had been subjugated by the dominant race, and, whether emancipated or not, yet remained subject to their authority."[6] Even before the founding of the country, blacks, according to the Court, "had for more than a century before been regarded as beings of an inferior order, and altogether unfit to associate with the white race, either in social or political relations; and so far inferior, that they had no rights which the white man was bound to respect; and that the negro might justly and lawfully be reduced to slavery for his benefit."[7]

Chief Justice Taney further ruled that there was no basic difference between free blacks and slaves. Citing various laws from both slave states and free states, he found "no distinction in this respect was made between the free negro or mulatto and the slave, but this stigma, of the deepest degradation, was fixed upon the whole race."[8] No blacks, slave or free, were entitled to the rights of citizenship; therefore, Dred Scott lacked the right even to bring his lawsuit in federal court. Chief Justice Taney then proceeded to invalidate the Missouri Compromise by ruling that slaves were property and that a slave owner's Fifth Amendment due process rights would be violated by a law that allowed the deprivation of a property interest simply because the property had been transported from a slave area to a free area.

The ignominious ruling in *Dred Scott*, underscored by scientific racism characterizing blacks as inferior beings, became one of the major landmarks along the road to southern secession and Civil War. The Reconstruction era that followed the war led to the addition of major amendments to the Constitution that abolished slavery (Thirteenth Amendment), secured equal voting rights for blacks (Fifteenth Amendment), and guaranteed equal protection and due process under law by the states (Fourteenth Amendment). Reconstruction-era federal civil rights legislation added to the legal guarantees of equality, even though the courts would later scale back several of those guarantees through narrow interpretations of the law. Scientific racism, however, would continue to thrive in the nineteenth century, fueled by new theories of biology and social science.

## Law and Nineteenth-Century Science

The late nineteenth century saw a confluence of major transformations in science and American jurisprudence. Following the Civil War, two intellectual movements influenced the incorporation of scientific thinking and contemporaneous science into judicial decision making. One was legal formalism, a movement in which academics and legal reformers worked to create a "science of law" that paralleled the methodologies of science and mathematics. The second was social Darwinism, which had powerful effects not only on the law but on an array of academic fields, including anthropology, sociology, and other nascent social sciences, by extending the theories of evolutionary biology to the social realm. Both movements reinforced the jurisprudence of the day, which defended laissez-faire economics, struck down much of the social welfare legislation that attempted to regulate business and conditions in the workplace, and upheld racial segregation as a legitimate exercise of state power.

### Formalism and "Legal Science"

During the nineteenth century, extraordinary developments took place in science, involving explanations of the workings of the natural universe as well as the remarkable expansion of technologies: the steam engine, steel manufacturing and construction, the harnessing of electricity, the telegraph, the telephone, and many others. Such growth in knowledge inspired strong confidence in the science of the day. Attempting to replicate scientific gains and to create systematic and universal principles of law, legal formalists applied methods of science and mathematical logic to law itself. Christopher Columbus Langdell, dean of the Harvard Law School during the late 1800s and a pioneer in university-based legal education, boldly declared in the preface to his 1871 casebook on contract law: "It is indispensable to establish at least two things, first, that law is a science; secondly that all the available materials of that science are contained in the printed books."[9] By characterizing law as a system composed largely of the decisions and opinions of courts, Langdell and other formalists proposed that legal "scientists" could analyze the law inductively and derive fundamental principles and axioms from the published court opinions. One formalist supposition was that, like the Linnaean taxonomies of animal and plant life, legal classifications and categories could be developed in a carefully disciplined and science-like process.

Extolled by its proponents as a dispassionate method through which law could be objectively analyzed and formal rules could be derived, formalism appealed strongly to legal academics and members of the judiciary. Critics, however, chastised formalism's disregard of actual social conditions and its abstract and sterile approach to solving legal controversies. Ironically, the "science" of law could be strongly anti-empirical because it treated the law as a closed system of appellate opinions and precedents. Social realities, moral and political values, and legislative intentions could easily be ignored or dismissed since they were not the subjects of legal-scientific inquiry.

As a practical matter, judges employing formalist logic might reject innovative legal theories or strike down progressive legislation because a strict adherence to formalism and its logical orderliness engendered rigidity and conservatism. For example, by assuming that employers and their individual employees possessed equal bargaining power (an assumption that was not at all reflected in the social reality of the time), courts could strike down legislation that attempted to regulate wages and hours by sustaining the tidiness of a system in which atomistic, free-thinking individuals had the liberty to bargain and enter into contracts with each other. At the same time, any extrinsic evidence of legislative intent or adverse effects on public health could be conveniently ignored.

### Social Darwinism

The publication in 1859 of Charles Darwin's *The Origin of Species* was not only a landmark in the history of science but also a major source of inspiration for nineteenth-century social and legal thinking. Darwin's theories of evolutionary biology transformed the natural sciences of the day, and the spillover effects in the worlds of philosophy and the nascent social sciences were powerful and widespread. Social Darwinism, or the extension of biological theories of natural selection to the realm of social theory, as seen in the writings of Herbert Spencer and other nineteenth-century thinkers, suggested that there was a natural state of human affairs in which government regulation should be curtailed or at least severely limited. Consistent with Spencer's concept of the "survival of the fittest," social Darwinists argued that inequalities should be treated as intrinsic to the natural order and that any interference with inherent social processes could hamper the evolution of the human species.

In post–Civil War America, social Darwinism became a dominant school of thought in fields such as economics, anthropology, and sociology, some of which were only in their infancy. As Paul L. Rosen observes, "the striking success of social Darwinism in the United States is attested to by the fact that it became practically synonymous with social science," yet "most nineteenth century social scientists adopted Darwinian biology as their paradigm for human behavior without considering that there might be a vital difference between the human species and animal species that precluded simplified comparison."[10] Nineteenth-century natural science and the burgeoning social sciences thus converged under an overarching theory predicated on competition, survival of the fittest, and evolutionary biology.

The impact of social Darwinism extended deeply into the law as well, leading Oliver Wendell Holmes, Jr., to comment that Herbert Spencer's influence was so great that he doubted that "any writer except Darwin has done so much to affect our whole way of thinking about the universe."[11] Social Darwinism had profound implications for the law, proscribing governmental regulation of business in favor of laissez-faire economics, emboldening the law's treatment of contract rights as sacrosanct, and justifying the unequal treatment of groups based on perceived biological characteristics, including race and gender. As Spencer himself wrote, "for the healthful activity and due proportioning of those industries . . . which maintain and aid the life of a society, there must . . . be few restrictions on men's liberties to make agreements with one another."[12] Deferring to the laws of nature—and simultaneously yielding to the interests of businesses and industrial growth—meant that the courts during the late nineteenth and early twentieth centuries could strike down most legislation that attempted to improve workplace conditions or infringed on the freedom to make and enforce contracts.

During the *Lochner* era, a period of reactionary judicial activity in the early twentieth century, the courts drew heavily on both formalist logic and social Darwinism to defend property and contract interests. In the 1905 case of *Lochner v. New York*, the Supreme Court struck down a New York state statute limiting the number of hours that bakers could work (a maximum of sixty hours per week or ten hours per day) as a violation of the "liberty to contract" under the due process clause of the Fourteenth Amendment.[13] The Court stated that "statutes of the nature of that under review, limiting the hours in which grown and intelligent men may labor to earn their living, are mere meddlesome interferences with the rights of the individual."[14] The Court showed minimal concern for the state's interest in the public health effects on workers and formalistically presumed the equal bargaining power of the employer and the individual employee in work contracts. But Justice Holmes, dissenting in *Lochner*, made clear that he disapproved of the Spencerian world view and theory of economics embodied in the majority's opinion: "This case is decided upon an economic theory which a large part of the country does not entertain. . . . The Fourteenth Amendment does not enact Mr. Herbert Spencer's Social Statics."[15]

### *Plessy v. Ferguson*

One of the clearest examples of the influences of social Darwinism on the law is *Plessy v. Ferguson*, the case that enshrined Jim Crow legislation as a legitimate and constitutional exercise of state power for nearly six decades. Although Justice Henry Brown did not explicitly cite social science findings in his 1896 opinion in *Plessy*, the opinion is imbued with references to biologically based racial differences, inherent social hierarchies, "racial instincts," and deference to a natural order in which other races were innately inferior to the white race. Racial subordination in the United States certainly did not begin with the writings of Darwin or Spencer, but it gained considerable traction through social Darwinism's power as an ideology that could explain and justify a legally sanctioned racial caste system.

The facts of *Plessy* are straightforward enough. Homer Plessy, classified under the blood quantum laws of the day as an "octoroon" (one-eighth black), refused to move from his seat in a whites-only railway car in a New Orleans train station and was consequently arrested and jailed for violating an 1890 Louisiana state law that required the segregation of white and black passengers on the rails. Punishment for violating the law was a fine of twenty-five dollars or a jail term of up to twenty days. Plessy challenged the law under both the Thirteenth Amendment, which prohibits slavery and involuntary servitude, and the Fourteenth Amendment. With only one dissenting vote, the U.S. Supreme Court upheld the constitutionality of the Louisiana statute as a valid exercise of state power and went out of its way to argue that racial separation did not imply racial inequality.

Framing the Fourteenth Amendment question as a consideration of whether or not the Louisiana law was reasonable, the Supreme Court ruled that the state was "at liberty to act with reference to the established usages, customs, and traditions of the people, and with a view to the promotion of their comfort, and the preservation of the public peace and good order."[16] The Court continued:

"Gauged by this standard, we cannot say that a law which authorizes or even requires the separation of the two races in public conveyances is unreasonable."[17] This language hints at a social Darwinist perspective by citing custom and tradition as justifications for reasonable legislation, implying that any interference with a natural social order might extend beyond the state's legitimate powers.

The opinion went even further. Early on, Justice Brown rejected Plessy's Thirteenth Amendment challenge: "A statute which implies merely a legal distinction between the white and colored races—a distinction which is founded in the color of the two races, and which must always exist so long as white men are distinguished from the other race by color—has no tendency to destroy the legal equality of the two races, or re-establish a state of involuntary servitude."[18] The Court's language assumed, consistent with social Darwinism, that race has a permanent, biological basis because of differences in skin color and that legal recognition of biological difference impugns neither the Thirteenth nor the Fourteenth Amendment. The Court's language is also formalistic, referring to segregation as a mere legal distinction that could somehow be divorced from any consideration of stigma or subordination inherent in the social realities of segregation. Rejecting the notion that racial separation implied racial inferiority, the Court went on to state, "If this be so, it is not by reason of anything found in the act, but solely because the colored race chooses to put that construction upon it."[19] The implication, based on the Court's own brand of amateur psychology, was that any feelings of harm or stigma were entirely self-imposed rather than a result of segregation.

Later in the opinion, the influence of social Darwinism became even more apparent. Dismissing any notion that nonsegregated facilities might be constitutionally mandated, Justice Brown wrote: "If the two races are to meet upon terms of social equality, it must be the result of natural affinities, a mutual appreciation of each other's merits, and a voluntary consent of individuals. . . . Legislation is powerless to eradicate racial instincts or to abolish distinctions based upon physical differences, and the attempt to do so can only result in accentuating the difficulties of the present situation."[20] Having recognized the white race as America's dominant one, the Court concluded: "If one race be inferior to the other socially, the Constitution of the United States cannot put them upon the same plane."[21]

The Supreme Court's references to "natural affinities," "racial instincts," and the permanence of "distinctions based on physical differences" reflect core tenets of social Darwinism. Racial separation was seen as a natural state of human affairs, and any legislative or judicial attempts to upend the inherent biological differences or to contradict innate instincts would be disruptive and futile. The *Plessy* opinion contained no citations to Spencer or to social scientists of the 1890s that would be comparable to footnote 11 in *Brown v. Board of*

*Education*, but no citations were needed. Social Darwinism's influence had become so pervasive that the Court's language and basic assertions sufficed.

Justice John Marshall Harlan's lone dissent in *Plessy* argued that "our constitution is color-blind, and neither knows nor tolerates classes among citizens."[22] Recognizing the inherent inequality of segregation, he continued: "The arbitrary separation of citizens, on the basis of race, while they are on a public highway, is a badge of servitude wholly inconsistent with the civil freedom and the equality before the law established by the constitution."[23] Yet like the majority opinion, Justice Harlan's dissent contains language that reveals support for the canons of social Darwinism. For instance, he prefaced his remarks on the Constitution's color blindness with these words: "The white race deems itself to be the dominant race in this country. And so it is, in prestige, in achievements, in education, in wealth, and in power. So, I doubt not, it will continue to be for all time, if it remains true to its great heritage."[24] And in highlighting the unequal treatment of blacks under segregation, Justice Harlan further reinforced biologically based racial hierarchies by comparing blacks to Chinese immigrants, a population whose presence in the United States had already been limited by exclusionary, race-based immigration laws upheld by the Supreme Court. He stated: "There is a race so different from our own that we do not permit those belonging to it to become citizens of the United States. Persons belonging to it are, with few exceptions, absolutely excluded from our country. I allude to the Chinese race. But, by the statute in question, a Chinaman can ride in the same passenger coach with white citizens of the United States, while citizens of the black race in Louisiana [would be criminally liable]."[25] Thus, "survival of the fittest," in Justice Harlan's opinion, might not justify the segregation of an inferior race in railway cars, but it could justify the exclusion of an even more inferior race from entering the country.

## Social Science and Legal Theory

Although their effects were broad and powerful, both social Darwinism and legal formalism spurred significant criticism during their ascendancies, and new movements in the social sciences and in jurisprudence developed in response. After the turn of the century, many social scientists shifted attention away from the biological determinants of behavior that populated social Darwinist theories to focus more on environmental determinants.[26] For instance, the work of Franz Boas, often called the father of American anthropology, focused not only on physical characteristics but on a full array of cultural attributes, including religion, art, history, and language. Boas's theories of "cultural relativism" suggested that no group was inherently superior to another, which directly contradicted many of the social Darwinist theories. Similarly, academics associated with the University of Chicago (members of the Chicago School of Sociology) examined social structures and behaviors through an environmentally deterministic lens, yielding findings on race that weakened biological theories and undermined some of the premises of *Plessy v. Ferguson* that social structures such as segregation did not affect an individual's sense of self. A related trend in the social sciences during the early twentieth century was a strong movement toward objective methods of investigation that would parallel scientific investigation in the physical and natural sciences. Building on nineteenth-century social thought such as the positivism of French philosopher Auguste Comte (who first coined the term *sociology*), many social scientists insisted that knowledge must be objective and based on concrete and verifiable data that could lead to the understanding of causal relationships.

The developments in the social sciences and ongoing discontent with legal formalism also engendered changes in legal theory and practice. Prominent figures such as Roscoe Pound, Oliver Wendell Holmes, Jr., and Louis Brandeis proposed that the overly abstract methods of formalism were too far divorced from the demands of the law as practiced and had to be replaced by a pragmatic jurisprudence that was more thoroughly grounded in social realities. Dean Pound called for a "sociological jurisprudence" that would "look to economics and sociology and philosophy, and cease to assume that jurisprudence is self-sufficient."[27] Holmes's proposals built on the epigram from his tract *The Common Law*: "The life of the law has not been logic: it has been experience."[28] Harvard law professor Felix Frankfurter called on lawyers to be social engineers who required an understanding of the social sciences to be successful, while a Frankfurter protégé, Charles Hamilton Houston, became dean of the Howard Law School and used social science as a major tool to direct the energies of a generation of black lawyers toward addressing social problems. "Legal realism," as the diverse, wide-ranging school of thought came to be known, marked a movement away from formalism's abstract, conceptual jurisprudence toward a more fact-based jurisprudence; the burgeoning social sciences were a ripe source for the economic and social data that could assist in developing this new jurisprudence. In the words of Columbia law professor Karl N. Llewelyn, a realistic jurisprudence recognized that there are many facets to the law and that "part of law, in many aspects, is all of society, and all of man in society."[29]

## The Brandeis Brief

An early illustration of the realist turn in legal advocacy and judicial decision making is the case of *Muller v. Oregon*, which involved a constitutional challenge to a 1903 Oregon law that limited the number of work hours for women employed in laundries to ten hours per day. Coming only three years after the Supreme Court struck down maximum-hour legislation in *Lochner v. New York*, *Muller* is a rare exception to the *Lochner*-era line of cases because of the Supreme

Court's unanimous ruling upholding the constitutionality of the Oregon law as a valid exercise of state power under the Fourteenth Amendment. Gender proved to be the key factor in the Court's decision upholding the state law, with a ruling that "legislation designed for [women's] protection may be sustained, even when like legislation is not necessary for men, and could not be sustained."[30]

*Muller v. Oregon* is most noteworthy for the content of the innovative brief submitted by Louis Brandeis on behalf of the state of Oregon. Rather than relying on legal argumentation and a recitation of Supreme Court precedents, the Brandeis brief cited only three cases and spent 113 pages focused on other sources of authority. The brief referred to state statutes and European laws that paralleled the Oregon law in limiting women's work hours as well as "extracts from over ninety reports of committees, bureaus of statistics, commissioners of hygiene, inspectors of factories, both in this country and in Europe, to the effect that long hours of labor are dangerous for women, primarily because of their special physical organization."[31] With copious extralegal sources, Brandeis argued that the "facts of common knowledge" established conclusively that there was a reasonable basis for a statute to limit laundry work hours for women to ten hours or less per day. [32]

The Supreme Court acknowledged the legitimacy of the Brandeis brief, citing many of the authorities in a lengthy footnote in the *Muller* opinion. The Court also made clear that it could consider matters of common knowledge that might be contained in the brief:

> The legislation and opinions referred to in the margin may not be, technically speaking, authorities, and in them is little or no discussion of the constitutional question presented to us for determination, yet they are significant of a widespread belief that woman's physical structure, and the functions she performs in consequence thereof, justify special legislation restricting or qualifying the conditions under which she should be permitted to toil. . . . We take judicial cognizance of all matters of general knowledge.[33]

In contrast to the more formalistic approaches that the Court had adopted in parallel cases involving wage and hour regulations, the *Muller* Court was at least willing to acknowledge that extralegal authorities had some relevance to its consideration of the constitutional issues at hand.

Whether the Court actually relied on the information in the Brandeis brief to reach its decision is not entirely clear, however. Language in the *Muller* opinion suggests that the Court also viewed gender differences and the inferiority of women as matters of common sense: "That woman's physical structure and the performance of maternal functions place her at a disadvantage in the struggle for subsistence is obvious. This is especially true when the burdens of motherhood are upon her."[34] Some of the Court's language also reflects a paternalistic endorsement of social Darwinism: "Still again, history discloses the fact that woman has always been dependent upon man. He established his control at the outset by superior physical strength, and this control in various forms, with diminishing intensity, has continued to the present. As minors, though not to the same extent, she has been looked upon in the courts as needing especial care that her rights may be preserved."[35]

In any case, whether it was the Brandeis brief, social Darwinism, or the justices' own notions of common sense that most strongly influenced the Court, *Muller v. Oregon* marked a distinct shift in the use of extralegal authorities to supplement precedent and logical deduction. The Supreme Court would not always be receptive to extralegal authorities: despite the introduction of similar evidence fifteen years later in *Adkins v. Children's Hospital*, the Court struck down a minimum-wage law for women, finding the economic data, expert opinions, and government reports to be "interesting, but only mildly persuasive."[36] A minimum-wage law was seen as less essential for a woman's protection than a maximum-hour law and therefore inconsistent with the "liberty of contract" so staunchly defended during the *Lochner* era. But with the Brandeis brief and the Supreme Court's ruling in *Muller v. Oregon*, the genie was out of the bottle; extralegal authorities would become commonplace in both written and oral arguments before the Court.

By contemporary standards, many of the authorities cited in the Brandeis brief were not products of science since they consisted of sundry reports by factory inspectors, miscellaneous compilations of government statistics, and even a recent State of the Union address by President Theodore Roosevelt. And even those authorities that might have been considered scientific at the time would probably not satisfy contemporary methodological standards. Nevertheless, the brief was revolutionary in its broad incorporation of social data, so much so that any brief that contains extensive social science findings or other extralegal information is today labeled a "Brandeis brief."

## The Science of Segregation

Only a few months after the Supreme Court issued its ruling in *Muller v. Oregon*, it handed down its decision in *Berea College v. Kentucky*, a case in which a private religious college had been found guilty of violating a 1904 Kentucky statute that made it unlawful to operate a college "where persons of the white and negro races are both received as pupils for instruction."[37] Coming only a few years after *Plessy v. Ferguson*, the Supreme Court's decision to uphold the conviction is not surprising. The Court focused largely on the state's power to regulate a state-chartered corporation, which the Court held was well within the powers of the state and the boundaries of the Fourteenth Amendment. What is notable about the case, however, is the brief that was filed on behalf of the state of Kentucky to justify its pro-segregation policy. Like the Brandeis brief filed in *Muller v. Oregon*, the Kentucky brief offered a compendium of factual evidence designed to support the state's interest in maintaining segregated schools. In many ways, it represented the state of "segregation science" up to that point in time.[38]

The Kentucky Attorney General requested that the Supreme Court take into account several scientific findings on race that were "so notorious and universally known as to form a part of the common information of mankind."[39] For instance, the brief cited the work of Dr. Sanford B. Hunt, a surgeon and specialist in the field of anthropometrics, the study of the physical characteristics of different races. Hunt's studies from the 1870s, like earlier studies by other anthropometrists such as Samuel George Morton, focused on differential brain sizes and cranial capacities among races. Hunt's data showed that on average a black person's brain weighed five ounces less than a white person's; moreover, a product of a mixed-race marriage—a "mulatto"—had a brain that was on average even smaller than a black person's brain. Combined with the assumption that brain weight positively correlated with intelligence, the implications were that blacks were less intelligent than whites and that racial intermarriage produced even less intelligent offspring. Moreover, because studies that examined cranial capacity from different centuries showed that the racial differences remained roughly the same over time, blacks had not progressed in catching up to whites, even over the millennia.

The Kentucky attorney general argued that, because of these and other studies, the state had a strong interest in maintaining racial segregation. There was a significant "mental gap" between whites and blacks, and the gap was "not the result of education, but [was] innate and God-given." Scientific research had demonstrated that "education, culture, refinement, and civilization are the result of the polishing of the inborn and God-given faculty. Training, culture, and education never produce faculty. All these are but the growth, the enlargement and expansion of inborn capacity."[40] Social interactions between the races—racial intermarriage, in particular—were to be seen as social evils that the state had a vested interest in prohibiting; combining students of different races in the classroom would be especially harmful because it would slow the progress of the more advanced white children.

In the final analysis, the Supreme Court did not need to address the legitimacy of the scientific evidence since it rested its decision on the state's powers to regulate corporations. But none of the studies cited in the Kentucky brief were indisputable. Herbert Hovenkamp suggests that there were three general positions on the nature of race in 1908.[41] A traditional position was anti-evolutionist and took the position that racial characteristics were innate, God-given, and immutable. Races were a permanent part of the natural order, and any inferiorities were fixed and unchangeable. This was likely the most popular position among the public and the easiest for Kentucky to substantiate through longstanding scientific literature. A second position, which enjoyed broad support among the scientific community in 1908, was evolutionist and focused on genetic theory and inheritance. Many scientists—evolutionary anthropologists, in particular—believed that characteristics such as intelligence could evolve over time; but because evolution could take thousands of years, differences between the races were, as a practical matter, permanent. Racial intermarriage was problematic because it could slow the progress of an advanced race and produce unhealthy offspring. A third position, which enjoyed far less support at the time, was environmentalist. These scientists were evolutionist and acknowledged the role of heredity, but they focused more on nonbiological influences. Education, economic status, and many other environmental factors were the more powerful determinants in their view. Genetic differences were not as great as many believed; therefore, racial mixing and interbreeding would not have any harmful biological consequences. Ultimately, it was segregationist science, whether evolutionist or anti-evolutionist, that was clearly the most potent force in 1908 and would continue to enjoy years of mainstream acceptance.

## Science or Common Sense?

The science of ethnology, with its focus on racial and cultural categorization, was a prominent field during the 1920s; but the Supreme Court encountered a conundrum when it was asked in two separate cases to resolve the question of whether particular applicants for naturalized citizenship were "white" under the law. The first federal naturalization law enacted in 1790 had limited naturalized citizenship to "free white persons." Consistent with other Reconstruction-era laws, the naturalization statute was amended in 1870 to make individuals of African nativity and descent eligible for naturalized citizenship. But because of strong anti-Asian sentiment, particularly against Chinese immigrants on the west coast, individuals of Asian descent were omitted from the 1870 amendments. Thus, the issue of who qualified as white under the naturalization law was extensively litigated during the late nineteenth and early twentieth centuries, with most decisions going against the immigrant petitioners.[42] In *Ozawa v. United States*, the Supreme Court was asked to determine whether a Japanese immigrant was eligible for naturalization as a white person.[43] A few months later, in *United States v. Thind*, the Court addressed whether an Asian Indian—a "high caste Hindu"—qualified as white under the law.[44] Not unexpectedly, the Supreme Court rejected both immigrants' claims. But the Court reached the same conclusion through different paths, relying in one case on scientific evidence of racial differences and in the other case on popular conceptions of race.

In *Ozawa*, the petitioner Takao Ozawa was a long-time resident of the

United States who had graduated from high school in Berkeley, California; had attended the University of California; spoke English in his home and with his family; and, if not for the racial bar on naturalization, would have been fully qualified for citizenship. In Ozawa's brief to the Supreme Court, he argued that "white" was at root a skin color, not an indicator of ancestry or national origin; therefore, Ozawa's light skin color meant that he fit within the statutory definition of white. Writing for the Supreme Court in 1922, Justice George Sutherland rejected this argument, turning to both lower court decisions and ethnological science, which indicated that "the words 'white person' were meant to indicate only a person of what is popularly known as the Caucasian race."[45] The Court admitted that the line between Caucasians and non-Caucasians might not be always clear; but in Ozawa's case, a negative conclusion was fully supported by both law and science: "The appellant, in the case now under consideration . . . is clearly of a race which is not Caucasian and therefore belongs entirely outside the zone on the negative side. A large number of the federal and state courts have so decided and we find no reported case definitely to the contrary. These decisions are sustained by numerous scientific authorities, which we do not deem it necessary to review. We think these decisions are right and so hold."[46] The *Ozawa* opinion, much like the opinion in *Plessy v. Ferguson*, ended with a disclaimer proposing that the Court was only recognizing differences, not endorsing racial subordination: "Of course there is not implied—either in the legislation or in our interpretation of it—any suggestion of individual unworthiness or racial inferiority."[47]

The case of Bhagat Singh Thind posed a puzzle for the Supreme Court, however, because according to numerous ethnological authorities, a person of "high caste Hindu stock, born in Punjab, one of the extreme northwestern districts of India" could be classified as a member of the Caucasian or Aryan race.[48] Thind was a U.S. army veteran of World War I and, like Takao Ozawa, had attended the University of California as a student. But unlike Ozawa, Thind was naturalized by a lower court, which had concluded that he was white under the law. Because of the scientific evidence that supported Thind, the Supreme Court was forced to confront the science and consequently developed a simple, if not disingenuous, solution: the Court found the scientific authorities to be ambiguous and opted instead to rely on common sense. "White" meant Caucasian, which by popular understanding, meant of European descent; and Thind was clearly not of European descent. Therefore, Thind was not white under the law.

Writing again for the Court, Justice Sutherland launched into a much more detailed survey of the ethnological literature, which now had to be either discredited or shown inconclusive in order for the Court to reverse the lower court's naturalization order. He concluded that the literature on the number of racial stocks was divided: "For instance, Blumenbach has five races; Keane following Linnaeus, four; Deniker, twenty-nine."[49] He also concluded that the

*Aryan* classification either had been discredited by scientists or referred to language origins rather than physical differences, thus making the category unusable. And the term *Caucasian* was not much better: "It is at best a conventional term, with an altogether fortuitous origin, which, under scientific manipulation, has come to include far more than the unscientific mind suspects."[50] Justice Sutherland concluded that the science was simply inconsistent with popular conceptions of race: "It may be true that the blond Scandinavian and the brown Hindu have a common ancestor in the dim reaches of antiquity, but the average man knows perfectly well that there are unmistakable and profound differences between them today."[51]

Justice Sutherland concluded the *Thind* opinion with a partial refutation of the Court's opinion in *Ozawa*, which was predicated on both law and ethnological science: "What we now hold is that the words 'free white persons' are words of common speech, to be interpreted in accordance with the understanding of the common man, synonymous with the word 'Caucasian' only as that word is properly understood." As he did in *Ozawa*, Justice Sutherland ended the opinion with a paradoxical statement on the meaning of its ruling: "It is very far from our thought to suggest the slightest question of racial inferiority or inferiority. What we suggest is merely racial difference, and it is of such character and extent that the great body of our people instinctively recognize it and reject the thought of assimilation."[52]

Both the *Ozawa* and *Thind* Courts glossed over the more fundamental question of whether the racial bar on naturalization amounted to racial subordination prohibited by equal protection or due process. Because the Court had ruled four decades earlier in *Chae Chan Ping v. United States (The Chinese Exclusion Case)* and other cases involving Chinese immigrants that racial discrimination in the federal immigration laws was beyond the power of the courts to review, it did not address the basic constitutionality of the race-based barrier to citizenship.[53] The Supreme Court simply denied any implication of racial inferiority, despite the obviousness of it. The Court remained in denial for many more years, and it took Congress close to thirty years to repeal the racial bar on naturalization in 1952.

Taken together, *Ozawa* and *Thind* demonstrate how the courts can manipulate facts—scientific authorities, in particular—to suit their purposes. The science itself had not changed in any meaningful way during the time between the *Ozawa* and *Thind* decisions: the two opinions were issued only three months apart. And there can be little doubt that the Court would have reached the same conclusion in *Ozawa* if it had ignored the scientific evidence since, by popular understanding, Japanese were, like Asian Indians, not white. But the scientific evidence was favorable for the *Ozawa* Court, so there was no need to ignore or question the evidence or to discuss it in any depth. In *Thind*, however, the Court had to address the ethnological evidence because it tended to cut in Thind's favor. Dismissing the science and relying on popular understanding was not the only option for the Court. In order to be consistent with *Ozawa*, it could have relied on the scientific evidence and upheld the naturalization of Thind. Also consistent with *Ozawa*, the Court could have turned to some of the scientific evidence and denied naturalization since not all of the ethnological literature would have supported Thind. Instead, the Court simply jettisoned evidence that did not fit its desired outcome and turned to commonsense notions of race as an alternative. After *Ozawa* and *Thind*, the biological definition of *white* did not need any greater clarity or precision since the term had become a legal construction informed by social facts. What the Court's analysis most seriously lacked was a consistent theory of fact finding that would enable it to employ scientific evidence as part of its process of reaching a legal conclusion, even if that meant not relying on the scientific evidence at all or using it only in a very limited way.

## Eugenics and *Buck v. Bell*

Despite the ascendancy of new biological and social science theories during the 1920s and 1930s, social Darwinism was still a force in both scientific and legal thought. One of the outgrowths of the social Darwinist movement of the nineteenth century was eugenics, an empirically rooted but fundamentally prescriptive theory that attempted to improve the human race through selective breeding. Relying on empirical tests developed early in the twentieth century, including measures of intelligence such as the IQ test, eugenicists proposed that the human race was divided into types that fell along a bell-shaped statistical curve, with superior members at the high end, inferior members at the low end, and the merely mediocre occupying the bulk of the middle of the curve. Most of the early empirical measures had serious cultural and class biases built into them, but that mattered little at the time. Many scientists and eugenicist advocates concluded that improvement of the human race would result from early and fruitful marriages among the superior, along with a curtailing of reproduction among the inferior.

As one would expect, eugenics provided powerful ideological support for racism, anti-Semitism, and anti-immigrant sentiment. Anti-miscegenation laws prohibiting intermarriage between whites and nonwhites had already been part of the legal landscape for decades; but revisions to the law such as Virginia's Racial Integrity Act of 1924 made "blood fractions" and multiple racial categories even more precise and explicit. By the 1920s, immigration laws had already restricted most immigration from Asia and the Pacific; but laws enacted in 1924 expanded the restrictions to include Japan and created new migration formulas that severely limited the entry of eastern and southern Europeans, who were viewed as less desirable than northern Europeans by eugenicist advocates.

Another set of public policies spurred by eugenicists was the segregation into state institutions of individuals who were considered "feeble-minded" or "mentally defective," along with their forced sterilization to prevent any replication of feeble-mindedness. In the 1927 case of *Buck v. Bell*, the Supreme Court addressed the constitutionality of a Virginia law that allowed Carrie Buck, a white woman who resided in Virginia's State Colony for Epileptics and Feeble Minded, to be sterilized.[54] State health officials had classified not only Carrie Buck as feeble-minded but her mother and her young daughter as well. The order for sterilization came via a court ruling that officials had obtained under the Virginia statute, which allowed sterilization of those "afflicted with hereditary forms of insanity" when doing so was in "the best interests of the [patient] and society." The Supreme Court upheld the statute as a valid exercise of state power under the Fourteenth Amendment's due process clause and equal protection clause.

Justice Holmes, one of the forerunners of legal realism, authored the *Buck* opinion. Although he did not refer to scientific evidence supporting the compulsory sterilization law, he was a known supporter of eugenics, having long admired the writings of the nineteenth-century political economist Thomas Malthus, who had advocated for population control measures as solutions to societal ills.[55] The language of the opinion—among the most inflammatory in Supreme Court history—is highly revealing and reflects Holmes's trust in contemporaneous science:

> We have seen more than once that the public welfare may call upon the best citizens for their lives. It would be strange if it could not call upon those who already sap the strength of the State for these lesser sacrifices, often not felt to be such by those concerned, in order to prevent our being swamped with incompetence. It is better for all the world, if instead of waiting to execute degenerate offspring for crime, or to let them starve for their imbecility, society can prevent those who are manifestly unfit from continuing their kind. The principle that sustains compulsory vaccination is broad enough to cover cutting the Fallopian tubes. Three generations of imbeciles are enough.[56]

As a legal realist, Holmes was a reformer who rejected formalist conservatism; in his view, sterilization of the feeble-minded was entirely consistent with an agenda that sought to improve society through control of some of its least desirable, and politically weakest members. With its roots in the science of the day, eugenics was a theory that Holmes and other members of the Court could fully endorse.

Fifteen years later, the Supreme Court was again asked to address the constitutionality of a forced sterilization program, this time involving an Oklahoma law that required the sterilization of habitual criminal offenders. In *Skinner v. Oklahoma*, the Court struck down the law as a violation of the equal protection clause; and recognizing the seriousness of sterilization and the fundamental interests at stake, the Court employed the elevated standard of review known as "strict scrutiny" to review the process.[57] Because the law applied unequally to similarly situated offenders (for example, someone who committed a second larceny involving more than twenty dollars was subject to sterilization, but someone who embezzled more than twenty dollars for a second time was not), the Court struck down the law as a violation of equal protection. Although the Court implicitly noted a eugenics preference in the law (larceny might be more likely to be committed by a poor or working-class person, compared to a white-collar crime such as embezzlement), it did not challenge the fundamental theory of eugenics underlying the law, which was that the criminal tendencies of certain offenders were inheritable. The Court had no evidence that the distinctions between the different types of offenders were meaningful: "We have not the slightest basis for inferring that that line has any significance in eugenics nor that the inheritability of criminal traits follows the neat legal distinctions which the law has marked between those two offenses."[58] The petitioner had offered scientific evidence disputing the basic link between repeat offenses and predispositions to commit crime, but the Court declined to address the kernel issue and looked exclusively at the equal protection question. Eugenics theory, even in the 1940s, still carried significant weight with policymakers and the courts; only the horrors of World War II and the Nazi death camps effectively halted the eugenics movement in the United States.

## Science and Loyalty

With changes in values and in the membership of the Supreme Court, the 1930s and 1940s saw a decline of the Court's restrictive *Lochner*-era approach to economic regulation and social welfare legislation. Most New Deal legislation received a judicial imprimatur, with the courts acknowledging the important public interests that would be served by the new laws. The expansion of social science into multiple disciplines, with full academic departments, professional associations, subdisciplines, and variegated methodologies, also blossomed during the pre–World War II era. American social science had already been moving in a strongly positivist and empiricist direction; and social scientists' methodologies closely paralleled the methods employed in the natural sciences and physical sciences, including experimentation, observational studies, and extensive statistical and mathematical analyses. Increasingly, social scientists were also turning their attention to addressing social problems such as poverty and discrimination. But not until after World War II, when shifts in racial attitudes began occurring throughout the country, were many of the social data addressing problems of inequality used by the courts in cases such as *Brown v. Board of Education.*

The role of science in the courts remained problematic through the World War II years, and there was no single theory of fact finding that the courts adopted to provide guidelines for when scientific evidence could and should be used. Much as they still do, the courts would often pick and choose evidence to suit their needs in a particular case. A powerful example is the Supreme Court's reliance on governmental evidence of disloyalty involving Japanese Americans during World War II. The result was the Court's upholding of laws that led to the internment of more than 110,000 Japanese Americans—two-thirds of whom were American citizens, with the remainder having been lawful permanent residents who were racially barred from citizenship.

During World War II, the Supreme Court was asked to address the constitutionality of different elements of the Japanese American exclusion from the west coast, which had been authorized by President Franklin Roosevelt's Executive 9066 and implemented by military leaders. In *Hirabayashi v. United States*, the Court addressed the constitutionality of a curfew order that required Japanese Americans to be off the streets during certain hours.[59] In *Korematsu v. United States*, the Court addressed the constitutionality of the exclusion of Japanese Americans from the west coast, which involved their forced uprooting from their homes and businesses and relocation to camps in the interior of the United States.[60] In both cases, the federal government argued that the threat of espionage and disloyalty among some Japanese Americans justified applying the policy to all of them.

In *Hirabayashi*, the government requested the Court to take judicial notice of several items of common knowledge, many of which were in fact highly disputable or presented an incomplete picture of reality. The government alleged disloyalty largely based on evidence implying that Japanese Americans had not assimilated into the population as a whole. Various evidence was offered: for example, children's after-school attendance at Japanese language schools, some of which were believed to be sources of Japanese nationalist propaganda; large numbers of children being sent to Japan for education; some Japanese American children's possessing dual citizenship; large numbers of permanent resident aliens occupying leadership positions with the Japanese American community, which might include associations with Japanese consulates; and, generally, a lack of social interaction between Japanese Americans and the white population.

Writing for a unanimous Court, Chief Justice Harlan Fiske Stone fully accepted the government's arguments and upheld the curfew order:

Viewing these data in all their aspects, Congress and the Executive could reasonably have concluded that these conditions have encouraged the continued attachment of members of this group to Japan and Japanese institutions. . . . Whatever views we may entertain regarding the loyalty to this country of the citizens of Japanese ancestry, we cannot reject as unfounded the judgment of the military authorities and of Congress that there were disloyal members of that population, whose number and strength could not be precisely and quickly ascertained.[61]

The Court employed a highly deferential legal standard and gave the government the benefit of the doubt when it came to the evidence. Rhetorically, the Court recognized that "distinctions between citizens solely because of their ancestry are by their very nature odious to a free people whose institutions are founded upon the doctrine of equality," but the government still satisfied the Court's deferential standard of review.[62]

Nevertheless, the *Hirabayashi* Court did have the opportunity to weigh other evidence of Japanese American assimilability and loyalty. The Japanese American Citizens League (JACL) filed an amicus curiae brief in the case that was essentially a 126-page Brandeis brief documenting that Japanese Americans were no different from any other immigrant group in seeking acceptance in American society. Drafted with the aid of a University of Chicago–trained anthropologist, the JACL brief cited Franz Boas's *The Mind of Primitive Man* and numerous accounts of the cultural assimilation of Japanese Americans.[63] The brief also countered the argument that disloyalty was a necessary outcome of ongoing discrimination against Japanese Americans:

It is said that since persons of Japanese ancestry have been discriminated against, legally and socially, in American life, they bear resentment against this country and would be likely to retaliate by betraying our west coast to an invader. . . . Fortunately the forces of evil, past and present, are not as all-powerful as the superficial would like to think. They have not succeeded in isolating these people or in alienating them from the main stream of American life.[64]

Yet the Supreme Court made no mention of the JACL brief or any of its social science findings in the unanimous *Hirabayashi* decision.

The *Korematsu* case, however, divided the Court because it involved a much more serious deprivation of civil liberties than did a curfew: the exclusion of all Japanese Americans from the west coast. Writing for the six-member majority, Justice Hugo Black established a heightened standard of review (a nascent form of the strict scrutiny standard that the courts now employ in reviewing race-conscious policies), but the Supreme Court still deferred to military judgment and upheld the exclusion as an acceptable exercise of the government's wartime powers. The Court noted that "all restrictions which curtail the civil rights of a single racial group are immediately suspect. That is not to say that all such restrictions are unconstitutional. It is to say that courts must subject them to the most rigid scrutiny. Pressing public necessity may sometimes justify the existence of such restrictions; racial antagonism never can."[65] Relying on the factual predicate of potential disloyalty established in *Hirabayashi*, the Court had no trouble justifying the exclusion: "Like curfew, exclusion of those of Japanese origin was deemed necessary because of the presence of an unascertained number of disloyal members of the group, most of whom we have no doubt were loyal to this country."[66] The Court recognized that the exclusion caused hardships, "but hardships are part of war, and war is an aggregation of hardships."[67]

The three dissenting justices in *Korematsu* excoriated the majority for its approval of the exclusion as an unwise deferral to military judgment and a sanctioning of governmental prejudice. Justice Frank Murphy argued that the "exclusion goes over 'the very brink of constitutional power' and falls into the ugly abyss of racism."[68] Citing social science studies demonstrating that "persons of Japanese descent are readily susceptible to integration in our society if given the opportunity," Justice Murphy directly attacked the military's evidence:

> A military judgment based upon such racial and sociological considerations is not entitled to the great weight ordinarily given the judgments based upon strictly military considerations. Especially is this so when every charge relative to race, religion, culture, geographical location, and legal and economic status has been substantially discredited by independent studies made by experts in these matters.[69]

Instead, Justice Murphy found the reasons for the exclusion "to be largely an accumulation of much of the misinformation, half-truths and insinuations that for years have been directed against Japanese Americans by people with racial and economic prejudices."[70] But the social science made no difference to the *Korematsu* majority, which found that military judgment during wartime sufficed.

Nearly forty years after the *Hirabayashi* and *Korematsu* decisions, researchers discovered governmental records revealing that the federal government had actually suppressed evidence of Japanese American loyalty and that the final military report presented to the Supreme Court had been altered to exclude information that might have led to the Court to reach a different outcome.[71] The individual convictions of the petitioners were eventually vacated by lower federal courts in the 1980s because of the government's misconduct. Nonetheless, the Supreme Court's original decisions and opinions remain precedents that can be used to justify race-based deprivations of civil liberties during times of war and national crisis.

SELECTIVELY SCANNING THE Supreme Court's treatment of science through the 1940s does not reveal any clear patterns, particularly when science itself was moving in different directions during the nineteenth and early twentieth centuries. But there is no question that science had an impact on judicial reasoning, if only because science and common knowledge often coincided under dominant ideologies such as scientific racism and social Darwinism. From a contemporary standpoint, it would be easy to dismiss scientific movements such as eugenics as misguided and not reflective of today's scientific values and standards, which would be accurate. But the science of the day was the science of the day, and the courts often invoked it. The courts' more recent uses of scientific research, made explicit in cases such as *Brown v. Board of Education*, do not reveal any clear and consistent patterns either—other than a generalized conclusion that, when it comes to science, the courts use it when they need it and ignore it when they don't. But American life dramatically changed after the *Brown v. Board of Education* decision, and the use of scientific research by advocates and the courts would never be the same.

# 3

# Desegregation and
# "Modern Authority"

In his book *Simple Justice*, widely considered to be the definitive history of the *Brown v. Board of Education* case, Richard Kluger suggests that Chief Justice Earl Warren's insertion of footnote II into the Court's *Brown* opinion was almost an afterthought. According to Kluger's account, the footnote, which cited several of the social science references included in the plaintiffs' briefs, was designed merely to add a modicum of support for the chief justice's response to the psychological musings of the majority opinion in *Plessy v. Ferguson*. In *Plessy*, the Supreme Court had proposed that any feelings of inferiority that blacks felt because of segregation were entirely self-generated and were not the product of the forced separation of the races. Kluger writes:

> To Warren, it had seemed an innocuous enough item to insert in the opinion. "We included it because I thought the point it made was the antithesis of what was said in *Plessy*," he later commented. "They had said there that if there was any harm intended, it was solely in the mind of the Negro. I thought these things—these cited sources—were sufficient to note as being in contradistinction to that statement in *Plessy*." Then he added, by way of stressing that the sociology was merely supportive and not the substance of the holding, "It was only a note, after all."[1]

Notwithstanding the chief justice's unassuming explanation of its genesis, footnote II has been far more than just a note. It is perhaps the most controversial footnote in the Supreme Court's long history of constitutional decision making, and by itself has generated as much commentary as any of the Court's full opinions. Although the studies cited in footnote II may not have strongly influenced the Court's reasoning in striking down educational segregation, they demonstrate that scientific research can play a major role in legal advocacy, judicial fact finding, and, perhaps most significantly, the rhetoric of judicial opinions.

In this chapter I continue the historical overview begun in chapter 2, initially examining the Supreme Court's post–World War II racial discrimination cases leading up to the landmark decision in *Brown v. Board of Education*. I then devote attention to several aspects of *Brown*, including the roots of the social science evidence cited in the case, the lower courts' assessment of expert testimony and scientific evidence, the Supreme Court's rulings in the consolidated desegregation cases, and the commentary generated in *Brown*'s aftermath. *Brown* is the primary focus of this chapter because social science played an unprecedented role in the case from start to finish—from the initial filings involving multiple lawsuits in separate states, to the trials and appeals, to the later implementation of desegregation orders by the lower courts. More than fifty years later, the impact of *Brown* and its uses of social science are still being felt. The chapter concludes by examining the use of scientific evidence in later desegregation cases and other major equal protection cases involving racial discrimination.

## Attacking Segregation

The separate-but-equal formula approved in the 1896 case of *Plessy v. Ferguson* became a deeply entrenched institution of American society during the first half of the twentieth century. Jim Crow legislation throughout the south segregated whites and non-whites in practically every aspect of life, including housing, employment, transportation, education, health care, and public facilities. Separate drinking fountains, separate public bathrooms, separate telephone booths, separate seats on buses and trains, separate lunch counters, separate theater seats, separate schools—these were just a few of Jim Crow's manifestations, most of which were never truly equal. Moreover, anti-miscegenation statutes banning interracial marriages with whites were among the most punitive of all of the Jim Crow laws, designed to maintain white racial purity at all costs.

The courts did little to change conditions under Jim Crow during the early decades of the twentieth century, and the U.S. Supreme Court reinforced the constitutionality of educational segregation in the late 1920s in *Gong Lum v. Rice*, a case involving a Chinese American student in Mississippi who challenged the legality of her exclusion from a whites-only school.[2] Concluding that it was addressing "the same question which [had] been many times decided to be within the constitutional power of the state Legislature to settle, without intervention of the federal courts under the federal Constitution," the Supreme Court ruled against Martha Lum, the Chinese American child represented in the litigation by her father Gong Lum.[3] Writing for a unanimous Supreme Court, Chief Justice William Howard Taft ruled that prior cases upholding the segregation of black students in separate schools were just as applicable to students of Chinese ancestry: "we cannot think that the question is any different, or that any different result can be reached . . . where the issue is as between white pupils and the pupils of the yellow races."[4]

But segregation certainly did not go unchallenged. Founded by W.E.B. Du Bois and other black leaders in 1909, the National Association for the Advancement of Colored People (NAACP) soon began developing legal campaigns in response to segregation, using litigation to address the harsh inequalities caused by Jim Crow laws. Strategies at first attempted to enforce the mandates of equality under separate-but-equal, with the goals of closing some of the major gaps between blacks and whites and avoiding a direct collision course with *Plessy v. Ferguson*, which was considered impregnable during the early years of legal challenges. Eventually, however, the strategies evolved into direct opposition to segregation, chipping away at its legal foundations until *Plessy* itself was overturned. Led by Thurgood Marshall and a corps of activist attorneys, many of whom had been trained at the Howard Law School under its dean Charles Hamilton Houston, the efforts of the NAACP's legal arm, the NAACP Legal Defense and Educational Fund, drew on many of the nation's leading legal experts and, in time, many of the leading social scientists studying race and racial prejudice.

During the 1940s, the NAACP obtained a number of important victories in the Supreme Court. In *Smith v. Allwright*, the Court struck down all-white primary elections as a denial of the right to vote under the Fifteenth Amendment.[5] In *Shelley v. Kraemer*, the Court declared racially restrictive covenants (court-enforced private agreements that prevented non-whites from obtaining real property) to be a violation of the Fourteenth Amendment.[6] Reflecting an evolving strategy of combining law and social science, the nearly one-hundred-page brief of the NAACP Legal Defense and Educational Fund in *Shelley v. Kraemer* merged legal arguments and Brandeis-brief data on the economic and social effects of housing segregation. The next steps in the Legal Defense Fund's litigation strategy led it to attack segregation in graduate school education, which was seen as a safer, less disruptive venue than education at the elementary and secondary school levels. In the late 1940s, two cases became the centerpieces of the strategy: one involved admission to the all-white doctoral program in education at the University of Oklahoma; the other, admission to the all-white University of Texas School of Law.

In *McLaurin v. Oklahoma*, a federal court ordered George W. McLaurin to be admitted to the Oklahoma doctoral program because there were no separate, let alone equal, facilities available. But the court order allowed certain restrictions on McLaurin's education; the department openly segregated McLaurin, forcing him to sit in his own row in the classroom, eat at his own table in the cafeteria, and occupy a separate desk in the library.[7] In *Sweatt v. Painter*, the Texas legislature had voted, before the trial, to accommodate Heman Marion ("Bill") Sweatt by creating a separate law school for blacks, a small three-room setting located across the street from the state capitol in Austin and staffed by a part-time faculty. Although Sweatt lost in the Texas courts, social scientists played an important role at trial by appearing as expert witnesses addressing the harms of segregated education. Despite opposition from the state on the relevancy of his testimony, Robert Redfield, the chair of the anthropology department of the University of Chicago, testified:

> Segregation has effects on the student which are unfavorable to the full realization of the objectives of education. . . . It prevents the student from the full, effective and economical coming to understand the nature and capacity of the group from which he is segregated. . . . Segregation has an unfortunate effect on the student . . . in that it intensifies suspicion and distrust between negroes and the whites, and suspicion and distrust are not favorable conditions either for the acquisition and conduct of an education, or for the discharge of the duties of a citizen.[8]

In June 1950, the U.S. Supreme Court ruled unanimously in both cases that the separate educational experiences provided by the institutions were not equal under the law. The Court declined, however, to rule on the fundamental question of separate-but-equal's constitutionality. Neither opinion cited social science evidence, but both concluded that the educational facilities provided to blacks were inferior. Writing for the Court in *Sweatt v. Painter*, Chief Justice Fred M. Vinson turned to both tangible and intangible differences between the separate law schools. The Negro law school had smaller facilities, fewer faculty, and an inferior library; more important, it lacked the same qualities of greatness such as "reputation of the faculty, experience of the administration, position and influence of the alumni, standing in the community, traditions and prestige."[9] In *McLaurin v. Oklahoma*, Chief Justice Vinson wrote that the restrictions placed on George McLaurin "were such that he had been handicapped in his pursuit of effective graduate education. Such restrictions impair and inhibit his ability to study, to engage in discussions and exchange views with other students, and in general, to learn his profession."[10] The University of Texas was ordered to admit Bill Sweatt to its law school, and the University of Oklahoma was ordered to remove the restrictions on George McLaurin. Both cases helped set the stage for the direct attack on school segregation that arrived in the Supreme Court as the consolidated cases known as *Brown v. Board of Education*.

## The Science of *Brown*

Like legal developments in the civil rights field, the science of race and racial prejudice changed significantly during the 1930s and 1940s. Because of methodological weaknesses in the regime of segregationist science, as well as shifts in thinking that coincided with the entry of more minorities into scientific fields and a growing repugnance toward white supremacy, mainstream social science began turning away from scientific racism to an anti-racism agenda that focused on pressing social problems.[11] As historian John P. Jackson, Jr., suggests, four lines of research embodied this rethinking of the science of race:

> First, social scientists began using the anthropological concept of "culture" to debunk the notion of innate superiority of the white race. Second, social scientists began conceptualizing "race prejudice" as a fundamentally irrational attitude. Third, social scientists began investigating the origins of racial attitudes in children in an attempt to prove that racial attitudes were not "natural kinds" but rather learned behaviors. Fourth, social scientists began sociological investigations of African American culture in order to investigate the "social pathology" of African Americans.[12]

Perhaps the single most important study that came out during the 1940s was Gunnar Myrdal's *An American Dilemma*, a sweeping work commissioned by the Carnegie Corporation that became an indictment of American racism and Jim Crow.[13] A Swedish economist who was also trained in law, Myrdal had prepared the 1944 study with the assistance of nearly fifty of America's leading scholars and experts on race. Combining sociological and economic analyses with sharp commentary, *An American Dilemma* attacked southern segregation, referring to widespread institutionalized racism in the United States as "America's greatest failure."[14] A work on American race relations written by a white, non-American social scientist, the book became one of the most important weapons in the litigators' arsenal in their assaults on segregation and had already been cited in the petitioners' brief in *Shelley v. Kraemer*, the 1948 case striking down racially restrictive covenants.

But litigators at the NAACP Legal Defense Fund also looked for evidence of specific injuries caused by segregation. Economic and sociological analyses could demonstrate aggregate inequalities and harms at a societal level, but psychological and psychiatric evidence could make the pain of segregation more individualized and concrete. One scientist studying the psychological effects of segregation on children was Kenneth B. Clark, a psychology professor at City College of New York. Along with his wife, Mamie Phipps Clark, Kenneth Clark had developed an experimental method involving "projective testing," a technique in which an individual answers questions about an object so that the researcher may obtain insights into the person's psychological makeup. One well-known example of a projective test is the Rorschach inkblot test, in which subjects are presented with a series of vaguely shaped inkblots and asked to describe what they see. Instead of inkblots, the Clarks employed a set of dime-store dolls, of which two were pink-skinned to represent whites and two were brown-skinned to represent blacks.

The Clarks collected data for their doll studies during the 1940s by interviewing 253 early-school-age children, of whom 134 attended segregated schools in the south and 119 attended integrated schools in the north. The children were presented with the diapered dolls, which were identical except for the differences in skin color, and asked a set of questions about them. Some questions were designed to reveal racial preferences: "Give me the doll that you like the best" or "Give me the nice doll." Others were designed to elicit racial identification: "Give me the doll that looks like a white child," "Give me the doll that looks like a colored child," or "Give me the doll that looks like a Negro child." A final question was designed to reveal self-identification: "Give me the doll that looks like you." The Clarks' results on racial identification were unremarkable, with the older children being more accurate than the younger children. But their findings on racial preferences were startling. Writing in a 1947 paper, the Clarks stated that "the majority of these Negro children prefer the *white* doll and reject the colored doll." Two-thirds of the children wanted to play with the white doll and thought it was the "nice" doll, and a similar percentage rejected the black doll. The Clarks' conclusion was that a black child's identification of the white doll as good and the black doll as bad indicated psychological damage to the child's self-esteem.[15]

The Clarks' data also revealed an unexpected geographic difference in the children's responses: the northern children had a slightly stronger preference for the white doll than did the southern children, and the southern children were significantly less likely to reject the black doll than the northern children were. The difference between northern and southern children was odd, especially if a core hypothesis was that segregation in the south would be expected to cause more serious psychological damage. And the difference persisted in other tests by the Clarks. One study involved a set of findings in which the Clarks had asked children to use crayons to color in various outlines, including a number of inanimate objects and a boy and a girl; the children were then asked which color of boy and girl they preferred. Once again, the northern children showed a stronger preference for white compared to the southern children. During cross-examination at one of the desegregation trials, Kenneth Clark tried to explain the differences by proposing that black children everywhere were influenced by their environment: many areas of the north were segregated despite the absence of legal mandates, and children were still exposed to the realities of segregation through mass media and other sources. The Clarks' doll studies were not the only scientific evidence employed in the litigation against segregation, but they became the lightning rods for criticisms concerning the courts' misuse of science—or, depending on the critique, the acceptance of pseudo-science.

In addition to the Clark studies, one of the most important studies for the desegregation plaintiffs was a survey conducted in 1947 by psychologist Isidor Chein, in which he surveyed nearly 850 social scientists and asked if they agreed that "enforced segregation has detrimental effects on members of racial and religious groups which are segregated, even if equal facilities were provided." The survey also asked a series of questions about the psychological effects on the groups that enforced the segregation, as well as the basis for the social scientists' opinions (the options were personal research, other social scientists' research, personal professional experience, and other social scientists' professional experience). The results were overwhelmingly critical of segregation: of the 517 social scientists who responded to the survey, 90 percent responded that segregation had detrimental effects on the segregated group, 83 percent responded that segregation had detrimental effects on the group that enforced the segregation, and 90 percent checked one of the four alternatives for the basis of their opinion. Joined by statistician Max Deutscher, Chein published the survey results in 1948 in the *Journal of Psychology*, and, like Kenneth Clark, served as an expert witness for the plaintiffs.

But using social science evidence in the legal challenges to segregation was controversial. Some civil rights attorneys embraced the scientific evidence as highly useful in proving that separate-but-equal education was inherently unequal, but others questioned whether scientific findings would be sufficiently convincing to judges, who would be more interested in traditional legal arguments. Some even derided the social science research, particularly the Clark doll studies, with one litigator quoted as saying, "Jesus Christ, those damned dolls! I thought it was a joke."[16] Ultimately, though, the decision was made to include the social science evidence in the trials as part of the full array of arguments presented to the courts for undoing *Plessy v. Ferguson*.

## The *Brown* Cases

In the early 1950s, seventeen states and the District of Columbia had segregated school systems, while four additional states permitted segregation at the discretion of local school districts.[17] Several cases challenging segregation eventually landed on the U.S. Supreme Court's docket and were consolidated into *Brown v. Board of Education*. *Brown* itself challenged the segregated school system in Topeka, Kansas. *Briggs v. Elliott* focused on Clarendon County in South Carolina. *Belton v. Gebhart* and *Bulah v. Gebhart* were challenges to segregated schools in Delaware. *Davis v. County School Board of Prince Edward County* attacked a school system's policies in Virginia, and *Bolling v. Sharpe* challenged school segregation in the District of Columbia. Only *Bolling v. Sharpe* was dismissed by the court before it could go to trial.

Two basic questions were at issue in the school segregation cases. First, were the separate schools equal in terms of physical facilities, transportation, curriculum, and other educational measures? In other words, was the "equality" element of separate-but-equal satisfied? Second, did separate schools cause other forms of inequality in addition to "tangible" factors? In other words, did segregation inherently cause injury to the black students and violate their constitutional rights under the equal protection clause? It was the second question, once answered affirmatively, that could undermine the factual predicate of *Plessy v. Ferguson*. Social science research and expert witnesses were put to work in answering both questions.

Kenneth Clark began working closely with the NAACP Legal Defense and Educational Fund well before the trials and became the lead expert witness for the plaintiffs, relying on his published doll studies as well as specific doll studies and interviews that he conducted within the local school districts. Isidor Chein testified in support of his survey of social scientists and related research. Various scientists testified at the different trials to discuss the social and psychological harms of segregation, including psychologists Helen Trager, Louisa Holt, and M. Brewster Smith; psychiatrist Frederic Wertham; sociologist John J. Kane; and, via the introduction of his prior testimony in *Sweatt v. Painter*, anthropologist Robert Redfield.

With precedent on their side, the defendant school districts did not rely on social science evidence, arguing instead that the scientific evidence was irrelevant and cross-examining the plaintiffs' witnesses to undermine their testimony. But in the Virginia case, *Davis v. County School Board*, which was one of the last to be tried, the defendants offered a much stronger attack on the plaintiffs' witnesses and offered several experts of their own. T. Justin Moore, lead attorney for the Virginia defendants, questioned Kenneth Clark thoroughly on the geographic anomalies in his doll studies and accused Isidor Chein of bias because he was "one-hundred percent Jewish" and at the time worked for the American Jewish Congress. Moore also offered three expert witnesses: a local psychiatrist and a local clinical psychologist, who testified on the unreadiness of the white population to accept desegregated schools; and Henry Garrett, chair of the psychology department at Columbia University, who testified on psychological testing. Although he was a known segregationist, Professor Garrett was also one of the nation's best-known academic psychologists and a former president of the American Psychological Association. Garrett attacked Chein's survey for having weak, almost unanswerable questions, a selective sample, and a predisposed bias to support the legal efforts to overturn segregation; Garrett also argued that no tests, including Clark's, could adequately gauge a student's attitudes toward segregation and that Clark's specific tests for Virginia were biased and had too small of a sample size.

The three-judge federal court in *Davis* found the scientific testimony on the inherent harms of segregation, taken as a whole, to be inconclusive; in effect, the expert witnesses had cancelled each other out. Concluding that there was "no hurt or harm to either race," the court upheld the segregation policy and ordered the physical facilities and curricula for black children to be equalized, but without a timetable.[18] In the other trials, the influence of the social science evidence was mixed. In the Kansas case, *Brown v. Board of Education*, the three-judge court accepted the evidence that segregation had harmful effects on children and issued an important finding of fact that echoed the plaintiffs' expert testimony:

> Segregation of white and colored children in public schools has a detrimental effect upon the colored children. The impact is greater when it has the sanction of law; for the policy of separating the races is usually interpreted as denoting the inferiority of the Negro group. A sense of inferiority affects the motivation of a child to learn. Segregation with the sanction of law, therefore, has a tendency to retard the educational and mental development of Negro children and to deprive them of some of the benefits they would receive in a racially integrated school system.[19]

Nevertheless, the court found the physical facilities of the schools to be substantially equal and upheld the constitutionality of the segregation policy, consistent with *Plessy* and *Gong Lum v. Rice*.

In the South Carolina case, *Briggs v. Elliott*, the three-judge court, by a two-to-one vote, essentially ignored the scientific evidence and upheld separate-but-equal schools. The court did, however, require the school officials to equalize their separate facilities and to report back in six months on their progress.[20] And in the Delaware cases, *Belton v. Gebhart* and *Bulah v. Gebhart*, the state court agreed with the social scientists that "the Negro's mental health and therefore, his educational opportunities are adversely affected by State-imposed segregation in education."[21] Nevertheless, the judge was compelled to abide by existing precedent. The Delaware judge did find, however, that the schools were not even close to being equal and that the plaintiffs' rights had been violated; consequently, he ordered that the children be admitted to the all-white schools.

Although the acceptance of social science evidence varied among the different courts, there was a clear distinction between the fact finding that the courts engaged in regarding the equality of physical facilities (*adjudicative* fact finding to determine if separate-but-equal had been satisfied under existing law) and the fact finding on the social and psychological harms caused by segregation itself (*legislative* fact finding on the question of whether separate-but-equal was inherently unequal). Some of the courts reached different conclusions on the adjudicative facts needed to order equalization, and only a few were willing to acknowledge the scientific evidence of psychological injury. But none of the courts was willing to go so far as to change the law because of legislative facts. That type of fact finding would be left for the U.S. Supreme

Court. Appeals were filed in the cases, and all of them eventually made it onto the Supreme Court's docket.

## Brown in the Supreme Court

Social science continued to play an important role in the Supreme Court appeals of the consolidated cases. The trial courts' findings of fact in the cases were available for the Supreme Court to rely upon, but both the plaintiffs' attorneys and the social scientists working with them decided that scientific authorities could also be included in the appellate briefs filed in the Supreme Court. A "Social Science Statement" signed by several of the leading researchers on race was attached to the main brief in Brown as an appendix, with Kenneth Clark and Isidor Chein leading the drafting and signature-gathering efforts.

### Social Science Statement

The appendix to the plaintiffs' brief in Brown carried the full title "The Effects of Segregation and the Consequences of Desegregation: A Social Science Statement."[22] The statement made clear at the outset that significant moral and legal issues were at stake and that social scientists had no special authority on these questions; however, the factual issues in the case fell within the purview of scientific researchers, and the scientific evidence could ultimately aid the Supreme Court's decision making. The statement then went on to offer two sets of arguments: first, segregation was psychologically damaging to both minority children and majority children; second, desegregation could proceed smoothly if ordered quickly and decisively by the Court.

To support the first argument, the statement cited several works, including Gunnar Myrdal's An American Dilemma and Kenneth Clark's 1950 fact-finding report to the Mid-century White House Conference on Children and Youth, which summarized several studies, including his own projective tests involving dolls.[23] The statement also included citations addressing how segregation created several serious problems: a distorted sense of reality; mutual suspicion, distrust, and hostility; the perpetuation of stereotypes; and a social climate in which violence could likely occur.[24] The statement further cited Chein's opinion survey of social scientists to show the widespread agreement on segregation's harmful effects.[25] To support the second argument that desegregation could be implemented without harmful effects, the statement cited studies by Otto Klineberg showing that blacks were not intellectually inferior to whites and therefore that desegregation would not harm the educational opportunities for white children.[26] The statement then went on to cite studies showing that desegregation had been successfully implemented in many settings without significant problems of racial tensions or violence.[27] In all, the statement had thirty-five footnotes containing supportive citations and a bibliography with well over fifty references. A total of thirty-two scientists, including two with medical degrees, signed the statement.

## Opposing Briefs

Although much of the plaintiffs' scientific evidence in the lower courts had gone unchallenged, the evidence was attacked in the legal briefs filed by the defendants in *Brown*. Kenneth Clark's doll studies, in particular, were scored for their methodological weaknesses and for the anomalous finding that northern children appeared to be suffering greater psychological injury than southern children. In comparing the Clarks' larger study from the 1940s to one of the specific studies conducted in the local school districts, the brief in *Briggs v. Elliott* stated: "While these experiments would seem to indicate that Negro children in the South are healthier psychologically speaking than those in the North, Dr. Clark appears to disagree. In any case, the results obtained in the broader sample of experiments completely explode any inference that the 'conflicts' from which Professor Clark's Clarendon County subjects were found to suffer are the result of their education in segregated schools."[28] The defendants' briefs further argued that scientific evidence, to the extent it was actually useful to the courts, suggested that segregated schools were in fact better for the students. "There is a large body of respectable expert opinion," one brief proposed, "to the effect that separate schools, particularly in the South, are in the best interests of children of both races as well as of the community at large."[29]

## Science in the Oral Arguments

The *Brown* cases went through the unusual process of having two rounds of oral arguments, in 1952 and in 1953, because the justices requested additional briefing and oral arguments on the legislative history of the Fourteenth Amendment and its relationship to segregated schools as well as on potential remedies if the Court were to strike down segregation. The delay in the Court's issuance of a final ruling in *Brown* was fortuitous for the plaintiffs because Chief Justice Fred Vinson, who apparently was equivocal on the school segregation question, died before the second round of arguments. President Eisenhower's appointee to replace the chief justice was Earl Warren, governor of California.

Much of the oral argumentation in the consolidated cases focused on the constitutional precedents—in particular, on the difficulties of trying to square *Plessy v. Ferguson* and *Gong Lum v. Rice* with a ruling striking down segregation. But Robert L. Carter, one of the NAACP Legal Defense Fund attorneys, made clear in his arguments in *Brown* that the harms of segregation were not limited to the inequality of tangible factors such as physical facilities and that the statements of expert witnesses were central to the plaintiffs' case:

It was testified that racial segregation, as practiced in the City of Topeka, tended to relegate appellants and their group to an inferior caste; that it lowered their level of aspiration; that it instilled feelings of insecurity and inferiority with them, and that it retarded their mental and educational development, and for those reasons, the testimony said, it was impossible for the Negro children . . . to secure, in fact or in law, an education which was equal to that available to white children.[30]

Early on in his arguments in *Briggs v. Elliott*, Thurgood Marshall also stressed his belief that the Supreme Court had to consider the social science that had been introduced at trial: "Appellees, in their brief comment, say that they do not think too much of [the plantiffs' expert witnesses]. I do not think that the District Court thought too much of them. But they stand in the record as unchallenged as experts in their field, and I think we have arrived at the stage where the courts do give credence to the testimony of people who are experts in their fields."[31]

Nonetheless, the defendants were prepared to contest the evidence in the Supreme Court. John W. Davis, a renowned appellate attorney, argued for the defendants in *Briggs v. Elliott* and spent several minutes attacking Clark's doll studies, the testimony of two other experts, and the value of social science evidence in general. In criticizing the overall evidence, Davis stated: "It seems to me that much of that which is handed around under the name of social science is an effort on the part of the scientist to rationalize his own preconceptions. They find usually, in my limited observation, what they go out to find."[32] Repeating arguments from the defendants' brief, he attacked the finding that northern students had found the white dolls preferable to black dolls more often than the southern students in segregated schools had. Davis went on to criticize other witnesses for lacking sufficient knowledge about the south and cited several authorities of his own who were more learned about the region and the desirability of segregated education. Davis even went so far as to quote NAACP co-founder W.E.B. Du Bois—largely out of context—as proposing that placing black children in safer, segregated environments was preferable to forcing them into unwelcome and hostile integrated environments.

Thurgood Marshall's rebuttal of these points focused on the fact that the defendants had not produced any expert witnesses of their own at trial and that there were no experts who could reasonably say that segregation did not cause any harms. In reply to a question from Justice Frankfurter on whether the plaintiffs would have had a different case if the opposing opinions of six professors had been introduced, Marshall stated: "You would, sir, but I do not believe that there are any experts in the country who would so testify. And the body of law is that—even the witnesses, for example, who testified in . . . the Virginia case, all of them, admitted that segregation in and of itself was harmful. . . . I know of no scientist that has made any study, whether he be anthropologist or sociologist, who does not admit that segregation harms the child."[33]

Justice Frankfurter made it clear during the *Brown* oral arguments that he was skeptical of social science evidence. In an exchange with Jack Greenberg, who was representing the plaintiffs in the Delaware case and arguing that the plaintiffs' expert witnesses had not been contradicted at the trial, Justice Frankfurter stated: "The mere fact that a man is not contradicted does not mean that what he says is so. . . . If a man says three yards, and I have measured it, and it is three yards, there it is. But if a man tells you the inside of your brain and mine, and how we function, that is not measurement, and there you are."[34] Frankfurter continued: "We are here in a domain which I do not yet regard as science in the sense of mathematical certainty. This is all opinion evidence. . . . I do not mean that I disrespect it. I simply know its character. It can be a very different thing from, as I say, things that are weighed and measured and are fungible. We are dealing here with very subtle things, very subtle testimony."[35]

Of course, neither the plaintiffs' attorneys nor any of their experts were arguing that social science could produce findings and conclusions with mathematical certainty; indeed, most scientific research findings can only be expressed in likelihoods and probabilities. Although he was correct to note that the social science evidence was of a different character than mathematical measurement of an object, Justice Frankfurter ultimately mischaracterized the legitimacy of social science as science. His expectations exceeded the explanatory potential of any social science evidence, favorable or unfavorable, that might have been introduced at trial.

## The *Brown* Opinion

On May 17, 1954, the Supreme Court issued its unanimous ruling in *Brown v. Board of Education* holding that segregated schools violated the equal protection clause of the Fourteenth Amendment. Intentionally worded to be understandable to the general public as well as to achieve unanimity within the Court itself, Chief Justice Earl Warren's opinion was unusually brief and devoid of extensive legal analysis and terminology. The opinion moved in three steps that led it to the conclusion that segregated schools were inherently unequal schools. First, the Court found that the legislative history of the Fourteenth Amendment, which the Court had asked the parties to flesh out in a second round of briefs and oral arguments, was inconclusive on the issue of school segregation. Moreover, at the time of the Fourteenth Amendment's passage, public education was in an immature and unsure stage of its development: "As a consequence, it is not surprising that there should be so little in the history of the Fourteenth Amendment relating to its intended effect on public education."[36] Thus, legislative history alone would not bind the Court or compel it to reach a certain conclusion.

Second, Chief Justice Warren argued that public education plays a central role in American life and must be examined in its present circumstances in order to determine if equal protection has been violated. The clock could not be turned back to 1868, when the Fourteenth Amendment was adopted, or even to 1896 with the issuance of *Plessy v. Ferguson*: "We must consider public education in the light of its full development and its present place in American life throughout the Nation."[37] Public education, the Court made clear, "is perhaps the most important function of state and local governments. . . . In these days, it is doubtful that any child may be reasonably expected to succeed in life if he is denied the opportunity of an education."[38] In this way, the Court set the stage for a conclusion that could avoid any direct conflicts with either the Fourteenth Amendment or *Plessy v. Ferguson*.

Finally, the Court addressed the basic question before it: "Does segregation of children in public schools solely on the basis of race, even though the physical facilities and other 'tangible' factors may be equal, deprive the children of the minority group of equal educational opportunities? We believe that it does."[39] Chief Justice Warren's opinion then mirrored the language of the expert witnesses on the harms of segregation: "To separate them from others of similar age and qualifications solely because of their race generates a feeling of inferiority as to their status in the community that may affect their hearts and minds in a way unlikely ever to be undone."[40]

The opinion went on to quote the finding of fact from the *Brown* trial court addressing the harms of segregation and then stated: "Whatever may have been the extent of psychological knowledge at the time of *Plessy v. Ferguson*, this finding is amply supported by modern authority." Footnote 11 of the opinion provided seven citations to support this proposition, most of which were contained in the "Social Science Statement" appended to the plaintiffs' brief:

> K. B. Clark, Effect of Prejudice and Discrimination on Personality Development (Midcentury White House Conference on Children and Youth, 1950); Witmer and Kotinsky, Personality in the Making (1952), c. VI; Deutscher and Chein, The Psychological Effects of Enforced Segregation: A Survey of Social Science Opinion, 26 J.Psychol. 259 (1948); Chein, What are the Psychological Effects of Segregation Under Conditions of Equal Facilities?, 3 Int. J. Opinion and Attitude Res. 229 (1949); Brameld, Educational Costs, in Discrimination and National Welfare (MacIver, ed., 1949), 44–48; Frazier, The Negro in the United States (1949), 674–681. And see generally Myrdal, An American Dilemma (1944).[41]

Ruling that "any language in *Plessy v. Ferguson* contrary to this finding is rejected," the Court then stated: "We conclude that in the field of public education the doctrine of 'separate but equal' has no place. Separate educational facilities are inherently unequal."[42] In grand, sweeping language that relied less on precedent or constitutional text than on present-day observations and factual assertions of social realities, the Supreme Court gave new meaning to racial equality under the Fourteenth Amendment.

As Richard Kluger suggests in *Simple Justice*, the inclusion of a footnote does not mean that the Court relied heavily on the social science to reach its final conclusion. If Chief Justice Warren had only been trying to undermine the *Plessy* Court's psychological assumption that any feelings of inferiority that blacks harbored because of segregation were self-generated, then his footnote succeeded. The studies, even if vulnerable to criticism, provided objective measurements of the subjective feelings of inferiority that were wrought by segregation. But was social science the basis for the Court's core holding? Perhaps in part, but the opinion does not elaborate on the social science; it merely cites it. And social science was not the only way to establish the factual predicate for the ruling. The Court's legal conclusion was based on the proposition that segregation causes a concrete harm: feelings of inferiority that affect a child's learning. Psychological findings simply confirmed what one might infer logically: if children are treated as inferior, then they will feel inferior. The social science citations were an openly visible part of the opinion, and they would thus become the target for the most commentary and the most criticism.

On the same day that it handed down the *Brown* decision, the Supreme Court issued a separate opinion in *Bolling v. Sharpe*, which struck down school segregation in the District of Columbia.[43] Because the text of the Fourteenth Amendment's equal protection clause only applies to state and local government and not to the federal government, the Court had to find a violation of the Fifth Amendment's due process clause in order to declare segregation in the District of Columbia to be unconstitutional. Chief Justice Warren concluded that the concepts of equal protection and due process were not mutually exclusive and that discrimination could be so unjustifiable that it violated due process.[44] Drawing on language from its opinion in *Korematsu v. United States*, the Court stated that "classifications based solely on race must be scrutinized with particular care, since they are contrary to our traditions and hence constitutionally suspect."[45] The Court then concluded that "segregation in public education is not reasonably related to any proper governmental objective, and thus it imposes on Negro children of the District of Columbia a burden that constitutes an arbitrary deprivation of their liberty in violation of the Due Process Clause."[46] In light of its decision in *Brown*, the Court noted that "it would be unthinkable that the same Constitution would impose a lesser duty on the Federal Government."[47]

## Critiques of *Brown*

As one would expect, the *Brown* and *Bolling v. Sharpe* decisions were greeted with resounding applause by opponents of segregation and with vehement scorn and resistance by proponents of Jim Crow. In Kluger's words, "the white-suprema-cists of the South were swift and shrill in their outcry." One critic proposed that the *Brown* decision had reduced the Constitution to a "mere scrap of paper," while another "called the decision 'the most serious blow that has yet been struck against the rights of the states in a matter vitally affecting their authority and welfare.'" A defiant leader stated that the south would "not abide by or obey this legislative decision by a political court" and that any effort to integrate the schools would lead to "great strife and turmoil."[48]

But even supporters of the decision were troubled by the Court's strong reliance on social science authorities. Writing the day after the decision, *New York Times* columnist James Reston stated: "Relying more on the social scientists than on legal precedents—a procedure often in controversy in the past—the Court insisted on equality of the mind and heart rather than on equal school facilities. . . . The Court's opinion read more like an expert paper on sociology than a Supreme Court opinion."[49] Law professor Alexander Bickel, who had clerked for Justice Frankfurter in the previous Supreme Court term, was critical of both the Clark doll tests and the inclusion of the social science simply through a footnote: "No matter how it had been done, no doubt, the enemies of the opinion were certain to seize upon it and proclaim the ruling unjudicial and illegal."[50] But Bickel also recognized the Court's need not to go too far in antago-nizing the many supporters of segregation, concluding that "Warren wanted to present as small a target as possible, and that was wise."[51]

Law review articles and commentaries that followed in the months after the *Brown* decision were just as critical of the footnote II citations, particularly the Clark doll studies. For instance, law professor Edmond Cahn attacked the methodological weaknesses and inferences of the doll experiments: "If Negro children say a *brown* doll is like themselves, [Clark] infers that segregation has made them conscious of race; yet if they say a *white* doll is like themselves, he infers that segregation has forced them to evade reality."[52] Thus, any result could have been interpreted to prove the hypothesis that segregation causes harm. Cahn also chastised the "Social Science Statement" appended to the plaintiffs' brief as "literary psychology," by which he meant "such psychological observations and insights as one finds continually in the work of poets, novel-ists, essayists, journalists, and religious prophets."[53] Expressing his concern that a change in scientific results could force a change in the constitutional meaning of equality, Cahn argued:

> Since the behavioral sciences are so very young, imprecise, and change-ful, their findings have an uncertain expectancy of life. Today's sanguine asseveration may be cancelled by tomorrow's new revelation—or new technical fad. . . . Today the social psychologists . . . are liberal and egali-tarian in [their] basic approach. Suppose a generation hence, some of

their successors were to revert to the ethnic mysticism of the very recent past; suppose they were to present us with a collection of racist notions and label them "science." What then would be the state of our constitutional rights?[54]

Although quick to dismiss social psychology—which he characterized as limited by a "recurrent lack of agreement on substantive premises" and a "recurrent lack of extrinsic, empirical means for checking and verifying inferred results"—Professor Cahn raised an important question about linking constitutional principles, which ideally should have an enduring life span, to scientific research, which by its very nature is prone to being revised by new data and findings.[55] Even without questioning the scientific studies themselves, one could criticize the Supreme Court's reliance on them. By placing even a small amount of weight on social science studies, the Court opened itself up to the charge that it went beyond its own judicial expertise and consequently could have misinterpreted or misapplied the social science evidence. More dangerously, the Court left a constitutional ruling in the precarious position of being toppled because new social science findings might undermine the base of social science findings on which the ruling had first been constructed.

The counterargument to Cahn's critique is that examining scientific evidence is only one method by which courts gather facts about the world, and there is nothing inherently wrong with a court changing the law because the world has significantly changed since a previous decision. Adapting to change is desirable, especially if one sees the Constitution as an evolving document designed to address the needs of a changing society. It may be unwise for a court to act as if it were a nine-member legislature and tweak the law every few years as new social data are presented, but there is no reason for the courts to ignore social realities that can be illuminated through valid and reliable scientific authorities. Social facts are only one part of a process of constitutional interpretation that also includes the analysis of text and precedents; turning to social science research is just one way of obtaining those facts. As Paul L. Rosen has observed, the Supreme Court "interprets the Constitution differently not only because society changes but also because its understanding of society changes in light of new knowledge. In other words, fact situations and the way in which the Court understands them lend color to the meaning of the Constitution."[56]

## Brown v. Board of Education II

What the Supreme Court avoided in its 1954 rulings in Brown and Bolling v. Sharpe was crafting a remedy to desegregate the schools. Concluding that the complexity of designing appropriate relief for segregation required more information and more deliberation, the Court postponed any decision until after the parties could again reargue the remedial questions. Reflecting the justices' concern that southern resistance could lead to violence if desegregation were implemented too quickly, the Court bought itself another year before it had to force a remedy on the south. Social science was again invoked in the briefs and rearguments (on both sides, since the southern interests had learned their lessons from the first ruling), but the impact of science was far less obvious than in the first *Brown* opinion.

The 1952 "Social Science Statement" had already cited several references to studies showing that integration could occur without major disruption if the courts quickly and firmly implemented desegregation orders. In addition, Clark had compiled a wide range of studies and commentaries on integration efforts and published a paper entitled "Desegregation: An Appraisal of the Evidence" in the *Journal of Social Issues*, which the plaintiffs' cited extensively in their brief. The plaintiffs also relied on Harry S. Ashmore's book *The Negro and the Schools*, which was published during the same month as the first *Brown* decision. Although Ashmore, an editor at the *Arkansas Gazette*, carried the byline, the book was a combined effort of more than forty scholars and commentators funded by the Ford Foundation. Supporting the plaintiffs' arguments that desegregation could and should move forward expeditiously, the Ashmore book found that it was frequently the case that "those who have had experience with integration—professional educators and laymen alike—have steeled themselves for a far more severe public reaction than they actually encountered."[57] Moreover, many school officials found gradualism to be far from ideal: "A markedly gradual program, . . . particularly one which involves the continued maintenance of some separate schools, invites opposition and allows time for it to be organized."[58]

Ironically, however, the Ashmore book was also extensively cited by the segregating states that had been invited by the Court to participate as amici curiae in the rearguments. One of the book's findings was that "community attitudes" were the most important factor in integrating school systems, based on experience outside of the south: "separate schools can be merged only with great difficulty, if at all, when a great majority of the citizens who support them are actively opposed to the move."[59] This conclusion was an invitation for southern gradualists to argue that desegregation needed to move slowly in order to accommodate the deeply held community attitudes that were resistant to change.

A basic question for the Supreme Court came down to whether community attitudes had to evolve before implementing desegregation or whether clear and expeditious desegregation efforts were needed to shift those attitudes. During the oral arguments in 1954, an exchange between Justice Frankfurter and S. Emory Rogers, the attorney for Clarendon County, crystallized the issue:

MR. JUSTICE FRANKFURTER: Would it not be fair to say that attitudes in this world are not changed abstractly, as it were, by reading something—that attitudes are partly the result of working, attitudes are partly the result of action?

MR. ROGERS: I think so.

MR. JUSTICE FRANKFURTER: Would that be a fair statement?

MR. ROGERS: Yes, sir, I think so. Our sociologists have had a very difficult time in saying what attitude comes from or how it can be changed. But it does have to be in the society as it works.

MR. JUSTICE FRANKFURTER: But you do not fold your hands and wait for an attitude to change by itself?

MR. ROGERS: No, sir. You cannot. That has not been done here. That is not being done in this district. We have made progress and greater progress will still be made, I am sure. But to simply say you have to change your attitude is not going to change it.[60]

Soon after the one-year anniversary of the first *Brown* opinion, the Court issued its second *Brown* opinion. Chief Justice Warren's opinion did not contain any citations to social science, nor did it contain a specific remedy to implement desegregation. Rather than create a single remedy, the Court punted the creation of remedies to the lower courts, which had the ability to engage in more localized fact finding. The Supreme Court openly recognized the need to reconcile the different interests involved: the students' interest in gaining access to nonsegregated schools as soon as possible as well as the public interest in moving at the appropriate pace to avoid disruption or violence. The result was language from the Court that provided guidelines for the lower courts to follow in implementing desegregation, such as considering a school's physical plant, the transportation system, personnel, school district lines and attendance zones, and local laws and regulations. But the Court imposed no deadline, nor even a general timeline, to implement desegregation. The district courts were authorized to "enter such orders and decrees . . . as are necessary and proper to admit to public schools on a racially nondiscriminatory basis with all deliberate speed the parties to these cases."[61] The phrase "with all deliberate speed," an oxymoron of sorts because deliberation is not typically speedy, proved to be a license for state and local officials to drag their feet or be openly obstructionist in desegregating the schools.

Whether the social science evidence actually influenced the Supreme Court in *Brown* II is difficult to divine. Since Chief Justice Warren cited no scientific evidence, the opinion itself provides no obvious clues, although one can speculate that the defendants' community attitudes evidence might have been more influential than the plaintiffs' evidence since the Court entered such an open-ended order. On the other hand, Kluger's description of the behind-the-scenes workings of the Court suggests that Chief Justice Warren did not want to mention psychological or sociological attitudes as part of the criteria that the lower courts should consider in formulating desegregation orders, which may have meant that Warren did not give much credence to the defendants' scientific evidence supporting gradualism.[62] In any case, science was certainly not needed to show that southern resistance would be a problem. The community attitudes that the defendants' had identified as entrenched were indeed very deeply entrenched, and massive resistance and violence were widespread throughout the southern states. In many areas, it would take years before school desegregation was achieved.

## Jim Crow's Collapse

*Brown v. Board of Education* dealt specifically with public education, and it was only one of the columns to fall in the lengthy but inevitable collapse of Jim Crow segregation. Laws requiring segregated public facilities and transportation eventually toppled as well. But the end of Jim Crow was not immediate, and court cases—as well as collective action engendered through the civil rights movement—were still necessary to ensure that state and local governments actually desegregated their public facilities. Social science played a more limited role in the expansion of the desegregation mandate after *Brown*, with the federal courts reasoning by analogy that if separate-but-equal was impermissible in public education, it was also impermissible when it came to beaches, parks, municipal golf courses, buses, restaurants, and courtrooms.

Which is not to say that state and local governments did not oppose desegregation or try to make the social science underpinnings of *Brown* an issue. In *New Orleans City Park Improvement Association v. Detiege*, for instance, the defendants argued that the trial court should have heard evidence to determine whether psychological harms were a significant problem in denying nonsegregated access to a city park, thus implying that plaintiffs would have to prove psychological harm in every area of life outside of public education. A federal appeals court flatly rejected this line of argument because of *Brown* itself and because of the Supreme Court cases decided soon after *Brown* that struck down segregation in the use of public beaches and golf courses.[63]

The Court did not elaborate on its reasons for striking down segregation in all of the areas outside of public education. In a set of decisions during the 1950s and 1960s, it issued a string of *per curiam* opinions (opinions on behalf of the full Supreme Court without a signed author) that were basic, one-page orders affirming the lower courts or, on rare occasions, reversing the lower court with specific orders to implement desegregation.[64] Scientific studies of psychological harms or adverse social effects were neither cited nor required by the Supreme Court or the lower appeals courts, which suggests either that the courts assumed that the psychological harms of segregation outside of education paralleled the harms of segregated education or, more simply, that the courts analogized the new settings to public education and decoupled the Supreme Court's underlying reliance on psychological injury in *Brown*. The social *meaning* of *Brown* was thus far more important than the social *science*.

Nevertheless, one of the concerns that commentators had raised about the social science predicates used to support the ruling in *Brown* actually came to fruition in a desegregation case in the early 1960s. In *Stell v. Savannah-Chatman County Board of Education*, a federal district court in Georgia denied the plaintiffs' request for an injunction that would have stopped the Savannah-Chatman schools from operating a segregated system because recently developed evidence presented in the case showed that segregation did not, contrary to the findings in *Brown*, cause harm to the minority students. Indeed, Judge Frank Scarlett found that integration actually caused more harm than good. Included in his findings of fact were the following:

SEGREGATION INJURY

18. Plaintiffs' assumption of injury to Negro students by the continuance of segregated schools is not supported by any evidence in this case. Whatever psychological injury may be sustained by a Negro child out of his sense of rejection by white children is increased rather than abated by forced intermixture, and this increase is in direct proportion to the number and extent of his contacts with white children.

19. Each study presented to the Court, confirmed by the opinions of the witnesses showed that the damaging assumptions of inferiority increase whenever the child is brought into forced association with white children. The principal author of the studies relied on by the Supreme Court in the *Brown* case came to the conclusion that compulsory intermixture rather than racial separation in school was the principal source of the damaging loss of race identification.[65]

The defendants in *Stell* offered several expert witnesses, all of whom the plaintiffs' conceded were authorities in their fields. Among them were Henry Garrett of Columbia University, R. T. Osbourne of the University of Georgia, Ernest van den Haag of New York University, and Clairette Garrett, a clinical psychologist from New York. Judge Scarlett even went so far as to rely on Kenneth Clark's work, in particular Clark's finding in his doll studies that southern children in segregated environments appeared to have fewer negative identifications than did northern children in integrated environments.

The plaintiffs in *Stell* objected generally to the defendants' expert witnesses: "The law is settled by the Supreme Court in the *Brown* case that segregation itself injures negro children in the school system. That is what the Supreme

Court's decision is all about, so we do not have to prove that."[66] But Judge Scarlett rejected this reasoning: "These are facts, not law. To make these findings the Kansas District Judge [in *Brown*] considered evidence—not cases."[67] The sense of inferiority and its effects on learning were "as much a subject for scientific inquiry as the braking distance required to stop a two-ton truck moving at ten miles an hour on concrete."[68] Consequently, Judge Scarlett ruled that the factual evidence in *Stell* led to the conclusion that the segregated schools in Savannah-Chatman County did not violate the plaintiffs' equal protection rights.

On appeal, the U.S. Court of Appeals for the Fifth Circuit unambiguously rejected Judge Scarlett's reasoning as a contravention of precedent, stating that "the District Court was bound by the decision of the Supreme Court in *Brown*. We reiterate that no inferior federal court may refrain from acting as required by that decision even if such a court should conclude that the Supreme Court erred either as to its facts or as to the law."[69] The appeals court continued: "We do not read the major premise of the decision of the Supreme Court in the first *Brown* case as being limited to the facts of the cases there presented. We read it as proscribing segregation in the public education process on the stated ground that separate but equal schools for the races were inherently unequal."[70] The Fifth Circuit thus recognized that the Supreme Court had articulated an enduring constitutional principle that was grounded in factual assertions about the general harms of segregation and was not dependent on the specific facts of *Brown* or its companion cases. The trial court had erred in treating the scientific evidence simply as adjudicative facts that could lead it to a particular decision in relation to the immediate parties, as opposed to legislative facts that could change the law. Because of precedent and the hierarchy binding the lower courts, the trial court was in no position to second-guess the Supreme Court's legislative fact finding in *Brown*. The Court declined to take the appeal of the *Stell* case and left the Fifth Circuit's ruling intact.

Notwithstanding the appellate court's rejection of the trial judge's analysis in *Stell*, the case illustrates the potential instability of a constitutional ruling that is at least partly based on social science findings that are subject to updating or repudiation in the future. In the proper venue, namely in the Supreme Court itself, and perhaps with the passage of enough time, the same evidence that had been introduced at trial in *Stell* could have been used to argue that *Brown* should be modified or reversed. In the same way that the *Brown* Court rejected *Plessy*'s factual assumptions and accepted modern psychological authority, there might be substantial evidence to assert that present conditions differ substantially from the time of *Brown* and that contemporaneous science supports a different outcome. A scenario such as this may seem highly implausible, particularly when egalitarian values have become so rooted in constitutional interpretation; but resting the law on potentially unstable predicates leaves open the possibility. The courts do not readily overrule well-established precedents, but on occasion they do. *Brown* itself is an example of a case in which facts were used to change the law.

## Anti-Miscegenation Laws and *Loving v. Virginia*

The abolition of one of Jim Crow's last remnants—anti-miscegenation laws prohibiting interracial marriages with whites—demonstrates the lasting impact of *Brown v. Board of Education*, not only on the substantive law of equal protection but also on the role of science in civil rights litigation. In its 1967 decision in *Loving v. Virginia*, the Supreme Court struck down Virginia's anti-miscegenation law, which, among other things, made it a felony punishable up to five years in prison for a white person to marry a non-white person, even if the couple had left Virginia to marry out of state and later returned to Virginia. Richard Loving, who was white, and Mildred Jeter, who was black and Native American, had left Virginia in 1958 to marry in Washington, D.C.; but after returning to the state, they were arrested, convicted, and sentenced to one year in jail in violation of the law. The judge suspended the jail sentence for twenty-five years on the condition that the couple leave Virginia and not return together for twenty-five years. The U.S. Supreme Court ruled unanimously that the anti-miscegenation law violated both the equal protection clause and the due process clause of the Fourteenth Amendment.

Chief Justice Earl Warren's opinion in *Loving* stated emphatically that "there is patently no legitimate overriding purpose independent of invidious racial discrimination which justifies this classification. The fact that Virginia prohibits only interracial marriages involving white persons demonstrates that the racial classifications must stand on their own justification, as measures designed to maintain White Supremacy."[71] In so ruling, the Court rejected the state's argument that "the scientific evidence is substantially in doubt and, consequently, [the Supreme] Court should defer to the wisdom of the state legislature in adopting its policy of discouraging interracial marriages."[72]

The Court did not cite scientific evidence in its opinion, but science was a major element of the dispute between the parties: in essence, contemporary science was pitted against the scientific racism that had justified anti-miscegenation laws for more than two centuries in the United States. Equal protection guarantees and state power were clearly at the center of the legal controversy, but competing scientific views of miscegenation were interspersed throughout the written briefs and the oral arguments. All of the briefs for the parties and for the amici curiae on both sides, except for the state of North Carolina's, contained scientific references to racial intermarriage. Even the amicus brief filed on behalf of several Roman Catholic bishops, which was composed primarily of statements of theological opposition to anti-miscegenation laws, contained citations to anthropological literature supporting racial intermarriage.[73] A recent statement by the United Nations Educational, Scientific and Cultural Organization (UNESCO) on the biological aspects of race, signed by several leading anthropologists, was also a key point of contention in the briefs; one of the justices quoted the UNESCO statement at length during the oral arguments: "The biological data . . . stand in open contradiction to the tenets of racism. Racist theories can in no way pretend to have any scientific foundation, and the anthropologists should endeavor to prevent the results of their researches from being used in such a biased way that would serve unscientific ends."[74]

Because the weight of scientific authority no longer considered racial intermarriage to be harmful for biological reasons, the state's argument focused on the social harms of intermarriage, including the psychological instability of individuals who entered into mixed marriages, high divorce rates, and the stigma suffered by interracial children. During oral arguments, R. D. McIlwaine defended Virginia by quoting a textbook by social anthropologist Albert Gordon: "It is my conviction that intermarriage is definitely inadvisable; that they are wrong because they are most frequently, if not solely, entered into under present-day circumstances by people who have a rebellious attitude toward society, self-hatred, neurotic tendencies, immaturity, and other detrimental psychological factors."[75] But Chief Justice Warren was clearly skeptical of any argument that relied on science to justify white supremacy, asking pointedly during oral arguments: "Didn't we, in the segregation cases, have also argued to us what was supposed to be 'scientific evidence' to the effect that the whites would be injured by having to go to school with the Negroes?"[76]

Rather than rely on scientific evidence, the North Carolina amicus curiae brief focused on law and history and, in a section titled "The So-Called Scientific Argument," offered commentary that was explicitly anti-science:

> We do not enter into the scientific realm on this question. There is no equalitarianism in the field of biology, anthropology and geneticism. There is no certitude or concrete exactness in this field. These so-called sciences have not yet reached the position or status of the exact sciences one hundred and fifty years ago. Usually the major emphasis in such books or discussions centers around the alleged sex jealousies of the white man and the alleged preference of the Negro man for white women. You can select books and treatises both pro and con on this question; one thing is sure and that is neither cranial measurements, intelligence quotients nor statistical averages will ever settle the question. This field is like expert witnesses in that you pay your money and take your choice.[77]

The attack on science itself no doubt reflected the marginalization by the 1960s of scientific racism that had supported anti-miscegenation laws for so long.

In the end, the Supreme Court found it unnecessary to delve into any lingering debates over the scientific justifications for anti-miscegenation laws. As it made clear in the *Loving* opinion, "Marriage is one of the 'basic civil rights of man,' fundamental to our very existence and survival. To deny this fundamental freedom on so unsupportable a basis as the racial classifications embodied in these statutes, classifications so directly subversive of the principle of equality at the heart of the Fourteenth Amendment, is surely to deprive all the State's citizens of liberty without due process of law."[78] Still, the role of science, made so explicit in *Brown*, had not been not lost upon the parties or their amici curiae. They could not risk excluding science from their legal arguments, even if, in its final analysis, the Court decided not to incorporate scientific evidence into its opinion.

## Beyond *Brown*

How much social science actually mattered in the Court's decision making in *Brown v. Board of Education* is still an ongoing debate. Writing in 1998, Scott Brewer observed that "*Brown* served as a remarkable culmination of the legal realist project of taming abstract legal propositions with the whip of social science—a process that began in the modern Supreme Court with the Court's acceptance of the 'Brandeis brief' in *Muller v. Oregon*."[79] Others have proposed that the Court was not particularly strategic about its use of scientific evidence and may have employed the social science studies simply because they were authoritative and intellectually fashionable at the time. For instance, Sanjay Mody wrote in 2002 that "the rise of social science as an accepted discipline of knowledge was a background condition that formed part of the Warren Court's perception of the world. The members of the *Brown* Court, from this perspective, were themselves seduced by the exalted claims of social science in the middle of the twentieth century. Footnote eleven was a consequence of ordinary human intuition, not grand strategy."[80] The conundrum may never be fully resolved, even with remarks from Chief Justice Warren himself, commenting that footnote 11 was "only a note."

Similarly, it is important to remember that, despite its power and mystique, the Supreme Court is still just a court. Even though members of that court rely on their own knowledge, values, and understanding of the law and the world, they still depend heavily on what is presented to them by the parties in order to make decisions. It was not the Court's idea to incorporate social science into the trial records in the desegregation cases; the lawyers for the plaintiffs chose to introduce scientific evidence in the litigation because it helped their case. Even then, it was a calculated risk. The acceptance of the evidence by the trial courts was decidedly mixed: the *Brown* trial court made a critical finding of fact about the harms of segregation that the Supreme Court quoted in its 1954 opinion, while the *Davis* and *Briggs* courts found the evidence to be inconclusive or ignorable. Might the Supreme Court have cited social science findings on its own initiative? Possibly, but other than Gunnar Myrdal's *An American Dilemma*, none of the studies in footnote 11 was particularly prominent outside of academic and research circles, and much of the research literature might have escaped the Court's review.

If the social science findings had been unsupportive of desegregation or highly ambiguous (and the research was certainly not invulnerable to attack, as the critics of the Clark doll studies demonstrated), the fight to end segregation might have been less potent, but it would not have been robbed of its moral force. The litigation would no doubt have gone forward without the scientific evidence. To say that black children in segregated schools were treated as inferior and less-than-equal citizens did not require a series of studies or expert witnesses. The final outcome in the Supreme Court might have been exactly the same, just without a quoted finding of fact from the *Brown* lower court or a footnote 11.

The Supreme Court had other ways of reaching the conclusion that educational segregation was unconstitutional. In *Brown*, it blithely dismissed the history of the Fourteenth Amendment as inconclusive on the question of public school segregation; but there was sufficient history for the Court to argue that the underlying purpose of the Fourteenth Amendment, like the Thirteenth and Fifteenth Amendments, was to guarantee equal citizenship to blacks and to eliminate state-enforced discrimination against them. The Supreme Court could easily have turned to cases decided soon after the ratification of the Fourteenth Amendment, such as *Strauder v. West Virginia*, where the Court struck down a statute that excluded blacks from jury service and concluded that the spirit and meaning of the Fourteenth Amendment barred state-sanctioned discrimination: "The words of the amendment . . . contain a necessary implication of a positive immunity, or right, most valuable to the colored race,—the right to exemption from unfriendly legislation against them distinctively as colored,— exemption from legal discriminations, implying inferiority in civil society, lessening the security of their enjoyment of the rights which others enjoy, and discriminations which are steps towards reducing them to the condition of a subject race."[81] If the *Brown* Court had articulated an anti-subordination theory of equal protection—an approach that was clearly evident in *Loving v. Virginia*, where the Court declared anti-miscegenation laws to be vehicles of white supremacy—the Court could have argued that segregated schools were inherently unequal because they imposed the stigma of inferiority on blacks, with no purpose other than signaling and maintaining white domination. Psychological harms, whether or not documented by scientific evidence, were merely symptomatic of the fundamental injury of being treated as inferior. The underlying social science findings of *Brown* were thus not as critical as the underlying values of equal protection: segregation was wrong in 1896 under *Plessy*, and it was still wrong in 1954.

The Court also had recent precedents from the 1940s and 1950s that allowed it to employ a strict scrutiny standard in *Brown*. The Court noted the World War II *Hirabayashi* and *Korematsu* cases in its opinion in *Bolling v. Sharpe*, which recognized the invidiousness of racial classifications and the need to treat legislation based on race as highly suspect. Relying on the language of strict scrutiny is exactly what the Court has done in developing its current tests to evaluate the constitutionality of race-conscious policies under the equal protection clause, but it took time for the Court to fully articulate its standards. Yet the Court already had the basic tools in 1953 and 1954 to employ strict scrutiny, an analysis that could have struck down segregation as failing to advance a compelling enough interest to justify racially separate schools.

In any case, speculating about what might have been does not help the enterprise of understanding *Brown*'s impact on the later use of social science in the courts. The courts' subsequent uses of social science are far from consistent, and the controversy generated by *Brown* and footnote 11 may actually have led some courts to be more circumspect about their use of scientific evidence to shape constitutional law. Perhaps the most important effects of *Brown* have not been on the courts but on legal advocacy and the scientific research that can support such advocacy. The attorneys at the NAACP Legal Defense and Educational Fund made scientific evidence a central part of their arguments in the desegregation cases, and in doing so they raised the bar for advocates seeking to influence the courts' development of constitutional law. Even within the *Brown* litigation itself, the defendants quickly learned that social science evidence could not go unanswered. When it came time to stand up for segregated schools in the *Stell v. Savannah-Chatman County Board of Education* case in the early 1960s, defendants were quite ready to employ their own battery of scientific studies and expert witnesses to defend their positions. Because of *Brown*, social scientists also have become well aware of the role their research might play in influencing court decisions and government policymaking in general. Almost every major civil rights case after *Brown* has scientific authorities appearing somewhere—in the trial record, in the parties' briefs, in amicus briefs, or in the court opinions themselves. The use of science in one form or another is nearly inescapable in contemporary civil rights litigation.

A concluding point: the science and law of *Brown* cannot be isolated from the ideological influences that characterized the Court's uses of scientific evidence (or common knowledge grounded in science) in earlier rulings such as *Plessy v. Ferguson* and *Ozawa v. United States*. The Supreme Court of the early 1950s, itself an all-white and all-male institution, both transformed and was transformed by evolving ideals regarding race and equality. Racial attitudes across the country had been shifting dramatically in the 1940s and 1950s; and lawyers, social scientists, and members of the Supreme Court were among those affected by such changes in attitudes. President Truman had ordered the desegregation of the armed forces six years before *Brown* and had made civil rights laws a key part of his legislative agenda; professional sports had begun its own headline-generating desegregation process with major league baseball's hiring of Jackie Robinson in 1947. Scientists such as Kenneth Clark and Isidor Chein were no less scientific for studying what they studied, but their research subjects and techniques reflected both their egalitarian values and the methodologies of a particular era. With advances in methods and technologies, contemporaneous science might be considered more "scientific" than the science of previous generations, but it can never be divorced from the time and the society in which it is produced.

# 4

# Science and
# Equal Protection

On May 3, 1954, two weeks before issuing its ruling in *Brown v. Board of Education*, the Supreme Court handed down its decision in *Hernandez v. Texas*, a case in which a Mexican American criminal defendant had challenged the systematic exclusion of Mexican Americans from serving on juries. The evidence revealed that, over a span of twenty-five years, none of the more than 6,000 individuals who had served as jurors in Jackson County, Texas, had ever been of Mexican descent. The state acknowledged the extreme statistical disparity but argued that no discrimination had occurred because Mexican Americans were classified as white. Because Hernandez was white and all of the jurors who indicted him were white, even if none happened to be Mexican American, the state argued that there was no constitutional violation. The Supreme Court disagreed. Writing for a unanimous Court, Chief Justice Warren stated:

> Throughout our history differences in race and color have defined easily identifiable groups which have at times required the aid of the courts in securing equal treatment under the laws. But community prejudices are not static, and from time to time other differences from the community norm may define other groups which need the same protection.... The Fourteenth Amendment is not directed solely against discrimination due to a "two-class theory"—that is, based upon differences between "white" and Negro.[1]

Since the 1950s, the Supreme Court has established an expansive equal protection jurisprudence, extending the law's reach to include special safeguards in cases involving not only racial classifications but also those based on national origin, gender, citizenship status, and legitimacy (affecting nonmarital children) and those implicating fundamental rights such as the right to vote or to travel between states. In recent years, the Court has also tackled difficult questions involving race-based affirmative action designed to benefit racial minorities as well as questions of discrimination involving sexual orientation. Much of this jurisprudence has been shaped by the Court's reliance on social facts, often obtained through scientific evidence introduced by the parties, through amicus curiae briefs summarizing empirical findings, and through the Court's own research. The Court has never articulated a clear theory of constitutional fact finding—the species of legislative fact finding that focuses on constitutional interpretation—to guide its use of science in developing constitutional principles; thus, its citation of scientific evidence is far from consistent. But the salience of scientific evidence in many leading equal protection cases is undeniable.

Both this chapter and chapter 5 explore the use of scientific evidence in the development of contemporary equal protection jurisprudence. I begin by examining the courts' general approaches to constitutional interpretation and the multi-tiered framework that the courts apply to governmental policies that implicate the Fourteenth Amendment's equal protection clause. In addition to the "strict scrutiny" standards applied to classifications based on race and national origin, the Supreme Court has established varying standards of scrutiny for classifications based on citizenship, gender, sexual orientation, and other categories. Scientific evidence has played roles in both developing the standards of review employed by the courts and ruling on the constitutionality of specific public policies. Epistemic questions—does, for example, scientific evidence provide the best avenue for judges to gain knowledge of the facts needed to interpret the constitution?—as well as issues of gatekeeping to regulate the admission of scientific evidence raise important concerns in constitutional interpretation, but a more detailed discussion of these problems is postponed until chapter 6. The focus of this chapter is on the courts' use of scientific evidence to develop constitutional standards rather than the underlying legitimacy of that evidence.

## Fact Finding and Constitutional Interpretation

A leading criticism of the *Brown v. Board of Education* opinion is that, by citing the conclusions of social science research, the Supreme Court loosened the law of equal protection from its moorings in traditional constitutional interpretation, which typically relies on adhering to constitutional text, examining the framers' original intent, deferring to earlier court precedents, analyzing a case through the lens of a constitutional theory, incorporating moral and policy values into opinions and judgments, or combining two or more of these interpretive techniques.[2] But science-based fact finding, like any fact finding, cannot be divorced altogether from the traditional tools of constitutional analysis. Facts provide context; facts determine the applicability of prior precedents; facts inform constitutional theories and value judgments. And scientific evidence often informs the core of judicial fact finding. There is no unanimity on the ideal tools to employ in constitutional interpretation; thus, fact finding is not necessarily any more or less legitimate than any of the other interpretive techniques that the courts employ.

### Constitutional Text

Fact finding is perhaps least significant in purely textual analyses of the Constitution and in examinations of the framers' original intent. Arguments from text are accepted as the most fundamental basis for informing judicial review, but much of the Constitution is written in general, sometimes vague language that does not provide ready guidance for the courts. Language in Article II requiring that the president of the United States be at least thirty-five years old and a native-born citizen provides ample specificity to limit who may run for the presidency, but the meaning of equal protection under the Fourteenth Amendment—"No State shall . . . deny to any person within its jurisdiction the equal protection of the laws"—cannot be explicated simply by reference to the text alone. Language may establish the basic parameters of constitutional interpretation (equal protection requires some exegesis of the meaning of *equality*), and constitutional text may specify the boundaries of what is *not* to be addressed in interpretive exercises: explications of the Fifteenth Amendment, for example, are limited to cases involving denials of voting rights based on race or color, not those based on age or gender. But interpretations of most constitutional passages rarely yield unique or conclusive results, and text by itself can provide only the starting point for most exercises in constitutional interpretation.

### Original Intent

Turning to the framers' "original intent" or "original understanding" provides a broader basis for comprehending the meaning of constitutional language. For instance, a general intention of the framers of the Fourteenth Amendment was to establish a legal regime applicable to state government in which whites and blacks received equal protection of the laws. But originalism has inherent limitations and may yield inconclusive results because of a scant or nonexistent legislative history that cannot identify the specific intentions of the framers. As Chief Justice Warren argued in *Brown*, for example, public education most likely was not on the minds of the framers of the Fourteenth Amendment; legislative history by itself provided insufficient guidance to inform the Court's judgment on the constitutionality of segregated schools.

Moreover, strict adherence to original intent can often lead to conservative, even reactionary conclusions because the courts must attempt to read the minds of framers who wrote many decades ago and most likely did not anticipate the contemporary problems and moral dilemmas that the courts must now address. Asking judges to divine the intentions of individuals who lived in 1787, when the original Constitution was adopted by convention, or in the late 1860s, when the Fourteenth Amendment was proposed and ratified, can produce outcomes rooted in values that may be greatly out of step with contemporary values. For example, since the 1970s, the Supreme Court has recognized that gender, like race, is a basis for heightened scrutiny of legislation reviewed under the equal protection clause, reflecting the changing attitudes and values regarding discrimination against women. Yet a strictly originalist interpretation of equal protection would find little or no support among the framers of the Fourteenth Amendment for addressing gender inequalities or for addressing other forms of inequality besides inequality based on race or color.

*Precedent*

Precedents offer the courts additional bases to resolve constitutional questions, and facts can be especially important in the process that courts employ when applying the facts and law of prior cases to current ones. With the hierarchy of federal courts, lower courts are bound by the precedents of higher courts when applying existing law to cases involving fact situations that are similar or analogous to the facts of prior cases. The Supreme Court, however, is not necessarily bound by its own prior decisions, even though in practice it typically relies on earlier cases for guidance and is reluctant to revise or overrule decisions without strong justification.

Fact finding can greatly affect the application of precedent because courts must draw parallels and analogies between the operative facts of a case and the facts of prior cases in order to apply an existing precedent; thus, adjudicative fact finding can lead a court to apply a prior decision with similar facts or to ignore a prior decision that is deemed too dissimilar. And if the evidence in a case engenders an entirely novel set of facts, the court may decide not to apply precedent at all. Moreover, assuming that some of the operative facts in a case trigger the application of precedent, additional facts may lead the court to reevaluate the predicates upon which the precedent was first established. The Supreme Court's *Brown* decision relied on a core set of facts—state-sanctioned segregation on the basis of race—that triggered the applicability of precedents such as *Plessy v. Ferguson* and *Gong Lum v. Rice*. But additional fact finding on the harmful effects of segregation led, ostensibly, to the Court's decision to repudiate its earlier rulings upholding racial segregation under the equal protection clause.

The overruling of prior cases, especially after the Court changes its membership and attitudes and values have time to evolve, occurs with some frequency; and fact finding is often critical to the establishment of new case law. For instance, the Court ruled in 2003 in *Lawrence v. Texas* that same-sex sodomy laws violated the due process clause of the Fourteenth Amendment and overturned its ruling of seventeen years earlier in *Bowers v. Hardwick* upholding the same types of laws as constitutional. Determining that the *Bowers* Court had overrelied on the historical treatment of homosexual conduct and had not taken into sufficient account the changing values toward the criminalization of many same-sex activities, the Court stated that "*Bowers* was not correct when it was decided, and it is not correct today. It ought not to remain binding precedent. *Bowers v. Hardwick* should be and now is overruled."[3] Similarly, the Supreme Court ruled in 2005 in *Roper v. Simmons* that the Eighth Amendment's ban on cruel and unusual punishment categorically prohibits capital punishment for crimes committed before the age of eighteen, effectively overturning its ruling sixteen years earlier that allowed the execution of individuals who committed crimes at the age of sixteen or seventeen.[4] In ruling that the juvenile death penalty did not reflect evolving standards of decency under the Eighth Amendment, the Court relied on the increasing disuse of the juvenile death penalty both in the United States and internationally as well as on scientific studies confirming that juveniles should not be classified among the worst offenders in the criminal justice system because "a lack of maturity and an underdeveloped sense of responsibility" among juveniles can "result in impetuous and ill-considered actions and decisions." Studies further confirmed that juveniles are not among the worst offenders because they are particularly prone to outside influences, including peer pressure, and because character traits are not as well formed in juveniles as in adults.[5]

*Constitutional Theory*

Fact finding can also strongly influence the development and application of a normative constitutional theory in a search for constitutional meaning. Constitutional theories can be both general, suggesting an overarching framework of constitutional interpretation and problem solving, and specific, suggesting more detailed analyses under a particular section or clause of the Constitution. An example of a more general constitutional theory is John Hart Ely's theory of judicial review developed in his work *Democracy and Distrust*, in which he proposes that, because the Constitution at its heart creates majoritarian political institutions, judicial review should be rooted in processes that correct the failings of majoritarian democracy.[6] Judicial solicitude for racial minorities via strict scrutiny of legislation under the equal protection clause, for instance, serves as a corrective measure for the historical deprivation and relative powerlessness of racially subordinated groups in the normal political process.

An example of a more specific constitutional theory is Kenneth L. Karst's theory of equal citizenship under the Fourteenth Amendment. According to Karst, "the principle of equal citizenship presumptively insists that the organized society treat each individual as a person, one who is worthy of respect, one

who 'belongs.' Stated negatively, the principle presumptively forbids the organized society to treat an individual either as a member of an inferior or dependent caste or as a nonparticipant. Accordingly, the principle guards against
degradation or the imposition of stigma."[7] A theory of equal citizenship would
thus have presumed the unconstitutionality of educational segregation and
other manifestations of Jim Crow that prevailed in the south during the nineteenth and twentieth centuries.

Constitutional theory can also take the form of a model of interpretive
techniques that the courts employ across a wide range of cases. For example,
balancing theory, as T. Alexander Aleinikoff describes it, is used in a wide variety of cases in which the court "analyzes a constitutional question by identifying
interests implicated by the case and reaches a decision or constructs a rule of
constitutional law by explicitly or implicitly assigning values to the identified
interests."[8] Most procedural due process cases reflect an explicit balancing of
interests between the government's interests in effective and efficient administration and an individual's life, liberty, or property interests, along with an
evaluation of the methods, such as a predeprivation notice or hearing, implicated in the case. Balancing models also appear frequently in equal protection
cases, where, for example, the court may balance the burdens placed on individuals who are not the direct beneficiaries of an affirmative action policy
against an underlying interest in remedying past discrimination or promoting
diversity. Policies that impose an undue burden on non-beneficiaries may be
struck down because the burdens significantly outweigh the benefits of the
policy.

Fact finding can play a role in informing many constitutional theories. A
process-oriented theory, for example, may turn to empirical inquiries about
whether a group has suffered past deprivations and has had inadequate access
to majoritarian political processes. Historical information and contemporaneous data could inform a decision on whether a group characteristic should trigger heightened judicial review of legislation under the equal protection clause.
Similarly, fact finding might be used to determine how a particular policy creates benefits and burdens that are assigned and assessed in a balancing calculus. A court might weigh, for example, the benefits of an affirmative action
program in determining whether the state's interest is sufficiently compelling
to satisfy strict scrutiny under the equal protection clause; at the same time, a
court could also attempt to measure the burdens, such as stigma or deprivations of access, on third parties to determine whether a policy was necessary to
serve the compelling interest. Although scientific evidence would not necessarily add any more precision to a court's cost-benefit analysis (the weight assigned
to any given interest is ultimately controlled by normative valuations, not scientific ones), it would provide some factual basis (compared to judicial speculation) for informing a balancing equation.

But if a constitutional theory is absolutist or categorical, in contrast to a balancing approach, then fact finding may play little or no role in informing the theory. For instance, if one applies a color-blind theory of equal protection to a race-conscious affirmative action program designed to promote diversity in the workplace, then no amount of legislative fact finding, scientific or nonscientific, may be able to overcome the presumption that there are no interests—other than remedying specific acts of past discrimination, which even strict advocates of color-blindness recognize as legitimate—that may be sufficiently compelling to justify a race-conscious policy. Nor would any policy be narrowly tailored to serve a compelling interest because any effects on non-minorities would be presumed to be unduly burdensome and therefore unconstitutional.

*Values*

Implicit in many normative constitutional theories are moral and political values that guide judicial decision making. Indeed, many legal analysts and political scientists subscribe to the view that constitutional decision making is driven largely by the judges' individual values and attitudes.[9] The mythology of judicial craft suggests just the opposite—that judges are supposed to be impartial arbiters who turn to legal principles rather than personal values to yield decisions. The reality, of course, is that no judicial process is value-free, although some decisions are more strongly animated by the judges' underlying values than other decisions are. A Supreme Court case involving the constitutionality of an abortion regulation, a race-based affirmative action program, or the rights of gays and lesbians is guaranteed to generate more heat and value-driven decision making than is an important but less passion-stirring case involving a disputed section of the Internal Revenue Code or the meaning of a federal rule of evidence. When interpreting the equal protection clause, judges cannot avoid addressing questions about the meaning of constitutional equality; their personal value judgments about justice and equality inevitably color their analyses.

The divided votes, as well as the vitriolic dissenting opinions, that often arise in Supreme Court cases and other multi-member court rulings are clear signs of how judicial values play major roles in controversial cases. For example, in Justice Anthony Kennedy's majority opinion in *Lawrence v. Texas*, he stated that allowing *Bowers v. Hardwick* to continue as a precedent "demeans the lives of homosexual persons" and that "the stigma [imposed by a sodomy law] is not trivial."[10] Compare that language with Justice Antonin Scalia's dissenting opinion proposing that the *Lawrence* decision is the product of a Court "that has largely signed on to the so-called homosexual agenda, by which I mean the agenda promoted by some homosexual activists directed at eliminating the moral opprobrium that has traditionally attached to homosexual conduct."[11]

Values are often deeply rooted and unchanging. No amount of fact finding, scientific or otherwise, may change an individual's views on controversial topics such as abortion or affirmative action. But fact finding can still play a role in informing value judgments that are less calcified. Facts, including scientifically generated ones, can certainly reinforce judicial predispositions. In the past, the findings of scientific racism and eugenics research no doubt underscored the justices' underlying values regarding the inherent inferiority of non-whites in decisions such as *Plessy* and *Gong Lum* that upheld segregation. More recent scientific research on the benefits of student-body diversity in higher education likely reinforced the values of members of the Supreme Court who supported affirmative action on principle and upheld its use in *Grutter v. Bollinger*. And fact finding might convince judges to change their minds about their underlying values. Some of the lower courts in the *Brown v. Board of Education* cases, for example, were receptive to the social science findings on the psychological harms of segregation and incorporated the findings into their opinions, even though they ultimately were compelled to rule against the plaintiffs because of the mandates of precedent.

## Functions for Science in Constitutional Fact Finding

As a manifestation of constitutional fact finding, the turn to scientific evidence can play multiple roles in constitutional interpretation, all of which may reinforce core constitutional norms and values. The most basic function is *informational*. By enlightening courts on he state of the world, scientific findings can shape theoretical perspectives and influence value judgments and even challenge deep-seated values and beliefs. Deborah Jones Merritt suggests, "As our understanding of society shifts, new social perceptions sometimes produce new constitutional meaning. . . . Good empirical work forces us to step outside of our own experience and examine the world from a different perspective. Acquiring that viewpoint greatly enriches constitutional theory. [Science] can alter social perceptions. Those perceptions, in turn, help forge constitutional theory."[12] Even though the Supreme Court in *Brown v. Board of Education* was not entirely reliant on social science for its core ruling that struck down segregation, the psychological and sociological evidence can certainly be seen as one of many informational influences that bore on the Court's decision making, along with evolving societal attitudes toward race; the recent memory of a war that had engendered stark racial conflicts and hypocrisies; and parallel civil rights advancements in the federal government, the private sector, and the world of professional sports.

A second and more controversial function for scientific evidence is serving an *authoritative* function. By acting as a source of authority, like constitutional text, precedent, theory, or contemporary values, a scientific finding can have a direct and powerful influence on constitutional meaning. Leading cases such as

*Brown* and *Roe v. Wade*, where the Supreme Court put empirical findings and scientific frameworks at the storm center of constitutional controversies, demonstrate the potency of empirical evidence. But *Brown*, *Roe*, and a number of lesser known cases also show that an authoritative use of scientific evidence—a source of authority on which the courts are on less solid ground because of their relative lack of expertise—can be perilous for both sound decision making and the courts' institutional legitimacy.

A third function for scientific evidence in constitutional fact finding is to serve an *illuminating* function. By framing constitutional questions to require fact finding and empirically rooted sources of information, courts reveal the underlying assumptions and values of the frameworks that guide their interpretations of the Constitution. For instance, if a court raises questions about whether the promotion of diversity in a given institution produces concrete benefits such as improved cross-racial relations or increased productivity, then it is clearly employing a balancing model to determine the strength of an interest in promoting diversity. On the other side of the equation, raising questions about the harms of a race-conscious policy involves considerations about whether or not the policy is sufficiently compelling and what undue burdens individuals might bear under the policy.

Even relegating some scientific evidence to a role of minor influence, or even irrelevancy, can have illuminating effects because doing so forces the court to articulate its reasons for devaluing the scientific findings and valuing other considerations in the case. In *Craig v. Boren*, for instance, when Justice William Brennan rejected the state of Oklahoma's statistical evidence on the incidence of drunk driving among males and females between the ages of eighteen and twenty-one as insufficient to support a distinction in the minimum purchasing age (twenty-one for males, eighteen for females), he made clear that heightened scrutiny for gender-based classifications imposed a much heavier burden on the state to prove its case. The constitutional scales were tipped presumptively against the state because of a newly emerging and countervailing value in having gender-neutral governmental policies.

A fourth function that scientific evidence can play is a *legitimating* role in constitutional interpretation. By invoking relevant scientific findings to guide their decision making, the courts can demonstrate thoroughness and circumspection in their analyses, even though normative judgments may ultimately be at the root of their decisions. Rather than relying on conjecture or factual assumptions that may be dubious, consideration and discussion of pertinent empirical literature show that a court has done its homework and is not neglecting its responsibilities in reaching an informed interpretation of the Constitution. Even if the courts take a highly skeptical approach to scientific literature, and even if they reject scientific findings as irrelevant or insubstantial, the process of constitutional fact finding can carry greater credibility and legitimacy when the courts go through the exercise of examining potentially relevant research and then reaching conclusions based on its utility for constitutional interpretation.

Finally, scientific evidence can play a *rhetorical* function in constitutional analysis, a function that inheres when the courts discuss science in their written opinions or invoke cite scientific literature as a source of authority. In an age when scientific and technological advancements are commonplace and applauded, the rhetorical use of scientific evidence can be particularly forceful because it suggests an independent expertise and trustworthiness that is untainted by the partiality of advocates. As Dean M. Hashimoto suggests, "the U.S. Supreme Court includes scientific facts in its constitutional law opinions mostly for their persuasive appeal and symbolic expression. Empirical results underscore the rightness of the legal rule announced by the Court. . . . The Court's increasing reliance on them suggests that the Court believes that this kind of rhetoric is effective in securing public acceptance of its constitutional interpretations."[13] Science, left unquestioned, thus becomes "truth" in constitutional analysis; scientific findings serve as "reassuring symbols to demonstrate that the legal rule is in harmony with our society's culture."[14] Footnote 11 in *Brown* was no doubt designed in part to augment the rhetorical power of the Supreme Court's desegregation ruling, even if critics of the opinion ultimately revealed the weaknesses in the underlying science and questioned the Court's interpretive methods. Of course, there is danger in using any authority, scientific or nonscientific, purely for rhetorical purposes: once the rhetoric is cast aside and the underlying reasons for a decision are unmasked, the entire process can undermine the legitimacy of a decision in particular and weaken the court's legitimacy as an institution in general.

Because the courts have not developed clear methodologies to engage in constitutional fact finding, all of these different roles for scientific evidence—informational, authoritative, illuminating, legitimating, and rhetorical—can be at play in a given case. Decision making by the U.S. Supreme Court is particularly opaque: there is limited information on the Court's decisional processes other than what the justices ask during oral arguments and write in their opinions, and notes from meetings or internal memoranda usually only appear in the papers of justices after they have left the Court or died. Thus, the actual influence of science in any particular case is difficult to measure. Scientific evidence might play a prominent role in briefing and in oral arguments, but the Supreme Court may not cite that evidence in its written opinion, as was the case in *Loving v. Virginia*. Or scientific evidence may first appear in the written opinion, based on the Court's own research, as was the case in *Roe v. Wade*. The Supreme Court's recent equal protection cases show that it does not invoke science in every case when articulating its jurisprudence of constitutional equality, but the Court still recognizes the utility of scientific evidence and often relies on that evidence to uphold its normative judgments.

## Tiered Model of Equal Protection

Like other Reconstruction-era amendments to the Constitution, the Fourteenth Amendment was originally designed to address the racial inequalities brought on by slavery and the *Dred Scott* decision and to extend constitutional coverage to actions by state and local governments. Since the 1950s, the Supreme Court has greatly expanded the scope of the Fourteenth Amendment's equal protection clause so that it has become the Constitution's primary vehicle for enforcing claims of discrimination and unequal treatment by governmental actors. The government constantly differentiates among classes of people, whether it is taxing them at different rates based on their incomes or regulating one type of business activity versus another. And most legislation goes forward without challenge. The courts, however, have developed elevated standards of judicial review to address legislation that is based on characteristics such as race or national origin, which the courts treat as inherently suspect, or legislation that infringes on fundamental interests such as the right to vote, regardless of who is burdened.

The Supreme Court's contemporary model of equal protection jurisprudence draws inspiration from a prominent footnote in twentieth-century case law, footnote 4 of *United States v. Carolene Products*, a 1938 case in which the Supreme Court upheld a federal prohibition on the interstate shipment of "filled" milk (skim milk combined with nonmilk fats) by presuming the statute's constitutionality and employing minimal scrutiny of the law. In footnote 4, Chief Justice Harlan Fiske Stone suggested potential exceptions to the normal course of judicial review, which would presume constitutionality, for a subset of cases: "Prejudice against discrete and insular minorities may be a special condition, which tends seriously to curtail the operation of those political processes ordinarily to be relied upon to protect minorities, and which may call for a correspondingly more searching judicial inquiry." [15] As Laurence H. Tribe suggests, heightened judicial scrutiny becomes appropriate for evaluating legislation that could injure groups in society that have occupied, "as a consequence of widespread, insistent prejudice against them, the position of perennial losers in the political struggle." [16] Racial minority groups are the quintessential examples of "discrete and insular minorities" deserving judicial solicitude.

The development of the strict scrutiny standard for "suspect" classifications draws on *Korematsu v. United States*, where the Supreme Court proposed that "all restrictions which curtail the civil rights of a single racial group are immediately suspect" and must be subjected to "the most rigid scrutiny." [17] Between the 1950s and the 1980s, the Court expanded the coverage of strict scrutiny to include legislation that implicated ancestry, national origin, and, if conducted at the state or local level, alienage or citizenship status. (Because the federal government has broad powers over immigration, citizenship distinctions created by Congress or the president are generally not subject to heightened review.) The Court also employed strict scrutiny when reviewing classifications that burdened particular fundamental rights or interests, such as the right to vote or to travel between states.

The basic test under strict scrutiny is to require that legislation be necessary and narrowly tailored to serve a compelling governmental interest. Thus, elements of strict scrutiny focus on both the ends and the means employed in legislation. First, the stated governmental interest must be very important and well documented: it must be constitutionally "compelling." Second, the policy that advances this interest must be carefully crafted and closely fit the interest: it must be "narrowly tailored." If a policy cannot satisfy these conditions, it violates the equal protection clause.

In recent years, the Supreme Court has established specific requirements under both the "compelling interest" and the "narrowly tailored" prongs that necessitate the introduction of empirical evidence. For example, the Court has ruled that a public institution that employs a race-conscious affirmative action program to promote opportunities for racial minorities can have a compelling interest in remedying its own past discrimination—an inherently valuable justification—but the institution must thoroughly document that discrimination. Consequently, the Court has imposed a requirement that an institution must have a "strong basis in evidence" to show that it has discriminated in the past and that the present effects of past discrimination continue to be a problem. To satisfy the "strong basis in evidence" requirement, institutions typically offer statistical analyses and other scientific evidence showing significant disparities between racial groups, as well as historical, documentary, and anecdotal evidence of past discrimination.

In addition, the Supreme Court has articulated a set of narrow tailoring requirements that institutions must satisfy under strict scrutiny, including demonstrating that the particular policy is efficacious and flexible, that it does not impose undue burdens on innocent third parties, that it has time limits, and that less discriminatory and race-neutral alternatives have been considered. In weighing factors such as the efficacy of a policy, the burdens imposed on third parties, and the effectiveness of alternative policies, the courts frequently insist on empirical evidence to determine whether or not institutions are complying with narrow tailoring. For instance, scientific analyses comparing the effects of a race-conscious university admissions policy with various race-neutral admissions policies can help determine whether a race-conscious policy is necessary to meet a university's compelling interest in promoting student-body diversity.

In contrast to strict scrutiny, when courts employ "rational basis" scrutiny, they presume the constitutionality of the statute and rely on a much more relaxed analysis of the ends and the means. The interest must be legitimate, and the means employed need only be rationally related to advancing the stated interest. As the Supreme Court has noted, when courts apply the rational basis standard, "a legislative choice is not subject to courtroom factfinding and may be based on rational speculation unsupported by evidence or empirical data."[18] The rational basis test is thus considerably more deferential than the strict scrutiny test is; consequently, most laws are routinely upheld if they are subjected to the lesser standard. Most economic and social regulations fall under the rational basis standard and pass constitutional muster as a matter of course.

During the 1970s and 1980s, the Supreme Court began employing a third category of review, an intermediate standard that falls somewhere between the strict scrutiny and the rational basis tests. The intermediate standard recognizes certain groups who have suffered discrimination or political powerlessness but also possess characteristics that might be less obvious than race or for whom government classifications might be acceptable in some circumstances. In cases in which the Court has decided not to extend full suspect classification status to a group but still chooses to impose a heightened standard of review, the Court will strike down statutes that are not "substantially related" to an "important governmental interest." The ends have to be important but not quite as important as a compelling interest, and the means have to be closely related but not necessarily a perfect fit. The Supreme Court has applied the intermediate standard to "quasi-suspect" classifications based on gender, illegitimacy (affecting nonmarital children), and undocumented immigrant status, at least in the context of allowing children access to elementary and secondary public education. The burdens on the state to produce empirical and other evidence are not as onerous under the intermediate standard as they are under the strict scrutiny standard; they are, however, significantly heavier than under the rational basis standard, which may involve the introduction of little or no empirical evidence by the state.

The three tiers of review are not mathematically precise, but they do make a significant difference in the likely outcome of a case. As a practical matter, the standard of review shifts the burdens between government and the individual or group challenging the policy. Under a rational basis test, the policy is presumed to be constitutional; the challenger bears the burden of proving that a policy is irrational and arbitrary, which is quite difficult to prove. Under a strict scrutiny test, the government bears the burden of demonstrating that its policy is compelling and narrowly tailored; the standard has often been applied so stringently that one leading constitutional scholar suggested that strict scrutiny was "scrutiny that was 'strict' in theory and fatal in fact."[19] The intermediate standard imposes more of a balance between the various interests; the government's burden is still sizable, and most classifications fail to satisfy the intermediate standard of review. The multi-tiered model of equal protection is not absolutely rigid, however, and reflects a general framework that has been more fluid in practice. For example, the Supreme Court employed some stringency in reviewing a classification that involved the mentally retarded, employing a rational basis test "with greater bite."[20] It has also employed a more relaxed and deferential version of strict scrutiny in the case of race-conscious affirmative action policies in higher education.[21] At the same time, it has used stronger language in intermediate-level scrutiny of gender-related policies, implementing a "skeptical scrutiny" test that requires government to show an "exceedingly persuasive justification" for a gender-based classification.[22]

## Intent Requirement

The Supreme Court has imposed a general requirement that equal protection challenges must demonstrate proof of intent to discriminate on the part of the government. While the discriminatory purpose of a racial segregation law has often been quite clear on the face of the law, most contemporary statutes that might have discriminatory effects are not facially discriminatory. In *Washington v. Davis*, the Supreme Court ruled that proof of discriminatory impact on a group would not suffice to show a violation of the equal protection clause, unlike civil rights statutes such as Title VII of the Civil Rights Act of 1964 that allow cases to go forward on the basis of discriminatory impact alone.[23] In *Washington v. Davis* itself, black applicants for Washington, D.C., police officer positions failed an ostensibly race-neutral written test at four times the rate of whites. Although proof of discriminatory impact could be a factor in determining intent, the Court ruled that impact alone was insufficient. In a later case, the Court eased the burden by ruling that a discriminatory purpose does not have to be the only purpose of statute in order to violate equal protection; if a discriminatory purpose is one motivating factor among a number of factors, then the intent requirement can be satisfied.[24]

Although the Supreme Court did not explore the empirical implications of imposing an intent requirement in equal protection cases, one of the underlying reasons for its ruling in *Washington v. Davis* was to prevent challenges to "a whole range of tax, welfare, public service, regulatory, and licensing statutes that may be more burdensome to the poor and to the average black than to the more affluent white."[25] It is not entirely clear that such a wide range of statutes might be invalidated by allowing disparate impact claims under the equal protection clause, but the intent requirement clearly imposes a heavy burden on plaintiffs seeking to challenge discriminatory laws and policies and runs counter to a view that the equal protection clause should be concerned more about the results of government actions than about motivations. As Laurence H. Tribe notes, "the goal of the Equal Protection Clause is not to stamp out impure thoughts, but to guarantee a full measure of human dignity for all. . . . The burden on those who are subjugated is none the lighter because it is imposed inadvertently."[26]

## Science and Equal Protection Standards

What role has scientific evidence played in the development of the regime of equal protection standards? The Supreme Court has on a number of occasions cited scientific literature to undergird a legal conclusion that a particular policy should be subject to heightened scrutiny. For example, in *Johnson v. California*, decided in 2005, the Supreme Court ruled that strict scrutiny rather than the deferential standard of review that is usually applied in cases involving prisoners' constitutional rights was the appropriate standard to evaluate a California cellmate assignment policy that temporarily segregated prisoners on the basis of race in order to prevent gang-related violence. [27] In doing so, the majority cited a scientific study of prison desegregation to highlight the potential of segregative policies to cause violence, thus making the need for strict scrutiny even more significant. The study found that over a ten-year period, the rate of violence between inmates segregated by race in two-person cells surpassed the rate among prisoners who were racially integrated.

On the other hand, some of the Supreme Court's recent rulings have been based purely on normative grounds without significant fact finding to inform a decision. For instance, in recent cases involving the constitutionality of race-conscious affirmative action programs, the Court, by a closely divided vote, has ruled that strict scrutiny should apply to *all* racial classifications, regardless of whether they are designed to subordinate racial minorities or to provide greater opportunities for minorities. The Court's judgment has been predicated on a theoretical principle of "consistency": "The standard of review under the Equal Protection Clause is not dependent on the race of those burdened or benefited by a particular classification."[28] Although the consistency principle is in tension with the reasoning in footnote 4 of *Carolene Products*, which suggests that strict scrutiny should attach to the protection of "discrete and insular minorities," it does align with the language of *Korematsu* proposing that classifications curtailing the rights of a single racial group are inherently suspect. Recent Supreme Court majorities have thus interpreted the equal protection clause to mandate strict scrutiny in cases affecting the rights of whites as well as those of racial minorities.

Similarly, in the "fundamental rights" strand of equal protection analysis (where the courts apply strict scrutiny because the interest at stake is fundamental, not necessarily because of a group's characteristics), heightened review has been limited to only a few rights that, in the Court's view, are either explicitly written into the Constitution or inherent in its framework. Rights that might be considered important because of contemporary values or because empirical findings might reinforce their worth do not necessarily fall under the rubric of a fundamental right. The Supreme Court has recognized fundamental interests such as the right to vote, the right to access the courts, and the right to travel between states. But it has rejected arguments that would recognize basic necessities such as housing, education, or welfare as fundamental rights deserving judicial solicitude. In *San Antonio Independent School District v. Rodriguez*, for example, the Court ruled that education, despite its significance in American life, is not a fundamental interest either explicitly or implicitly in the Constitution and proceeded to uphold a wealth-based school financing scheme that disadvantaged students in poorer school districts.[29]

Nevertheless, scientific evidence has played and can continue to play a role in addressing two sets of constitutional questions that are informed by legislative or constitutional facts. One set of questions revolves around whether a particular government classification should be subject to heightened review under either strict scrutiny or intermediate scrutiny. Within this set of questions, specific inquiries focus on defining the nature of a category and identifying characteristics or problems suggesting that a classification should be suspect or quasi-suspect. Assuming that the standard of review has been properly aligned with a public policy, a second set of questions revolves around whether the policy satisfies the equal protection standard. Within this set of questions, specific inquiries focus on whether a governmental interest is compelling, important, or rational; inquiries can also focus on whether a policy is appropriately tailored to advance the state's interest.

## Defining Classifications

Although some governmental classifications are relatively easy to define without resort to scientific evidence (most differences between males and females, for example, can usually be discerned through common knowledge), other classifications may require greater refinement. The definitions and nuances of race, color, national origin, and ancestry form one such area. Recall that in the 1920s the Supreme Court was asked to clarify, in *Ozawa v. United States* and *United States v. Thind,* the statutory definition of *white* under the federal naturalization laws; the Court had little trouble concluding that neither Japanese nor Asian Indian immigrants were white under the law. More recently, the Court ruled in the 1987 case of *Saint Francis College v. Al-Khazraji* that an Arab American (an individual classified as white under contemporaneous racial categories) was nevertheless protected under 42 U.S.C. section 1981, a Reconstruction-era statute that prohibits racial discrimination in the making and enforcement of contracts.[30] In a detailed opinion replete with citations to scientific literature, Justice Byron White traced the history of ethnology and racial classifications from the enactment of section 1981 soon after the Civil War through the present day. Focusing on recent scientific findings, Justice White noted that traditional notions of race, predicated on biological differences, no longer enjoyed a consensus among contemporary scientists:

Many modern biologists and anthropologists . . . criticize racial classifications as arbitrary and of little use in understanding the variability of
human beings. . . . Clear-cut categories do not exist. The particular traits
which have generally been chosen to characterize races have been criticized as having little biological significance. It has been found that differences between individuals of the same race are often greater than the
differences between the "average" individuals of different races. These
observations and others have led some, but not all, scientists to conclude
that racial classifications are for the most part sociopolitical, rather than
biological, in nature.[31]

Justice White concluded that the prohibition on racial discrimination under
the law was fluid and was designed to include protections for "identifiable
classes of persons who are subjected to intentional discrimination solely because of their ancestry or ethnic characteristics."[32]

More than thirty years earlier, in *Hernandez v. Texas*, the Supreme Court
clarified that the equal protection clause also protects members of national origin minority groups, not just racial minority groups.[33] As discussed, *Hernandez*
involved a challenge to a Texas policy that systematically excluded individuals
of Mexican descent from becoming jury commissioners, members of grand juries, and members of petit juries. Because the Supreme Court had ruled in 1880
in *Strauder v. West Virginia* that blacks as a class could not be excluded from jury
membership, precedent invalidating an invidious racial classification would
apply if Mexican Americans were also classified as racial minorities. The state of
Texas argued, however, that Mexican Americans were white, not members of a
racial minority group.

Petitioner Pete Hernandez countered this argument, not by disputing the
racial classification of Mexican Americans but by asserting that discrimination
against Mexican Americans as a distinct class violated the equal protection
clause. In support of this argument, Hernandez's brief documented the widespread discrimination against Mexican Americans in jury selection as well as in
education, housing, property ownership, employment, and access to public facilities. In an appendix not unlike the "Social Science Statement" in the *Brown v.
Board of Education* petitioners' brief, Hernandez's brief referred to government
reports and social science studies that chronicled longstanding discrimination
against Mexican Americans in Texas. The brief stated: "Not only is the Mexican-
American commonly regarded as a class apart, but by every objective measurement—from biological makeup to deaths from tuberculosis and from infantile
diarrhea—he *is* a class apart."[34]

Writing for a unanimous Supreme Court, Chief Justice Warren stated:
"When the existence of a distinct class is demonstrated, and it is further shown
that the laws, as written or as applied, single out that class for different treat-

ment not based on some reasonable classification, the guarantees of the Constitution have been violated."[35] The Court concluded that the exclusion of otherwise eligible persons from jury service because of their ancestry or national origin was prohibited by the Fourteenth Amendment.[36] Noting a number of social science studies, as well as the testimony of public officials and community members, it decided that a distinct class of Mexican Americans did exist in Texas. Then, turning to statistical evidence demonstrating the disparities between the large pool of potential jurors and the absence of any jurors with Spanish surnames (the method for exclusion), the Court concluded that the policy violated the Constitution: "Circumstances or chance may well dictate that no persons in a certain class will serve on a particular jury or during some particular period. But it taxes our credulity to say that mere chance resulted in their being no members of this class among the over six thousand jurors called in the past 25 years."[37]

## Facially Neutral Classifications

A more recent juror exclusion case involved another Hernandez—Dionisio Hernandez, a criminal defendant who argued that New York state prosecutors had violated his equal protection rights by striking Spanish-speaking Latino individuals from his jury panel. In 1991, a plurality of the Supreme Court ruled in *Hernandez v. New York* that a *language*-based action did not necessarily serve as a proxy for race or national origin discrimination.[38] In raising his equal protection challenge, Hernandez relied on the legal theory developed in *Batson v. Kentucky* that establishes a case for discrimination if prosecutors intentionally remove minorities from jury panels through "peremptory challenges" (procedures allowing lawyers to remove potential jurors without having to argue a cause for their removal) and the prosecutors do not have a race-neutral purpose for doing so. In Hernandez's case, the prosecution had removed Spanish-speaking Latinos from the panel but offered the reason for exclusion as the need to eliminate jurors who might second-guess the Spanish-language translator during the trial, a determination that was purportedly based on both an individual's bilingualism and his personal characteristics. The Court accepted the prosecutor's reasons as sufficiently race-neutral, even though it had the disproportionate effect of excluding Latino jurors.

Hernandez's argument was predicated on showing that there was an inextricable tie between language and national origin and that therefore the prosecution's rationale was not race-neutral. An amicus curiae brief filed on behalf of the Mexican American Legal Defense and Educational Fund and the Department of Puerto Rican Community Affairs in the United States contained extensive summaries and citations to sociolinguistic literature demonstrating that bilingualism is tightly bound with Latino ethnicity and that jury strikes on the basis of membership in a language group would therefore implicate the equal protection clause. Justice Kennedy, who announced the judgment of Court, acknowledged the sociolinguistic evidence and cited some of the literature when he stated that "language permits an individual to express both a personal identity and membership in a community, and those who share a common language may interact in ways more intimate than those without this bond. Bilinguals, in a sense, inhabit two communities, and serve to bring them closer."[39]

Nevertheless, the plurality accepted the prosecutors' rationale for the peremptory challenges. Justice Kennedy did state, however, that the Court "would face a quite different case if the prosecutor had justified his peremptory challenges with the explanation that he did not want Spanish-speaking jurors." He concluded that it may well be, for certain ethnic groups and in some communities, "that proficiency in a particular language, like skin color, should be treated as a surrogate for race under an equal protection analysis." Moreover, he added, "a policy of striking all who speak a given language, without regard to the particular circumstances of the trial or the individual responses of the jurors, may be found by the trial judge to be a pretext for racial discrimination."[40]

The decision in *Hernandez v. New York* is consistent with a number of cases in which the Supreme Court has ruled that evidence of a disproportionate impact on a group is not by itself sufficient to trigger a suspect or quasi-suspect classification. During the 1970s, the Supreme Court rejected equal protection claims in which scientific evidence was presented to show a close link between facially gender-neutral classifications and adverse effects on women. In *Personnel Administrator of Massachusetts v. Feeney*, the Supreme Court upheld a state law that created hiring preferences for military veterans, even though it had a clear discriminatory impact on women.[41] Statistical evidence showed that more than 98 percent of the veterans in Massachusetts were male, while less than 2 percent were female. The Court then concluded that nothing in the record demonstrated that the veterans' preference was designed as it was because it would accomplish the goal of keeping women in stereotypical roles in the Massachusetts civil service.[42]

In *Geduldig v. Aiello*, the Supreme Court ruled that a state law excluding pregnancy-related problems from coverage under a California disability insurance system was not a gender-based classification and upheld the exclusions under the more deferential rational basis test.[43] The record in the case, as well as numerous amicus curiae briefs, highlighted extensive statistical and medical evidence on the problems of pregnancy-related disabilities; but the Supreme Court employed a curious logic to rule that pregnancy-related exclusions did not amount to a gender classification. Justice Potter Stewart wrote: "The program divides potential recipients into two groups—pregnant women and non-pregnant persons. While the first group is exclusively female, the second includes members of both sexes. The fiscal and actuarial benefits of the program thus accrue to members of both sexes."[44] Under this reasoning, because women who were not pregnant also benefited from the lower insurance costs that resulted from excluding pregnancy-related disabilities, the Court ruled that there was no discrimination against women as a class. Writing in dissent, Justice William Brennan applied a different line of reasoning: "In effect, one set of rules is applied to females and another to males. Such dissimilar treatment of men and women, on the basis of physical characteristics inextricably linked to one sex, inevitably constitutes sex discrimination."[45] Science itself was less central to *Geduldig*'s core holding (the fact that only women can become pregnant did not require much scientific documentation), and it was the majority's odd logic that prevailed.

## Group Characteristics and Heightened Scrutiny

Another use of scientific evidence in constitutional fact finding has been to inform the court's determination of whether a group classification should receive heightened scrutiny. In one recent case, the Supreme Court summarized its criteria for establishing suspect classification status: in order to form a suspect class, a group should, as a historical matter, have been subject to discrimination; have exhibited obvious, immutable, or distinguishing characteristics that define members as a discrete group; and be either a minority or politically powerless.[46] The Supreme Court has typically relied on commonsense notions or historical evidence to address these criteria, but it has occasionally turned to scientific evidence to accept or reject classifications as eligible for heightened scrutiny.

### Immigrant Inequalities

Alienage, for example, is one area that the courts have readily analogized to race. Historically, citizenship discrimination has been intertwined with racial discrimination, and noncitizens are especially vulnerable in the political process because they are routinely denied the right to vote. Because of the longstanding bar on naturalization that prohibited non-whites from becoming naturalized citizens, laws were often written in language that was silent on race but designed to subordinate racial minorities. For example, several western states passed "alien land laws" in the 1920s to prohibit the ownership or transfer of land to individuals who were ineligible for citizenship; the targets of these laws were Asian immigrants who were subject to the racial bar on naturalization. In 1948, the Supreme Court struck down a California law that denied commercial fishing licenses to individuals who were ineligible for citizenship. In *Takahashi v. Fish and Game Commission*, the Court stated that the equal protection clause protects "'all persons' against state legislation bearing unequally upon them either because of alienage or color" and that "the power of a state to apply its laws exclusively to its alien inhabitants as a class is confined within narrow limits."[47]

In 1971, the Supreme Court held in *Graham v. Richardson* that "classifications based on alienage, like those based on nationality or race, are inherently suspect and subject to close judicial scrutiny. Aliens as a class are a prime example of a 'discrete and insular' minority . . . for whom such heightened judicial solicitude is appropriate."[48] Concluding that the state's interest in preserving its limited welfare benefits for citizens was not compelling, the Court struck down an Arizona law that imposed a fifteen-year residency requirement on lawful permanent resident aliens before they could become eligible for welfare benefits. In later cases, the Court struck down a number of state classifications based on citizenship status, including restrictions on eligibility to be a state civil servant, to practice law, to become a licensed engineer, to obtain financial aid for higher education, and to become a notary public.[49]

The Supreme Court relied on historical rather than scientific evidence to aid its decision making in *Graham v. Richardson*. In *Plyler v. Doe*, however, the Court turned to the statistical and social science evidence that had been introduced by the parties and various amici curiae in applying heightened scrutiny to determine the rights of undocumented immigrant children to attend public schools.[50] Both sides of the dispute submitted extensive evidence on the economic and social costs of educating or, as was the case in Texas, of *not* educating many thousands of undocumented children, as well as on the more general problems of undocumented immigration in the United States. Data estimates on the economic costs for the state were in the millions, but studies also showed that government revenues were higher because of the taxes paid by undocumented immigrants and their other contributions to the economy; expert testimony on the social costs of failing to educate the children suggested that they would become overrepresented in the criminal justice system, in the welfare system, and among the unemployed. There was no consensus generated by the body of scientific evidence, and the Supreme Court itself divided on a five-to-four vote in developing a constitutional framework that applied heightened scrutiny to the problem.

After initially clarifying that undocumented immigrants were indeed covered by the Fourteenth Amendment, Justice Brennan's majority opinion cited statistics that indicated the gravity of the undocumented immigration problem, noting the existence of "a substantial 'shadow population' of illegal migrants—numbering in the millions—within our borders."[51] Justice Brennan then proposed that the situation raised "the specter of a permanent caste of undocumented resident aliens" and that "the existence of such an under-class presents most difficult problems for a Nation that prides itself on adherence to principles of equality under law."[52] Turning specifically to the problems faced by undocumented children who might be deprived of an education, he wrote:

> Illiteracy is an enduring disability. The inability to read and write will handicap the individual deprived of a basic education each and every day of his life. The inestimable toll of that deprivation on the social, economic, intellectual, and psychological well-being of the individual, and the obstacle it poses to individual achievement, make it most difficult to reconcile the cost or the principle of a status-based denial of basic education with the framework of equality embodied in the Equal Protection Clause.[53]

The Court recognized that treating undocumented immigrants as a suspect class would be inconsistent with their lack of legal immigration status. But it ruled that an intermediate level of scrutiny would be appropriate because the children constituted a discrete class being penalized for conditions outside their control (that is, unlawful status caused by their parents' actions) and because public education has played an important role in American society. "In determining the rationality of [the law], we may appropriately take into account its costs to the Nation and to the innocent children who are its victims. In light of these countervailing costs, the discrimination . . . can hardly be considered rational unless it furthers some substantial goal of the State."[54]

Applying heightened review to the law, the Court relied on several facts, underscored by social science findings, to reject the state's interests in preserving its scarce resources and protecting itself from the effects of an influx of undocumented immigrants. The Court found no evidence in the record suggesting that undocumented immigrants imposed a significant burden on the state's economy: "To the contrary, the available evidence suggests that illegal aliens underutilize public services, while contributing their labor to the local economy and tax money to the state fisc."[55] The Court also cited a lack of evidence in rejecting the state's argument that educating undocumented children would hurt the quality of education, as well as the argument that undocumented children would leave the state after gaining the benefits of an education. Ultimately rejecting the state's interests and method of classification as insubstantial, the Court concluded: "It is difficult to understand precisely what the State hopes to achieve by promoting the creation and perpetuation of a subclass of illiterates within our boundaries, surely adding to the problems and costs of unemployment, welfare, and crime. . . . [W]hatever savings might be achieved by denying these children an education, they are wholly insubstantial in light of the costs involved to these children, the State, and the Nation."[56]

*Plyler* is an exceptional case, one of the few in which the Supreme Court has addressed the rights of undocumented immigrants; and the Court has not been asked to extend a similar set of protections to undocumented immigrants outside of K–12 education. Scientific evidence clearly played important informational and illuminating roles in the *Plyler* majority's analysis, even though the full body of evidence presented to the Court was not unequivocal. Both sides offered economic and social data to support their arguments, and expert witnesses for each side figured prominently in the lower court fact-finding processes. The Court employed a balancing test to weigh the various interests, with social science findings informing both sides of the inquiries. The justices' underlying values may have been at the heart of the final decision in *Plyler* (Justice Brennan's description of the adverse costs as "inestimable" may not have been the term that one might expect an economist to use), but social science certainly reinforced the policy judgments that the Court generated in response to the problem of undocumented immigration in general and the problem of educating undocumented children in particular.

### Age, Mental Retardation, and the Rational Basis Test

The majority opinion in *Plyler v. Doe* exemplifies how the Supreme Court can employ social science literature to inform a normative judgment on the meaning of constitutional equality. Nevertheless, the Court has not always relied favorably on scientific evidence in deciding whether to apply elevated standards of review. In ruling that age-based classifications do not engender heightened scrutiny, it discounted a significant body of medical and social science evidence that demonstrated both the long-term ability of elderly citizens to contribute to society and the adverse effects on the elderly of removing them prematurely from the workforce. In *Massachusetts Board of Retirement v. Murgia*, the Supreme Court ruled that a state policy that imposed a mandatory retirement age of fifty on uniformed state police officers only had to be reviewed under a rational basis test. In a *per curiam* opinion, the Court stated: "While the treatment of the aged in this Nation has not been wholly free of discrimination, such persons, unlike, say, those who have been discriminated against on the basis of race or national origin, have not experienced a 'history of purposeful unequal treatment' or been subjected to unique disabilities on the basis of stereotyped characteristics not truly indicative of their abilities." [57] The Court noted commonsensically that everyone inevitably ages, so it is difficult to treat the elderly as a category needing special constitutional protection. The Court did acknowledge evidence that there was not a perfect alignment between age and physical ability to perform police work; but because it employed only a rational basis test, the Court upheld the Massachusetts policy.

Writing in dissent, Justice Thurgood Marshall argued that age should form the basis for heightened scrutiny, citing both historical evidence of discrimination against the elderly as well as medical and clinical evidence: "Mandatory retirement poses a direct threat to the health and life expectancy of the retired person, and these consequences of termination for age are not disputed by appellants. Thus, an older person deprived of his job by the government loses not only his right to earn a living, but, too often, his health as well."[58] Ultimately, the Court's decision in *Murgia* reflected a normative judgment that many age-related classifications are appropriate for government to enact and that subjecting them to a higher standard of review, notwithstanding scientific evidence of the harms that these policies might cause, would not serve the best interests of sound public policymaking.

In *City of Cleburne v. Cleburne Living Center*, the Supreme Court addressed the constitutionality of a Texas city's denial of a special use permit for the operation of a group home for the mentally retarded.[59] The Court declined to extend suspect or quasi-suspect classification status to the mentally retarded but still struck down the policy as unconstitutional. Although numerous amicus curiae briefs were filed on behalf of medical authorities, mental health professionals, disability rights organizations, and scientific research associations, the Court majority was not swayed by the extensive findings in the briefs and decided to use a rational basis test for reviewing the city's actions. Writing for the majority, Justice Byron White concluded that the "mentally retarded" classification was quite broad and amorphous and, as empirical findings showed, was composed of many subclasses with individuals of different abilities and needs; moreover, the mentally retarded were not politically powerless and had had no trouble gaining the attention of lawmakers.

Perhaps most important for the *Cleburne* Court, there was a strong policy reason for limiting heightened review: extending quasi-suspect classification status might inhibit the enactment of legislation that could address the special and varied needs of the mentally retarded. The Court went on to recognize that past and ongoing discrimination against the mentally retarded was a serious problem; in applying the rational basis test with more rigor than usual, the Court concluded that the city's denial of a permit rested on "an irrational prejudice against the mentally retarded" and was therefore unconstitutional.[60] In contrast to the majority's analysis, Justice Marshall's dissenting opinion drew heavily on the historical and scientific evidence—and even cited the Court's prior decision in *Buck v. Bell*, which upheld forced sterilization against the "feeble-minded"—to argue that the mentally retarded should be accorded quasi-suspect classification status: "As the history of discrimination against the retarded and its continuing legacy amply attest, the mentally retarded have been, and in some areas may still be, the targets of action the Equal Protection Clause condemns."[61]

As in the *Murgia* case, the justices' varying approaches to the scientific evidence in *Cleburne* illuminated the different normative judgments that they had developed in deciding whether to employ an elevated standard of review. Scientific evidence on the problems facing the mentally retarded no doubt played a role in informing the decisions; even portions of the majority opinion recog-nized the vulnerabilities of the mentally retarded and the harms caused by prejudice and discrimination. But it was the policy values of the Court majority that led them down the road to review the state's actions under a rational basis test; at the same time, those values guided their recognition that a policy subor-dinating the mentally retarded was fundamentally irrational and could not pass even the lowest standard of review.

SCIENTIFIC EVIDENCE HAS played an occasional but nonetheless influential role in the development of standards for equal protection review. Clearly, evolving attitudes and values toward subordinated groups, whether they are racial minorities, women, immigrants, or the disabled, have led to important develop-ments in civil rights laws and the Supreme Court's equal protection jurispru-dence. Scientific findings have informed a number of these decisions; but they have also failed to sway the values of justices in some cases, even though the justices may have been sympathetic to the interests advanced through both le-gal arguments and scientific findings. As chapter 5 reveals, scientific evidence is frequently used to prove, and to defend against, violations of the equal protec-tion clause. Nevertheless, the courts' receptivity to scientific evidence remains checkered and value-driven.

# 5

## Proving Discrimination

In 1880, the San Francisco Board of Supervisors passed an ordinance that required all operators of laundries in the city to obtain a business permit if their laundries were located in buildings not built of brick or stone. Anyone operating a laundry without a permit could face a fine, jail time, or both. On its face, the law appeared to be neutral and fair; requiring a permit for laundries in wooden buildings, which were common in the city, could be justified on health and safety grounds. But the board's administration of the law was neither neutral nor fair. About 320 laundries were operating in San Francisco in 1880, and about 310 were constructed of wood. Of the total number, roughly 240 were owned and operated by Chinese immigrants. Following passage of the ordinance, more than two hundred Chinese laundry operators applied for permits; not one was granted. Because most of the Chinese owners depended on their laundries for their livelihoods, they continued to operate the businesses without permits. Most of them were fined or spent time in jail; a typical penalty was either 10 dollars up front or one night in jail for every dollar of the fine that could not be paid. Except for one application, all of the permit applications from non-Chinese laundry operators (a total of eighty) were granted. The Board of Supervisors admitted to the discriminatory administration of the ordinance but offered no explanation for it.

These were the basic facts presented to the U.S. Supreme Court in *Yick Wo v. Hopkins*, a landmark case in which the Court ruled that the equal protection clause is fully applicable to noncitizens and that discriminatory administration of a law, even one that is neutrally written, can violate equal protection. The Court stated: "Though the law itself be fair on its face, and impartial in appearance, yet, if it is applied and administered by public authority with an evil eye and an unequal hand, so as practically to make unjust and illegal discriminations between persons in similar circumstances, material to their rights, the denial of equal justice is still within the prohibition of the constitution."[1] The Board of Supervisors made no admission of discriminatory motive or intent, but the smoking gun was clear: Chinese laundry operators were routinely denied permits and later fined or jailed, and practically all of the non-Chinese laundry operators were granted permits.

*Yick Wo* was a case that turned on numbers. No mathematicians or social scientists were needed as expert witnesses because the statistical data pointing to racial discrimination were so glaring that the Supreme Court could infer the board's discriminatory motives. *Yick Wo* was not a "disparate impact" case in the contemporary sense. The Board of Supervisors had every intention of discriminating against Chinese laundry owners, as the numbers showed. Board members simply chose not to explain themselves or to write "Chinese need not apply" into the ordinance itself.

*Yick Wo* is not often cited as a case in which scientific evidence played a role in Supreme Court decision making. Nevertheless, it illustrates the kind of numerical data, even if rudimentary, that the courts accept as evidence of discrimination. Theories of discrimination have multiplied and statistical methodologies have grown much more sophisticated since the 1880s, but the courts are still most responsive when the statistics reveal fundamental and inescapable disparities between groups.

This chapter examines the role of scientific evidence in proving and defending against claims of discrimination under the equal protection clause. In some areas of civil rights law, particularly employment discrimination claims under Title VII of the Civil Rights Act of 1964 and voting rights claims under the Voting Rights Act, statistical analyses and social science evidence are routinely accepted and typically form the core of a party's case. But in equal protection litigation, the courts have been more wary of scientific evidence and in some instances have discarded scientific data and findings because of countervailing constitutional values. Moreover, many of the Supreme Court's most recent equal protection cases have not involved challenges to policies that harm historically subordinated groups. What increasingly occupy the federal courts' equal protection dockets are challenges to race-conscious affirmative action programs, claims of unfair legislative districting plans that favor minority voters, and lawsuits contesting the constitutionality of voluntary desegregation policies designed to promote racially integrated student bodies.

## Constitutional Violations

Because of the multi-tiered framework that the Supreme Court has imposed on equal protection claims, the type and volume of evidence that it reviews in cases can vary significantly. In strict scrutiny cases, the burden on the government is high, and presumptions of unconstitutionality run against the challenged legislation. In rational basis cases, the burden falls more heavily on the plaintiffs, and presumptions of constitutionality run in favor of the challenged legislation. Intermediate scrutiny is not a true middle ground, and the burdens on government remain high, although not as considerable as in strict scrutiny cases. Both plaintiffs and defendant governments have employed scientific evidence in leading equal protection cases; not surprisingly, though, the Supreme Court has not developed consistent rules on the types of scientific evidence that it will accept or on the proper use of scientific evidence in its own fact finding. In setting some of the ground rules for adjudicative fact finding by the lower courts, the Court has developed preferences for certain types of scientific evidence, as when it requires a statistical analysis of disparities to demonstrate discriminatory intent in jury selection cases. The Court has also identified cases in which it expects "a strong basis in evidence," as in most cases challenging race-conscious affirmative action plans; the government must produce extensive statistical and historical evidence if it expects to maintain its policy.

But even if the type of empirical evidence that the Court accepts is unambiguous, the standards by which it adjudicates a constitutional claim may still be opaque. In its "one person, one vote" line of cases, for example, the Supreme Court has required that legislative districts must be substantially equal in population size in order to guarantee the equal weighting of votes: if districts are substantially unequal in population, individual votes in districts with high populations are diluted because they carry less weight than do votes in districts with low populations. To determine whether reapportionment plans satisfy the constitution, the Court has turned to basic census data on the population sizes of districts and the deviations among districts. Since the 1970s, the Court has consistently examined the "maximum percentage deviation," a figure that measures the spread of the largest and smallest districts from an ideally populated district. The maximum percentage deviation can be obtained using the following formula:

$$\text{Maximum percentage deviation} = \frac{MP - MP}{IP} + \left| \frac{LP - IP}{IP} \right|$$

where    IP = population of the ideal district
         MP = population of the most populous district
         LP = population of the least populous district

For example, if 2 million people live in a state, and there are twenty legislative districts, the ideal district population would be 100,000. If the largest district contains 110,000 people, while the smallest district contains 90,000 people, the maximum percentage deviation would be 20 percent.[2]

Despite its consistent use of population deviation figures, the Supreme Court has not adopted a clear set of numerical benchmarks to decide whether a districting plan actually complies with its "one person, one vote" principles. In *Mahan v. Howell*, a 1973 case, the Court stated: "Neither courts nor legislatures are furnished [with] any specialized calipers that enable them to extract from the general language of the Equal Protection Clause of the Fourteenth Amendment the mathematical formula that establishes what range of percentage deviations is permissible and what is not."[3] The Court has distinguished its constitutional requirements for congressional districts (requiring almost absolute population equality) from its requirements for state legislative districts (allowing higher deviations, ostensibly because of a state's interest in maintaining the integrity of county and other local boundaries and because an absolute equality requirement would "impair the normal functioning of state and local governments.")[4] In general, the courts have allowed state legislative plans that contain maximum deviations below 10 percent to pass constitutional muster; plans with greater deviations have been examined with a more careful eye but can still be upheld. Applying these general principles, the Supreme Court in one case struck down a congressional districting plan in which the maximum percentage deviation was less than 0.7 percent.[5] In another case, however, it upheld a Wyoming state legislative plan with a maximum percentage deviation of 89 percent—a plan justified by the state's interest in offering each county in the state at least one state representative.[6]

## Problems of Proving Intent

*Yick Wo v. Hopkins* is an example of a case in which statistical evidence could easily be used to infer discriminatory intent because the skewed administration of the San Francisco ordinance was obvious: no Chinese applicants were granted permits, and almost no other applicants were denied permits. Another glaring example is *Gomillion v. Lightfoot*, a 1960 case that involved a challenge to the redrawing of city boundaries in Tuskegee, Alabama, which effectively excluded blacks from participating in city elections.[7] The boundaries were changed from a square into a twenty-eight-sided figure, and 395 of the 400 blacks in the city were placed outside the new city boundaries while none of the whites were excluded. Ruling that the redrawing violated the right to vote under the Fifteenth Amendment, the Court stated that "the conclusion would be irresistible, tantamount for all practical purposes to a mathematical demonstration, that the legislation is solely concerned with segregating white and colored voters by fencing Negro citizens out of town so as to deprive them of their preexisting municipal vote."[8]

But since its 1976 ruling in *Washington v. Davis*, the Supreme Court has consistently ruled that statistical disparities by themselves are usually not sufficient to maintain a plaintiff's claim for an equal protection violation because proof of discriminatory intent, not just proof of discriminatory impact, is required. Although the Court did clarify in later cases that a discriminatory purpose does not have to be the sole motivation in adopting a law (simply one motivating factor), the burden on plaintiffs to show even partial motives is difficult. In *Personnel Administrator of Massachusetts v. Feeney*, the Court upheld a Massachusetts law that created a set of veterans' preferences that clearly had adverse effects on women since only 1.8 percent of the state's veterans were female and more than 98 percent were male.[9] The Court acknowledged the statistical disparities but found them insufficient to demonstrate discriminatory intent. It stressed that proving discriminatory purpose means showing that the government has adopted a policy "because of" its adverse effects on a particular group, not "in spite of" its adverse effects. According to the *Feeney* Court, nothing in the record showed that the veterans' preference was adopted because it would also subordinate women.

Yet in one case, *Castaneda v. Partida*, the Court opened the door for the use of statistical evidence to establish a presumption of discriminatory intent, at least in jury selection cases.[10] Previous Supreme Court cases had concluded that major disparities between eligible juror pools and jury venires (the large panels from which individual juries could be drawn) could prove purposeful discrimination. In the long history of one case, no black juror had ever served before the early 1960s, despite the fact that 45 percent of the county's population in 1960 was black; even after the parties had made two additional trips to the Supreme Court, the disparities between the percentage of blacks on the eligibility list and the percentages on the jury venires were still striking: blacks were 27.1 percent of the individuals on a tax digest list but only 9.1 percent of the grand jury venire and 7.8 percent of the petit jury venire.[11] The Court concluded that intentional racial discrimination was at work.

In *Castaneda*, the evidence revealed that the population of Hidalgo County, Texas, was 79.1 percent Mexican American but that during the eleven years between 1962 to 1972 only 39 percent of the individuals summoned for grand jury service were Mexican American. Further, the statistical evidence was unrebutted by any government evidence that race-neutral qualifications resulted in the low proportion of Mexican Americans grand jurors. In an unusually detailed opinion highlighting specific statistical methodologies, Justice Blackmun established a basic legal test for criminal defendants to show that a selection procedure has resulted in the substantial underrepresentation of their racial or national origin group. First, they must establish that the group is a recognizable, distinct class singled out for different treatment. Second, they must demonstrate the degree of underrepresentation by comparing the proportion of the group in the total population to the proportion called to serve as grand jurors over a significant period of time—a method of proof sometimes called the "rule of exclusion." Third, they must show that the selection procedure is susceptible to abuse or not racially neutral. Once defendants have shown substantial underrepresentation of their group, they have made out a prima facie case of discriminatory purpose; the burden then shifts to the state to rebut the case. Applying this test to the facts of *Castaneda*, Justice Blackmun ruled that the defendant's equal protection rights had been violated.

In a series of technical footnotes running throughout his majority opinion, Justice Blackmun highlighted a specific statistical test—a "binomial distribution" model—and even offered different scenarios to answer the concerns of the dissenting justices. Examining different pools of potential jurors to determine expected outcomes and comparing them with percentages in the actual jury venires, Justice Blackmun's calculations yielded figures suggesting that the odds of the various results occurring by chance were, depending on the starting values, between $1$ in $10^{25}$ and $1$ in $10^{140}$, results that would permit an inference to be drawn that racial discrimination was at work in the jury selection process. Although *Castaneda* itself was limited to jury selection, the statistical test that Justice Blackmun identified in the case also became the test that is a primary metric for proving intentional, group-targeted employment discrimination in more frequently litigated Title VII cases.[12]

Scientific evidence appeared in the *Castaneda* case in another way. In ruling that Castaneda's equal protection rights had been violated, Justice Blackmun made clear that the fact that Mexican Americans occupied many elected positions and judgeships in Hidalgo County, a point raised by Justice Powell in dissent, did not undermine the strength of the constitutional claim. Citing several studies, Justice Marshall underscored the majority's view in his concurring opinion: "Social scientists agree that members of minority groups frequently respond to discrimination and prejudice by attempting to disassociate themselves from the group, even to the point of adopting the majority's negative attitudes towards the minority."[13] Moreover, he noted that "such behavior occurs with particular frequency among members of minority groups who have achieved some measure of economic or political success and thereby have gained some acceptability among the dominant group."[14]

In the 1986 case of *Batson v. Kentucky*, the Supreme Court also endorsed the use of statistical evidence in claims of racial discrimination in the use of peremptory challenges, which allow prosecutors and defense attorneys to remove a potential juror without having to show cause for the removal.[15] The *Batson* case marked a significant change in the law because the Court had previously required that any equal protection challenges to peremptory strikes demonstrate that they were a recurrent problem that had appeared in "case after case," a standard that posed an almost insurmountable burden on defendants.[16] *Batson* allowed criminal defendants to challenge peremptory strikes in their individual trials. Like the *Castaneda* framework, criminal defendants must first show that the challenges are directed against an identifiable group; then they must establish that the prosecutor used peremptory challenges to discriminate against the group. To show a pattern, a defendant can offer quantitative evidence, which does not need to be an elaborate study but can involve basic statistical models as well as testimony and other evidence. If the defendant establishes a prima facie case, the prosecutor then must articulate a neutral reason for the challenges. Statistical evidence can thus play a central role in creating an inference of prosecutorial intent to discriminate.

But one year later, in *McCleskey v. Kemp*, a different Supreme Court majority, by a five-to-four vote, limited the use of statistical evidence to demonstrate intentional discrimination in criminal sentencing.[17] McCleskey's challenge revolved around the death penalty sentence arising from his murder conviction for the killing of a white police officer. McCleskey, who was black, challenged the sentence on both equal protection and Eighth Amendment ("cruel and unusual punishment") grounds by introducing a set of statistical studies, compiled from more than 2,000 murder cases in Georgia during the 1970s, that showed disparities in sentencing based on the murder victim's race and, to a lesser extent, on the defendant's race. Produced by law professor David C. Baldus and other researchers, the Baldus study, as it came to be known, employed regression models that permitted the analysis of up to 230 variables that could be used to explain the disparities on nonracial grounds. Findings based on a thirty-nine-variable model showed that, on average, a defendant's odds of receiving the death penalty increased by a factor of 1.1 when the defendant was black and by a factor of 4.3 when the victim was white. Black defendants who were convicted of killing white victims thus carried the highest risk.

McCleskey's Eighth Amendment claim was arguably the stronger of the two claims because the law up to that point was concerned with the systemic *risk* of "arbitrary and capricious" sentencing, and the Baldus study clearly identified risks in the system. But McCleskey's equal protection claim was also viable, particularly after the Court's ruling in *Castaneda v. Partida*, where the Court approved a much simpler statistical model to infer discriminatory intent in jury selection. Writing for the majority in *McCleskey*, Justice Lewis Powell assumed that the Baldus study was methodologically valid but proceeded to reject both McCleskey's equal protection claim and his Eighth Amendment claim. The risk of "arbitrary and capricious" sentencing under the Eighth Amendment was addressed by changing the law to shift the focus away from systemic risk to the individual's particular case, effectively nullifying the relevance of the study.

In rejecting the equal protection claim, Justice Powell tried to distinguish *Castaneda v. Partida* (and Title VII statistical analyses) on several grounds. First, he argued that there are many more entities involved in death penalty decisions, thus making it difficult to isolate the discriminatory intentions. Second, individual juries are unique in composition, and their determinations are based on many factors. In contrast, a venire is composed of a more general group that is limited by only a few qualifying factors (such as being a voter and a resident of the county). Thus, because of all of these factors, Justice Powell proposed that there was no common standard on which to evaluate a death penalty case. Third, the state would not have a meaningful opportunity to rebut an analysis like the Baldus study since jurors cannot be called to testify about their decision making and prosecutors need to be given enough discretion in their decision making in death penalty cases. Fourth, death penalty sentencing is a fundamentally discretionary activity at "the heart of the criminal justice system" and therefore requires a much higher level of proof than do other processes.

Both critics and the dissenting justices attacked Justice Powell for relying on faulty assumptions and creating distinctions without any meaningful differences: first, even with many entities, sophisticated-enough statistical models could isolate the underlying criteria for decisions; second, it is not necessarily true that death penalty cases lack common standards or that employment decisions always have common standards; third, the state need not use the statements of jurors or prosecutors, which can be self-serving, to rebut a case, since it could attack the statistical evidence directly or produce its own statistical analyses; and fourth, death penalty cases are not uniquely at the heart of the criminal justice system, any more than having a representative jury is at the heart of the system.[18] Notwithstanding the weaknesses in Justice Powell's analysis, the bottom line is that, after *McCleskey*, statistical analyses, regardless of their sophistication, cannot create inferences of discrimination in individual death penalty cases.

Aside from the minutiae of the statistics-related arguments, both Justice Powell and the dissenting justices raised more basic concerns about the trade-offs and values inherent in maintaining the integrity of a death penalty system while also trying to keep racial discrimination out of the system. Justice Powell's proposal to privilege death penalty cases above other criminal justice processes because they go to "the heart of the criminal justice system" reveals a value judgment favoring the death penalty, just as language in Justice Brennan's dissent reveals his values in trying to eliminate racial discrimination from the system: "to reject McCleskey's powerful evidence . . . is to ignore both the qualitatively different character of the death penalty and the particular repugnance of racial discrimination."[19] And Justice Stevens' dissent was even more explicit, posing that "the Court's decision appears to be based on a fear that the acceptance of McCleskey's claim would sound the death knell for capital punishment in Georgia."[20]

## School Desegregation and Resegregation

In the more than fifty years that have passed since the Supreme Court's ruling in *Brown v. Board of Education*, segregation in elementary and secondary school education remains an intractable problem throughout the country, not just in the south. Yet the Supreme Court has shown a greater tolerance for evidence of discriminatory effects in the area of school desegregation, upholding school policies as constitutional that maintain high levels of segregation or even lead to greater segregation. The reams of data analyses that are typically produced in desegregation cases—including statistical metrics such as a "dissimilarity index," which typically runs on a scale of 0 (indicating full integration) to 100 (indicating full segregation), or an "exposure index," which provides numerical measures of cross-racial interaction on a scale of 0 (no interaction) to 1 (maximum interaction)—offer clear measures of segregation within school districts. The results are often sobering and discouraging.[21] Recent studies suggest that many northern and western school districts are among the most segregated in the country, while southern school districts are actually among the most racially integrated, primarily because of previous or ongoing desegregation orders.[22] The integration ideal engendered by *Brown* has not been abandoned altogether, but the Supreme Court's willingness to extend desegregation mandates has both expanded and contracted over time. Notwithstanding the extensive statistical and social science evidence that is introduced in desegregation cases to demonstrate problems of racial isolation, the Court in recent years has allowed school districts to be released from their previous obligations to desegregate. The result has been the resegregation of many school districts.

During the 1960s and early 1970s, the Supreme Court established specific guidelines requiring schools with de jure (intentional and legally mandated) segregated school systems to desegregate. The Court prohibited certain types of transfer plans that were employed after school boards rezoned their assignment districts to create desegregated schools because the transfer plans would inevitably lead back to segregation.[23] It also rejected the closure of public schools and the funding of new whites-only private schools with tax credits and subsidies when the clear intent of the closures was to avoid desegregation.[24] In *Green v. County School Board*, the Court ruled that segregated school systems must be dismantled "root and branch," with the goal of obtaining a "unitary" and nonracial school system in which desegregation is achieved not only in student assignments but also in facilities, staff, faculty, extracurricular activities, and transportation.[25]

In *Keyes v. School District No. 1*, the Court concluded that northern schools could commit de jure segregation even if segregation had not been mandated by statute. With ample statistical and historical evidence that the district had gerrymandered attendance zones and used construction policies to keep one part of the district segregated, the Court presumed the discriminatory intent of the school board and imposed the burden on the board to show that the remainder of the district was not intentionally segregated.[26] And in *Swann v. Charlotte-Mecklenburg Board of Education*, the Court endorsed an array of court-ordered remedies to address de jure segregation, such as redrawing attendance zones

(Including pairing or clustering zones that were not contiguous with each other) and ordering busing, so long as the time and distance was not so great that it posed a risk to students' health or interfered with the learning process.[27]

But the Court also made clear in its 1971 *Swann* decision that de facto segregation (unintended segregative effects) that might arise through changing demographics and residential patterns could not be addressed by court order, regardless of the severity of the racial imbalance in the schools. The de jure–de facto distinction that limits court-ordered remedies to intentional segregation, along with changes in the membership and values of the Supreme Court since the mid-1970s, have led to cases that have significantly diluted desegregation mandates. The Court curtailed the power of federal courts to order integration across city-suburb district lines and limited the use of magnet schools that draw students from the suburbs to the urban core unless the school segregation originally caused "white flight" to those suburbs.[28] And in *Board of Education v. Dowell*, the Court ruled that, when a school district has complied in good faith with a desegregation order and the vestiges of de jure segregation have been eliminated to the extent practicable, a district will be relieved of its desegregation responsibilities.[29] Despite statistical analyses in the *Dowell* case showing that thirty-three of the sixty-four elementary schools in the district would become hypersegregated by being more than 90 percent black or white, the Court ruled that the court-ordered desegregation order could be lifted. It has also ruled that as long as a district has achieved unitary status along only one of the dimensions described in *Green v. County School Board*, such as facilities or transportation, it can petition to have that portion of court-order lifted and be freed of its obligations.[30]

Clearly, these recent decisions in the desegregation arena illustrate major shifts in the values of members of the Court. There has been ample statistical evidence, both national and district-specific, to show that school segregation is severe in many communities, sometimes even reaching the levels found during the 1940s and 1950s, when the *Brown* litigation was initiated. But the Supreme Court has chosen to weigh the interest in obtaining desegregated schools against the concerns of school districts and the practicability of their policies; several Court majorities have been willing to tip the balance in favor of school districts, despite problems of resegregation. Scientific evidence of racial isolation has abounded in desegregation litigation, but the federal courts have been willing to give school districts the benefit of doubt and put an end to decades-old court orders when the schools are acting in good faith. Instead of addressing ongoing problems of segregation, much of the litigation being generated in the early twenty-first century has involved challenges by white plaintiffs to voluntary integration plans, paralleling the developments in higher education, where advocates of color-blind constitutionalism have actively litigated against university affirmative action programs.[31]

## Redistricting and "Expressive Harms"

One area in which the Supreme Court seems to have relaxed the intent requirement, or at least has offered a novel method of demonstrating intent, is in the area of race-conscious redistricting: it has recently allowed constitutional challenges to redistricting plans when districts are so bizarrely shaped that only racial considerations can account for the line drawing. *Shaw v. Reno* was a 1993 Supreme Court case involving a challenge to the decennially drawn congressional districts in North Carolina, some of which had been drawn to concentrate the electoral power of black voters in order to comply with the requirements of the federal Voting Rights Act. Because of longstanding patterns of residential segregation and voting behavior that closely tracks race (there is often a "black vote" and a "white vote,") voting rights are frequently tied to geography and the drawing of legislative lines. Vote dilution can occur when populations of minority voters are split between districts or when they are overconcentrated in one district and could have been divided more strategically across multiple districts in order for them to have the opportunity to elect additional representatives of their choice.[32]

Because the Supreme Court ruled in 1980 that the Fifteenth Amendment, like the equal protection clause, contains an intent requirement, Congress amended the Voting Rights Act in 1982 to allow claims based on discriminatory effects; thus, the act has been a major source for litigation challenging districting plans and electoral systems that may result in minority vote dilution.[33] Moreover, most of the southern states, as well as many counties in other parts of the country, are required under the Voting Rights Act to comply with special requirements when redrawing their lines or updating their election systems because of their long histories of racial discrimination in the electoral process.

With its many layers of evidence, voting rights litigation is the area of civil rights law that is perhaps most dependent on statistical and social science evidence because claims require proof of cohesive minority voting and strong oppositional voting as well as analyses of local populations, residential patterns, voting histories, and past discrimination. Techniques such as "homogeneous precinct analysis" and "ecological regression" are typically employed to show racial bloc voting. Because the Constitution requires that districts must be close to equal in population size, census data sets and advanced mapping software are commonly used to aid in line drawing and in constructing alternative districts.[34] As a consequence of the many lawsuits filed in the 1980s and early 1990s, along with the high costs of having to defend themselves with their own battery of experts, many state governments created majority-minority districts to avoid potential liability under the Voting Rights Act.

*Shaw v. Reno* was thus a novel and surprising constitutional claim because the Supreme Court itself had endorsed and set the parameters for vote dilution litigation in the 1980s.[35] Before 1992, no black person had ever been elected to Congress from North Carolina; after the creation of two majority-minority districts following the 1990 census, two black Democrats were elected to the House of Representatives. White voters challenged the North Carolina districting plan that had created the two districts, which were especially inelegant and multi-sided. One district was compared to a "Rorschach ink-blot test" and a "bug splattered on a windshield"; the other was considered even more oddly shaped—a snake-like configuration that tracked much of the length of an interstate highway.[36] As products of multiple interests, both partisan and nonpartisan, as well as highly politicized processes, electoral districts rarely conform to perfect geometrical forms. Yet the Supreme Court ruled in a five-to-four vote in *Shaw* that the line drawing itself triggered strict scrutiny and ultimately violated the equal protection clause. Writing for the majority, Justice O'Connor stated that "redistricting legislation that is so bizarre on its face that it is 'unexplainable on grounds other than race' . . . demands the same close scrutiny that we give other state laws that classify citizens by race."[37] She continued:

> Put differently, we believe that reapportionment is one area in which appearances do matter. A reapportionment plan that includes in one district individuals who belong to the same race, but who are otherwise widely separated by geographical and political boundaries, and who may have little in common with one another but the color of their skin, bears an uncomfortable resemblance to political apartheid. It reinforces the perception that members of the same racial group—regardless of their age, education, economic status, or the community in which they live—think alike, share the same political interests, and will prefer the same candidates at the polls.[38]

Yet what the scientific evidence from prior vote dilution litigation had shown was that members of the same racial group very often did share the same political interests and did prefer the same candidates at the polls. In creating a new constitutional claim based on appearances—the non-compactness of an electoral district—Justice O'Connor appeared to be placing a higher value on individualism and the undermining of racial stereotypes than on the realities of racial bloc voting. A *Shaw* claim apparently does not require that plaintiffs demonstrate their own vote dilution or other specific injury. Instead, the *Shaw* Court recognized an "expressive harm" that attaches more broadly to the injection of race into the political process and the automatic labeling of voters and districts by race.[39]

In subsequent cases, the Supreme Court has offered an alternative to the *Shaw* model that focuses less on geography than on whether race is the predominant factor in the districting process.[40] Also, a bizarrely shaped district or a plan in which race predominates is not per se unconstitutional; it triggers strict scrutiny, and a state can defend itself by demonstrating that the plan is narrowly tailored to satisfy a compelling interest, such as remedying past discrimination in the electoral process. Preventing a violation of the Voting Rights Act, if well documented, is also likely to be upheld as a compelling interest. Vote dilution claims are still available under the Voting Rights Act, but *Shaw* and its progeny have created a tension in which redistricting bodies must walk a fine line between using race just enough to comply with the Voting Rights Act but not so much that it could violate the equal protection clause. Scientific evidence will continue to be a major source of information and evidence in voting litigation, whether under the Voting Rights Act or in *Shaw v. Reno* claims. How the Court votes in future cases will determine whether the values of color-blindness and individuality predominate over the values of color-consciousness and group rights.

## Science in Remedial Affirmative Action

Affirmative action is one area in which plaintiffs have had no problems proving that the use of race is intentional; clearly, many policies designed to increase opportunities for racial minorities are not at all facially neutral. Before the Supreme Court's 1995 ruling in *Adarand Constructors, Inc., v. Peña*, the standard of review for race-conscious affirmative action policies was unsettled. Some earlier Court cases had upheld affirmative action programs by the federal government under an intermediate scrutiny test, while others cases addressing state and local policies applied a strict scrutiny test. The *Adarand* case made clear that strict scrutiny is applied in all cases involving race-conscious policymaking at the federal and state levels and regardless of whether racial minorities are burdened or benefit from a policy. [41]

Like other race-conscious policies, affirmative action policies must be narrowly tailored to a compelling governmental interest. Through 2003 the Supreme Court had recognized two compelling interests in the affirmative action arena: (1) remedying the present effects of past discrimination and (2) promoting student-body diversity in higher education. The Court did not turn to fact finding or scientific evidence to demonstrate the value of remedying past discrimination; in the eyes of the Court, it is inherently compelling. Remedying past discrimination is, however, a closely confined interest. It does not apply to remedying broad societal discrimination, which the Court has ruled is too amorphous to be constitutionally compelling. Instead, the past discrimination must be specific to a governmental institution, and both the past discrimination and its present effects must be thoroughly documented. Thus, an institution must demonstrate that it has a "strong basis in evidence" to show that it has discriminated in the past and that there are lingering effects of past discrimination. In addition, the Supreme Court has imposed specific narrow tailoring criteria that institutions must satisfy, including demonstrating that the particular policy is flexible, that it does not impose undue burdens on innocent third parties, that race-neutral alternatives have been considered, and that it has time limits. Fact finding is thus central to determining whether a remedial affirmative action program is constitutional.

The burden on government to justify a race-conscious policy is indeed heavy, and the policy must be carefully crafted and specific. For example, in *City of Richmond v. J. A. Croson Co.*, decided in 1989, the Supreme Court assessed the constitutionality of a minority set-aside program for publicly funded construction contracts and found the city's evidence to be insufficient to justify its interest in remedying past discrimination.[42] Among other things, the Court concluded that there was no evidence that the city itself had acted discriminatorily in the past; even though less than 1 percent of the past contracts had gone to African American contractors, there was no sign that the number of qualified minority businesses exceeded this percentage (that is, no evidence of disparities between those actual contracted and the potential pool of applicants); and congressional findings of nationwide discrimination did not indicate the degree of discrimination in the Richmond area itself. In addition, the Court concluded that Richmond's affirmative action policy was not narrowly tailored for a number of reasons, including the lack of consideration of race-neutral alternatives and the overinclusiveness resulting from the policy's inclusion of several racial and ethnic minority groups for whom there had been no history of discrimination in Richmond.

But the "strong basis in evidence" rule is not insurmountable. For instance, in *Concrete Works of Colorado v. City and County of Denver*, a case that the Supreme Court declined to review in 2003, the U.S. Court of Appeals for the Tenth Circuit addressed the constitutionality of a construction contractor program that established participation goals for minority- and women-owned firms.[43] The evidence offered by Denver was massive and produced a trial record that was more than 10,000 pages long. In presenting its defense, Denver relied on statistical studies and expert witness testimony that identified major disparities between the availability of minority-owned and women-owned businesses and Denver's use of them. A basic measure was calculating a disparity index by dividing the percentage of minority- and women-owned participation in city contracts by the percentage in the relevant population of local construction firms; an index of 1 would show full participation, while an index closer to 0 would show underuse. A number of the indices were stark: in 1985 housing bond projects, for example, the disparity indices were 0.43 for minority businesses and 0.09 for women-owned businesses. The studies also found that minorities in the construction industry were less likely to be self-employed in Denver; when they were self-employed, they made less money than whites did. In addition, the city offered anecdotal evidence, including testimony regarding racial graffiti, verbal and physical harassment on job sites, and widespread stereotyping against sub-contractors. Finding Denver's program to be narrowly tailored to its compelling interest in remedying past discrimination in the local construction contracting market, the Tenth Circuit upheld the program as constitutional.

## Higher Education Admissions

Beyond setting the evidentiary requirements that may guide the introduction of statistical and other scientific evidence in equal protection cases, the Supreme Court engages in its own science-based fact finding to aid its decision making. In the area of higher education admissions, the Supreme Court has not imposed the same heavy evidentiary burden as in its remedial affirmative action cases. The Court adopted a more deferential version of strict scrutiny in *Grutter v. Bollinger*, decided in 2003, when it recognized the promotion of student-body diversity in university settings as a compelling interest. Since institutions of higher learning hold a special place in the Court's constitutional tradition be-cause of the academic freedoms that they enjoy under the First Amendment, the Court ruled that the University of Michigan Law School's "educational judg-ment that such diversity is essential to its educational mission is one to which we defer."[44] Not only did the Court decline to impose its "strong basis in evi-dence" requirement on the university; it did not impose any specific evidentiary requirements at all. The Court did, however, turn to the trial record, amicus curiae briefs, and a number of social science studies on the benefits of student-body diversity to help support its conclusion that promoting diversity is a com-pelling interest. The Court also cited briefs submitted by retired military officers, several leading corporations, and educators to show the importance of diversity. Because the Court reached a general conclusion of law on the value of student-body diversity as a compelling interest—in the same way that the harms of segregation led to a general conclusion of law in *Brown v. Board of Education*—schools are not required to establish individual factual predicates to claim that their interest in promoting diversity is compelling, unlike remedial cases in which the government must always demonstrate its particular need to remedy past discrimination.

Narrow tailoring, however, is nearly as stringent in the higher education context as it is in remedial cases. The *Grutter* Court made clear that universities must adopt policies that are flexible and do not impose quotas or special tracks for minority students, do not impose undue burdens on non-minority students, contain time limits, and be weighed against race-neutral alternatives. The university's law school admissions policy—a "whole file review" policy that weighed applicants holistically and counted race as only one of many factors—satisfied the Court's multipronged narrow tailoring test. In the *Gratz v. Bollinger* case, however, the Supreme Court struck down the University of Michigan's undergraduate admissions policy because its point system, which allocated 20 points out of a possible total of 150 to underrepresented minority group members, was not sufficiently flexible and practically guaranteed admission to minority students.[45]

In addition to being cited in the *Grutter* Court's compelling interest inquiry, scientific evidence appeared in the Michigan opinions in various forms. In *Grutter,* dissenting justices used statistical data on admissions at the law school to try to undermine the school's argument that it was not employing a quota in trying to attain a critical mass of underrepresented minority students—a flexible goal designed to produce numbers that exceeded token numbers. Although the dissents' numbers were revealing (the percentages of various minority groups applying and admitted over a six-year period were fairly consistent), the *Grutter* majority countered by pointing to its own statistics showing that minority student enrollment figures varied significantly over time, suggesting that a quota was not at work. (Justice O'Connor's counterargument is not especially strong, however, because *enrollment* figures, compared to *admissions* figures, are subject to other influences outside of the admissions process; moreover, many top students are likely to have been admitted to other schools that they can choose to attend.) Dissenting justices also pointed to social science research to underscore various points. Justice Thomas's dissent in *Grutter* cited social science studies addressing potential disadvantages to diversity in education that tended to undermine the majority's compelling interest requirement, and Justice Ginsburg's dissent in *Gratz* cited extensive social science evidence to chronicle ongoing problems of racial inequality in the United States and to criticize admissions policies that might be used as alternatives to race-conscious admissions.

Because the *Grutter* Court relied on a less-strict strict scrutiny analysis, it is not clear how influential the social science evidence actually was—or how much it needed to be in order to make a difference in the case. Without question, scientific evidence informed and illuminated the Court's decision making and played small authoritative and rhetorical roles along with other sources that the Court cited to underscore the compelling interest argument. But the science may have fallen short as well: it did not provide clear answers to some empirical questions that were important and problematic, such as what *critical mass* might mean in specific terms. In any case, because of the controversies inherent in an issue such as race-conscious affirmative action, a host of interpretive tools were at play in the Michigan cases: precedents, constitutional theories of color-consciousness and color-blindness, contemporary values regarding racial equality, and constitutional fact finding. Thus, there is no ready answer to what counted most. The next affirmative action case that appears on the Supreme Court's docket will no doubt be just as complicated and controversial.

## Compelling Interests and Necessary Measures

The compelling interest inquiry in strict scrutiny analysis is essentially a value judgment on the importance of a governmental interest. Some interests require little discussion of their merits: remedying past discrimination, for example, is an inherently important interest that is consistent with a core principle of the civil justice system—past injuries should be remedied. Protecting national security during time of war is another interest that most people would agree is compelling, although many might disagree about the means used to advance the interest in a given case. But other governmental interests have not been so indisputably important and have been challenged in litigation. A university's interest in promoting diversity within its student body is just one example of a hotly contested state interest.

*Grutter v. Bollinger* is an important case, not only because the Supreme Court provided guidance on diversity-based admissions but because the *Grutter* Court made clear that remedying discrimination is not the only type of interest that can be compelling—in contrast to what the *Grutter* plaintiffs and some lower courts had argued. In doing so, the *Grutter* case opened the door to a wide variety of interests whose value, if sufficiently documented, might satisfy the compelling interest requirement. Although it is not clear if the stringent "strong basis in evidence" requirement imposed in remedial cases must apply to all cases outside of diversity-based admissions in higher education, the courts will require some quantum of evidence to justify race-conscious policies. Scientific evidence on the value of particular programs has been, and will likely continue to be, an important element whenever government takes account of race.

A number of lower courts have already turned to social science findings to support their upholding of compelling interests involving the use of race in elementary and secondary public education. For example, the U.S. Court of Appeals for the Ninth Circuit upheld the constitutionality of a race-conscious admissions policy for a laboratory school based at the University of California, Los Angeles, that had been engaged in research on urban education. Relying on the expert testimony of educators and psychologists who discussed the pressing problems of urban education, including race relations, and the importance of research in the field to improve the quality of education, the Ninth Circuit concluded that the "interest in operating a research-oriented elementary school" was a compelling interest.[46] Lower federal courts have also upheld the compelling interest in promoting racial diversity and reducing racial isolation in elementary and secondary education. In cases involving voluntary transfer policies that considered race as a factor, the courts have looked to a body of social science research on segregation and desegregation that had been developed in the aftermath of the *Brown* decision and desegregation efforts as well as more recent survey research and case studies on the benefits of racial diversity in contemporary K–I2 settings.[47]

Another area in which a nonremedial interest has been ruled constitutional is in serving the operational needs of law enforcement. In *Wittmer v. Peters*, the U.S. Court of Appeals for the Seventh Circuit upheld a hiring policy that favored black applicants for correctional officer positions at a prison "boot camp" because of the operational need to have guards whose race matched the race of the majority of prisoners.[48] The Seventh Circuit concluded that the race-conscious hiring plan was necessary to serve the inherently compelling interest in effective prison administration. Based on expert testimony, the Seventh Circuit concluded that "the black lieutenant is needed because the black inmates are believed unlikely to play the correctional game of brutal drill sergeant and brutalized recruit unless there are some blacks in authority in the camp."[49]

Although the court found the defendants' experts to be credible and helpful and the plaintiffs' expert testimony to be largely inconclusive, the social science evidence was not very extensive because little research on boot camps had been conducted up to that point in time. The Seventh Circuit adopted a deferential approach, arguing that it could not wait for science to catch up with a much-needed policy. Judge Richard Posner's opinion stated:

> It is true, as the district court pointed out, that the defendants' expert witnesses had had little experience with boot camps and that the social scientific literature on which they relied does not focus on such institutions. The reason is that these institutions are too recent to have been studied exhaustively, given the leisurely pace at which most academic research proceeds. If academic research is required to validate any departure from strict racial neutrality, social experimentation in the area of race will be impossible despite its urgency.[50]

The court did, however, caution that future research on the benefits of the policy would be vital to its being sustained: "We do not hold that after correctional boot camps have been around long enough to enable thorough academic (or academic-quality) study of the racial problems involved in their administration, prison officials can continue to coast on expert evidence that extrapolates to boot camps from the experts' research on conventional prisons."[51]

The Seventh Circuit's *Wittmer* decision showed an unusual degree of tolerance for governmental experimentation in the use of race to serve operational needs. And some of that tolerance can likely be attributed to the judges' intuitive or commonsense approval of the prison guard policy since the science itself was not conclusive. It is not entirely clear whether other federal courts or the Supreme Court will be willing to endorse innovative or experimental policies in later cases without a more considerable measure of empirical evidence. But regardless of how courts might rule in the future, the *Wittmer* case sends a signal that scientific research on race and social problems will continue to be needed in formulating public policies and assessing their constitutionality. One can expect that specific lines of scientific research will be developed to help demonstrate operational needs in areas of policing and employment as well as to show the benefits of racial diversity in sectors outside of higher education.

## Gender Stereotypes and Scientific Defenses

Scientific evidence has been used prominently in equal protection cases involving gender classifications, but the Supreme Court has been far less tolerant of statistical and other scientific evidence that has been used to defend policies that only reinforce stereotypes against women. If a policy is not predicated on "archaic and overbroad generalizations" about women, it is more likely to be upheld by the courts. But the Supreme Court has also recognized, with little resort to science, that fundamental biological differences do exist between men and women, and the differences have been especially important when reproductive biology is tied to a state's interest, such as an interest in preventing teen pregnancies or in ensuring parental status in order to confer U.S. citizenship on an out-of-wedlock child.[52]

For most of the nation's history, equality for women has been elusive; and the Supreme Court did little to apply constitutional protections to women. In *Bradwell v. Illinois*, decided in 1872, the Supreme Court upheld the denial to women of a license to practice law under the Fourteenth Amendment.[53] Justice Joseph Bradley, concurring in the decision, expressed a commonly held view of women under the law: "The civil law, as well as nature herself, has always recognized a wide difference in the respective spheres and destinies of man and woman. Man is, or should be, woman's protector and defender. The natural and proper timidity and delicacy which belongs to the female sex evidently unfits it for many of the occupations of civil life."[54] One hundred years would pass before the Supreme Court decided to extend the special protections of the Fourteenth Amendment through heightened review to gender-based classifications.

### Intermediate Scrutiny and Stereotyping

The Supreme Court came close to making gender a suspect classification in the early 1970s: in *Frontiero v. Richardson*, four votes were cast in a plurality opinion that employed strict scrutiny for the first time to strike down a gender classification, specifically an armed forces policy that discriminated against a female officer who sought the same benefits for her spouse that male officers received for their dependents.[55] Citing several social science studies that chronicled stereotyping and longstanding discrimination against women, Justice Brennan wrote: "Women still face pervasive, although at times more subtle, discrimination in our educational institutions, in the job market and, perhaps most conspicuously, in the political arena."[56]

But other members of the Court preferred the less searching rational basis test; consequently, in 1976, a majority of the Court settled on an intermediate level of scrutiny as the appropriate standard of review in gender cases. In *Craig v. Boren*, the Court addressed the constitutionality of an Oklahoma law that prohibited the sale of 3.2 percent beer, which was supposed to have limited intoxicating effects, to males under the age of twenty-one and to females under the age of eighteen.[57] The equal protection claim focused on the denial of rights to males in the age range of eighteen to twenty. Requiring that "classifications by gender must serve important governmental objectives and must be substantially related to achievement of those objectives," the Court accepted the state's interest in promoting traffic safety as important but rejected the relationship between the interest in traffic safety and the law's gender classification as insubstantial.[58]

Oklahoma's defense of its policy rested on a number of statistical studies that showed significant differences between men and women in alcohol use, drinking-related accidents, and arrests for driving while intoxicated. Justice Brennan highlighted the findings of one study that he considered most relevant to the case: 2 percent of males in the eighteen-to-twenty age range were arrested for drunken driving, while only 0.18 percent of females in the same age range were arrested. Stated another way, males were eleven times more likely than females in the relevant age range to be arrested for drunken driving. Nevertheless, Justice Brennan found the statistical evidence to be insufficient, stating that, "while such a disparity is not trivial in a statistical sense, it hardly can form the basis for employment of a gender line as a classifying device."[59] He proposed that using gender was not an effective proxy for drinking and driving because only 2 percent of the male population had been arrested; even assuming that the statistical studies were not methodologically suspect, none of them focused specifically on the use of 3.2 percent beer, which was supposed to be nonintoxicating anyway. Moreover, the law only prohibited the *sale* of 3.2 percent beer, not the actual drinking of beer, which the young men might have obtained through other means. Justice Brennan concluded that "the principles embodied in the Equal Protection Clause are not to be rendered inapplicable by statistically measured but loose-fitting generalities concerning the drinking tendencies of aggregate groups."[60] And in a more general statement about the limitations of statistical evidence, Justice Brennan added: "There is no reason to belabor this line of analysis. It is unrealistic to expect either members of the judiciary or state officials to be well versed in the rigors of experimental or statistical technique. But this merely illustrates that proving broad sociological propositions by statistics is a dubious business, and one that inevitably is in tension with the normative philosophy that underlies the Equal Protection Clause."[61]

While Justice Brennan's language is overly dismissive of scientific evidence as a general matter—statistical evidence cannot offer definite proof, only likelihoods that suggest inferences to a decision maker—his critiques of the *relevance* of the individual studies were sufficient to undermine the substantiality of the state's policy. Moreover, his language reveals how he chose to place normative values above scientific inquiry in his hierarchy of interpretive tools. More focused and relevant statistical evidence might have altered his perspective on the case, but it seems likely that Justice Brennan would still have found the law to be normatively objectionable and therefore unconstitutional under the heightened scrutiny standard.

### Scientific Defenses

But the Supreme Court has not always maintained an aversion to stereotyping in its gender discrimination cases. Consider *Rostker v. Goldberg*, a 1981 case in which the Court upheld the federal government's males-only selective service registration program for the military draft.[62] Empirical evidence abounded in the case on both sides. Amicus curiae briefs addressed questions of military readiness, the harms of stereotyping, and the question of whether or not women were capable of serving in the military, including in combat. The majority opinion written by Justice Rehnquist acknowledged some of the data offered on stereotyping against women and noted their ability to serve in the military; the Court nonetheless yielded to Congress's authority in military affairs and the fact that women were not eligible for combat positions in any case, thus making a males-only registration process acceptable. Writing in dissent, Justice Marshall criticized the majority's deference to Congress and its upholding of stereotypes and chided the Court for placing "its imprimatur on one of the most potent remaining public expressions of 'ancient canards about the proper role of women,'" and upholding a statute that "categorically excludes women from a fundamental civic obligation."[63]

More recent cases suggest, however, that the Court is unlikely to uphold gender classifications if there are any hints of stereotyping, even if statistical and scientific data might suggest some substantiality between the gender classification and the state's interest. In *Mississippi University for Women v. Hogan*, the Supreme Court addressed a male applicant's challenge to the women-only admissions policy of the School of Nursing at the state-operated Mississippi University for Women.[64] Putting the burden on the state to show an "exceedingly persuasive justification"—a restatement of the requirement that the policy be substantially related to an important interest—Justice O'Connor's majority opinion rejected the state's interest in remedying past discrimination against women since women had long predominated in the nursing profession and had had no trouble gaining entry to the field. The Court concluded that the policy of excluding males from the nursing school only perpetuated the stereotyped view of nursing as an exclusively woman's job. And since the school already permitted men to audit classes at the school, any substantial relationship between having only women at the school and advancing the school's educational goals was undermined.

Writing in dissent, Justice Powell proposed a less searching standard of review and advanced an additional interest that the majority did not acknowledge: providing women with additional educational choices, including single-sex learning. Justice Powell then cited an extensive literature tracing the history of women's colleges and showing the advantages of single-sex educational environments. Quoting one study, Justice Powell noted that "both [male and female] single-sex colleges facilitate student involvement in several areas: academic, interaction with faculty, and verbal aggressiveness. . . . Men's and women's colleges also have a positive effect on intellectual self-esteem. Students at single-sex colleges are more satisfied than students at coeducational colleges with virtually all aspects of college life."[65] The majority, however, was unpersuaded by Justice Powell's argument, countering that he was begging the question of whether the plaintiff or any other male applicant had the opportunity to attend the school of *his* choice, which he did not because of the nursing school's single-sex admissions policy.

In 1994, in *J.E.B. v. Alabama ex rel. T.B.*, the Court addressed the question of whether gender-based peremptory challenges violate the equal protection clause and, paralleling its prior reasoning in *Batson v. Kentucky*, held that gender, like race, is an "unconstitutional proxy for juror competence and impartiality."[66] The state proposed that men might be more sympathetic to the arguments of a man alleged in a paternity action to be the father of an out-of-wedlock child, while women might be more sympathetic to the arguments of the complaining witness who had given birth to the child. Writing for the majority, Justice Blackmun ruled that the peremptory challenges were based on stereotypes and generalizations about women's and men's attitudes. Specifically rejecting a study that the state offered in support of its "quasi-empirical claim that women and men may have different attitudes about certain issues justifying the use of gender as a proxy for bias," Justice Blackmun countered that "the majority of studies suggest that gender plays no identifiable role in jurors' attitudes."[67]

## United States v. Virginia

In 1996, the Supreme Court addressed the constitutionality of a single-sex program at the Virginia Military Institute (VMI), a males-only military college founded in 1839. The state of Virginia sought to defend its policy by arguing that VMI's males-only environment, which employed an "adversative" model of education that featured "physical rigor, mental stress, absolute equality of treatment, absence of privacy, minute regulation of behavior, and indoctrination in desirable values," would be undermined by the admission of women. One prominent feature of the model was the entering students' "rat line," which was "an extreme form of the adversarial model comparable in intensity to Marine Corps boot camp." Rather than compromise the model through the admission of women, the state tried to create a comparable but less rigorous program for women at a nearby private women's college. The basic interest put forward by the state was the interest in providing educational diversity within its state system, part of which would be a military college with VMI's unique features. The case went through an extensive trial, and the testimony of numerous expert witnesses was introduced into the record. Some experts focused on the integrity of VMI's adversarial model; some testified on the value of single-sex schools, both male and female; and some addressed the capability of women to function and succeed in military environments. Nearly twenty amicus curiae briefs were filed in the case, and a number of science-laden briefs supplemented the record with additional studies and research addressing empirical questions in the case.

In *United States v. Virginia*, the Supreme Court in a seven-to-one decision ruled that the VMI policy violated the equal protection rights of women and that the newly created women's program was not a sufficient substitute.[68] Applying a "skeptical scrutiny" standard that seemed to elevate the intermediate-level scrutiny applied in previous cases, the Court rejected the claim that the VMI program would be undermined by the admission of women. Writing for the majority, Justice Ruth Bader Ginsburg rejected the contention that promoting educational diversity in the Virginia state system was the true motivation of the state since there were no women-only programs that would balance the diversity of the system. While acknowledging that many, if not most, women might prefer a more cooperative learning environment—a point that the state's expert witnesses had suggested and on which the trial court had made findings of fact—Justice Ginsburg argued that this was a generalization and did not mean that the women seeking admission to VMI were not willing and able to participate in the adversarial program. Other research suggested that women were quite capable of surviving and excelling in military environments. Justice Ginsburg concluded that there was "no reason to believe that the admission of women capable of all the activities required of VMI cadets would destroy the Institute rather than enhance its capacity to serve the 'more perfect Union.'"[69]

In dissent, Justice Antonin Scalia criticized both the elevated skeptical scrutiny standard employed by the majority and Justice Ginsburg's disregard for the trial court's findings. Justice Scalia noted that, as an initial matter, the state had demonstrated at trial that "a substantial body of contemporary scholarship and research supports the proposition that, although males and females have significant areas of developmental overlap, they also have differing developmental needs that are deep-seated."[70] Moreover, the district court had found that "students of both sexes become more academically involved, interact with faculty frequently, show larger increases in intellectual self-esteem and are more satisfied with practically all aspects of college experience (the sole exception is social life) compared with their counterparts in coeducational institutions." In particular, Justice Scalia emphasized: "Attendance at an all-male college substantially increases the likelihood that a student will carry out career plans in law, business and college teaching, and also has a substantial positive effect on starting salaries in business. Women's colleges increase the chances that those who attend will obtain positions of leadership, complete the baccalaureate degree, and aspire to higher degrees."[71]

Justice Scalia's reliance on fact finding and scientific evidence in his dissent is ironic when compared to the more dismissive tone of his dissenting opinion in *Grutter v. Bollinger*, decided seven years after the VMI case. In *Grutter*, he criticized the majority for its constitutional fact finding regarding the educational benefits of diversity in higher education, even going so far as to argue that cross-racial understanding "is not, of course, an 'educational benefit' on which students will be graded on their Law School transcript . . . or tested by the bar examiners."[72] Scientific evidence—or Justice Scalia's dismissal of it in one case versus another—thus played a far more rhetorical role than the typical informational or authoritative role that it may have played in the majority opinions in either *United States v. Virginia* or *Grutter v. Bollinger*.

### Reproductive Biology and Gender Discrimination

Notwithstanding the recent line of cases striking down gender classifications that appear to rely on stereotyping, even when predicated in part on empirical evidence of gender differences, the Court has upheld gender classifications where the distinction between men and women is rooted in basic biological and reproductive differences between the sexes. In the 1981 case of *Michael M. v. Superior Court*, for example, the Supreme Court upheld a statutory rape law that applied only to male defendants because of the state's important interest in preventing unwanted teenage pregnancies, a particularized interest that would not be similarly advanced by applying the law to female defendants and male victims.[73]

More recently, in *Nguyen v. Immigration and Naturalization Service*, a 2001 case involving a challenge to a federal immigration law that imposed additional requirements on fathers of out-of-wedlock children to prove parenthood for purposes of conferring American citizenship on a child, the Supreme Court ruled that the extra requirements for fathers, which had to be completed before the child turned eighteen, were substantially related to the government's interests in ensuring a genuine biological parent-child relationship and making sure that a real and practical relationship exists between the child and the citizen parent and, in turn, the United States.[74] Arguing that biological and practical relationships between a mother and child are self-evident by the event of birth but not self-evident in the case of a father (even with scientific proof of paternity through DNA testing, there is no guarantee that a practical relationship will develop between the child and the father), the five-member majority in *Nguyen* concluded that gender stereotyping was not at the root of the government's policy.

Writing for the four dissenting justices in *Nguyen*, Justice O'Connor chastised the majority for failing to scrutinize the statute adequately by inquiring more deeply into whether the two cited interests were in fact the government's true interests; she also criticized the majority for upholding policies that were based not on genuine biological differences but on gender stereotypes. Justice O'Connor argued that the federal policy stereotypically presumed that fathers could not form the same caring relationships as mothers and that DNA testing could easily establish the fundamental biological relationship without resort to the statute's more onerous and time-limited requirements; moreover, gender-neutral alternatives that imposed the same burdens on fathers and mothers could just as readily satisfy the government's interests.

IF WE VIEW the 1973 *Craig v. Boren* decision and the 2001 *Nguyen* case as bookends for an evolving gender jurisprudence, we can see that scientific evidence seems to play an important role in Supreme Court decision making when it undermines gender stereotypes but may also be ignored or cast aside by the majority when it seems to reinforce stereotypes. Scientific evidence has not been unanimous or unquestioned, and both advocates and the justices have no doubt framed their arguments around the most supportive studies. One exception may be when governmental classifications are based on reproductive differences; in these instances, scientific evidence may play a subordinate role to commonsense—and potentially stereotypical—notions of biological differences between men and women. Ultimately, judicial values, as well as the changing membership of the Court, are the important determinants of gender discrimination decisions, not scientific evidence per se. The additions of Justice O'Connor and Justice Ginsburg, who was one of the leading litigators who brought the first major sex discrimination cases before the Court in the 1970s, have unquestionably shifted the balance of power and interests in gender cases; the skeptical scrutiny approach developed in the VMI case likely reflects that changing balance. Gender may not be a suspect classification in formal terms, but it appears that the Court will treat it as suspect as long as gender stereotyping remains a problem.

## Science and Irrationality

Although the rational basis test (the lowest level of equal protection review) usually leads to the upholding of legislation, it is not a rubber stamp that the Supreme Court applies automatically and without regard to the underlying purposes and methods employed in a policy. When the Court reviewed the City of Cleburne's denial of a permit that would have allowed the construction of a home for the mentally retarded in *City of Cleburne v. Cleburne Living Center*, the justices applied a searching rational basis inquiry and struck down the policy because it was fundamentally irrational. Scientific evidence often appears in both challenges and defenses of the rationality of public policies.

### Mental Retardation and Mental Illness: Rational Distinctions

In *Heller v. Doe*, a 1993 case involving a set of Kentucky statutes that permitted the state to involuntarily commit individuals who were found to be a danger to themselves or others, the U.S. Supreme Court upheld the constitutionality of a distinction between the mentally retarded and the mentally ill that provided greater procedural protections to mentally ill individuals.[75] Under the Kentucky laws, the burden of proof on the government to commit mentally retarded individuals was a "clear and convincing evidence" standard, a lower legal standard than the "beyond a reasonable doubt" standard required to commit mentally ill individuals.

In a five-to-four decision, the Court concluded that the distinction satisfied the rational basis test. Confirming that "a legislative choice is not subject to courtroom factfinding and may be based on rational speculation unsupported by evidence or empirical data," the Court ruled that the state of Kentucky had offered more than enough evidence to justify the differences in treatment between the mentally retarded and the mentally ill.[76] Justice Anthony Kennedy's majority opinion cited reference manuals from the American Psychiatric Association and the American Association on Mental Retardation as well as a range of scientific studies documenting key differences between the two groups in terms of conditions, treatments, and risks of misdiagnosis—all of which could justify the state's affording greater protection to the mentally ill. Moreover, he noted that "the law has long treated the classes as distinct, [which] suggests that there is a commonsense distinction between the mentally retarded and the mentally ill."[77]

In his dissenting opinion, however, Justice David Souter proposed that the Kentucky laws failed to satisfy even the low-level rational basis test. While acknowledging important differences between mental retardation and mental illness, he cited numerous research studies that demonstrated that the mentally retarded were also at significant risk of invasive treatments involving psychotropic drugs and serious psychiatric measures: "The same sorts of published authorities on which the Court relies . . . refute the contention that '[t]he prevailing methods of treatment for the mentally retarded, as a general rule, are much less invasive than are those given the mentally ill.'" Justice Souter concluded that "there are no apparent differences of therapeutic regimes that would plausibly explain less rigorous commitment standards for those alleged to be mentally retarded than for those alleged to be mentally ill."[78]

Because the Court had already ruled in the *Cleburne* case that the mentally retarded were not a suspect or quasi-suspect class, the rational basis test provided more than enough leeway for the five members of the *Heller* majority to rule that the Kentucky law complied with equal protection mandates. Even if the scientific evidence might not have been overwhelmingly conclusive, the relaxed legal standards provided sufficient room for the Court to defer to legislative judgments; as Justice Kennedy made clear, "the problems of government are practical ones and may justify, if they do not require, rough accommodations—illogical . . . and unscientific."[79]

### Rationality and Citizenship

As a general rule, the Supreme Court applies strict scrutiny to state and local government classifications based on citizenship status. But in 1973, it announced an important exception to the general rule whenever an alienage classification involves government jobs that "perform functions that go to the heart of representative government."[80] In *Sugarman v. Dougall*, the Court applied strict scrutiny to strike down a law limiting civil service jobs to citizens but also noted that some positions, such as those involving elective office and important non-elective positions dealing with policymaking, should be treated differently. Once categorized as falling within the *Sugarman* exception, a classification is subject to only minimal scrutiny and is routinely upheld. Over time, the *Sugarman* exception has grown so much that the exception has threatened to swallow the general rule. The Supreme Court has ruled, for example, that jobs such as state police officers and deputy probation officers fall within the exception and can be limited to citizens only.[81] Scientific evidence has played two supporting roles in these types of cases: (1) demonstrating whether or not a classification should fall within the exception; and (2) if it does, whether or not employing the classification is rational.

In *Ambach v. Norwick*, a five-to-four decision, the Court addressed the constitutionality of a New York state law that limited public school teacher positions to U.S. citizens and lawful permanent residents who intended to become citizens.[82] Taking into consideration the importance of public education and the degree of responsibility and discretion that teachers exercise in fulfilling their roles, the Court ruled that public school teachers perform a "governmental function" and therefore fell within the *Sugarman* exception. Citing a number of research studies, Justice Powell found that "perceptions of the public schools as inculcating fundamental values necessary to the maintenance of a democratic political system have been confirmed by the observations of social scientists."[83] Justice Powell later noted that studies "reinforce the common-sense judgment, and the experience of most of us, that a teacher exerts considerable influence over the development of fundamental social attitudes in students, including those attitudes which in the broadest sense of the term may be viewed as political."[84] Applying minimal scrutiny to the state's interest in providing education that imparts democratic values, the Court upheld the classification as entirely rational.

Writing in dissent, Justice Blackmun questioned both the categorization of public teachers within the governmental function exception and the rationality of the citizenship classification. After discussing the historical roots of the New York statute as one of several nativist laws enacted at the beginning of World War I, Justice Blackmun proposed that public school teachers fell well within the boundaries of those positions that should be open to noncitizens. Arguing against the law's rationality, he added a more commonsense objection: "Is it better to employ a poor citizen teacher than an excellent resident alien teacher? Is it preferable to have a citizen who has never seen Spain or a Latin American country teach Spanish to eighth graders and to deny that opportunity to a resident alien who may have lived for 20 years in the culture of Spain or Latin America?" Justice Blackmun concluded that "the State will know how to select its teachers responsibly, wholly apart from citizenship, and can do so selectively and intelligently."[85]

*Sexual Orientation*

Evolving attitudes toward homosexuality have made litigation in the area of gay and lesbian rights among the most intriguing and emotionally charged areas of constitutional and civil rights law. For instance, the state court decision in *Goodridge v. Department of Health*, the 2003 case in which the Massachusetts Supreme Judicial Court ruled that the state's failure to offer marriages to gay and lesbian couples violated the Massachusetts constitution, is among the most prominent and controversial court decisions in recent decades.[86] Although the history of discrimination against gays, lesbians, and bisexuals is lengthy and persistent, sexual orientation has not been ruled to be a either a suspect or quasi-suspect classification; and it is unlikely to be accorded heightened review status by the U.S. Supreme Court any time soon. Yet in recent equal protection and due process cases, the Court has developed a jurisprudence that is increasingly skeptical of legislation predicated on homosexual status or behavior. Scientific evidence has not played an authoritative role in the Supreme Court's recent decisions, at least if measured by arguments and citations in the Court's majority opinions. But scientific evidence has appeared in the records of cases and amicus curiae briefs to demonstrate the harms of stereotyping and to undermine biological and psychological misconceptions of homosexuality. These studies seem likely to have informed at least some of the justices' values and opinions.

The evolution of changing attitudes and values toward homosexuality in recent years is demonstrated by the Supreme Court's reversal of its 1986 ruling in *Bowers v. Hardwick* by its 2003 ruling in *Lawrence v. Texas*. The Court ruled in *Lawrence* that anti-homosexual sodomy laws violated a basic liberty interest under the Fourteenth Amendment's due process clause, even though the *Bowers* precedent was only seventeen years old and had reached exactly the opposite conclusion. But the issue of gay rights is clearly a divisive one. In *Boy Scouts of America v. Dale*—a case decided in 2000 in which the Court ruled that the Boy Scouts' associational freedoms under the First Amendment were violated by a state anti-discrimination law that barred the Boy Scouts from excluding gays as members—the justices divided on a five-to-four vote. The decision generated some strongly worded dissents that both chronicled the history of discrimination against gays and lesbians and articulated the changing attitudes toward homosexuality.[87]

The Supreme Court's major equal protection case in this area is *Romer v. Evans*, a 1996 case in which the Court ruled by a six-to-three vote that a Colorado constitutional amendment that would have prohibited the state or any Colorado cities from enacting anti-discrimination laws to protect gays and lesbians violated the equal protection clause.[88] The Court applied a rational basis test and did not address the question of whether heightened review was appropriate. Rejecting the state's argument that Amendment 2 was designed to protect the freedom of association of other Colorado citizens, Justice Kennedy's opinion concluded that the amendment was "inexplicable by anything but animus toward the class that it affects."[89] The bare desire to harm a politically unpopular group was a not legitimate interest according to the Court; the amendment was designed to make gays and lesbians "unequal to everyone else," which the Constitution clearly forbids. The *Romer* case dealt specifically with the rights of gays and lesbians as a class, but the case has implications for any group that may be disadvantaged in the political process because of discriminatory animus toward the group.

Leading professional associations such as the American Psychological Association, the American Psychiatric Association, and the American Public Health Association have been regular players in these cases through their amicus curiae briefs. They have contributed summaries of scientific literature dealing with the harms of stereotyping and discrimination, the minimal public health effects of anti-sodomy laws, and the misconception that homosexuality is a mental defect or disease. And their contributions have been cited by members of the Court: for example, in his dissenting opinion in *Boy Scouts of American v. Dale*, Justice Stevens considered the American Psychological Association's and the American Psychiatric Association's removal of *homosexuality* from their respective lists of disorders to be an important indicator of how attitudes toward gays and lesbians have changed in significant ways; Justice Blackmun made a similar observation in his *Bowers v. Hardwick* dissent.

Scientific findings may not have had an overriding influence on the Supreme Court's reasoning in these cases, but they were part of the large corpus of constitutional facts that informed the justices' decision making. Religious and moral traditions have factored heavily into views of homosexuality; yet scientific findings have, at least in recent decades, run counter to these beliefs. As Justice Stevens observed, the consensus among health professionals is that homosexuality is not a mental disorder; but that was not always the position of many scientists, and scientific attitudes have changed just as much as general attitudes within society and among judges and lawyers. Whether science leads or follows is perhaps not as important as the fact that it informs and is informed by changing societal values.

## Science and Constitutional Values

Are there any clear patterns indicating when and how the Court will use scientific evidence in making constitutional decisions? Empirical studies of the Supreme Court's uses of social science have revealed a few trends, but none are especially surprising. For instance, in a 1998 study examining thirty-five of the Supreme Court's gender-related cases, including sex discrimination cases, Rosemary J. Erickson and Rita J. Simon offered the not-unexpected conclusion that the Court gives more weight to its past rulings than to social science data. Erickson and Simon also found that the Court's use of social science does not depend on whether it was introduced in the lower courts; the frequency of the use of data does not depend on whether an opinion is a majority or dissenting opinion; certain kinds of social science data do not carry more weight than others; and data are used in court consistent with legal standards, not social science standards.[90]

Examining the Supreme Court's equal protection jurisprudence of recent decades suggests that scientific evidence often plays an informational role for justices, confirming and legitimizing their value-driven decision making. When addressing basic normative questions, such as whether a governmental interest is sufficiently weighty to be "compelling," scientific evidence can reinforce value judgments, such as when the Supreme Court cited social science evidence on the benefits of student-body diversity in higher education. When cases have required assessing multiple interests and various costs and benefits in a balancing test, the Court can turn to constitutional facts, including scientific evidence, to inform and support its judgments. In *Plyler v. Doe*, the 1982 case involving the rights of undocumented immigrant students, the majority drew heavily on economic data and social science testimony contained in the record to weigh the costs and benefits of employing a heightened standard of review and the substantiality of the state's interests and classifications. But the balancing test was not a simple mathematical equation, where the Court could plug in numbers for cost and benefit variables. The weighting of studies and expert opinions was a product of both evidence and judicial norms and values: the meaning of equality when applied to a state deprivation of rights against a particularly vulnerable population.

But even if there is evidence that supports a possible justification for maintaining a group difference, such as gender differences or racial bloc voting, the Court does not always heed the outcomes of scientific evidence. Again, judicial values predominate. Recent gender discrimination cases have illuminated the justices' strong adherence to an anti-discrimination principle that prohibits differential treatment that is based in or maintains stereotypes about women and men. A related current has developed in the racial gerrymandering cases, where a majority of the court has been willing to recognize constitutional claims that run counter to studies on voting behavior, largely to advance a more individualistic, color-blind agenda that minimizes the use of race in public policymaking. Similar values have appeared in the Court's recent affirmative action cases but usually with one or two justices tipping the balance in a different direction to allow some degree of race-consciousness. Members of the Court have been attentive to constitutional fact finding; the more thoroughly developed opinions, majority or dissenting, reflect that attentiveness. But fact finding rarely gets in the way of overriding norms and values. In setting the basic ground rules for many constitutional claims, whether imposing difficult standards that may preclude even the most sophisticated statistical analyses from showing discriminatory intent or requiring a "strong basis in evidence" for institutions trying to defend remedial affirmative action programs or redistricting plans, some justices have demonstrated their less-than-enthusiastic interest in addressing ongoing problems of racial discrimination and their skepticism for any policy that takes race into account.

# 6

## Science, Advocacy,
## and Fact Finding

During a series of individual interviews with three of the nine sitting justices on the Supreme Court, conducted not long after the conclusion of the Court's 2002–3 term, law professor David L. Faigman posed several questions focusing on the Court's constitutional fact finding. The three justices—Stephen Breyer, Sandra Day O'Connor, and John Paul Stevens—offered a set of revealing, sometimes incongruous responses to Faigman's queries, confirming some of his presuppositions about "the haphazard way constitutional facts come to the Court's attention."[1] Justice Breyer, for example, cited amicus curiae briefs submitted directly to the Court as a leading source of information for the justices in obtaining legislative facts since it was "very rare that facts will be found in lower courts in constitutional cases in ways that are specific or [that] we would have to reconsider."[2] Justices Stevens and O'Connor, on the other hand, were less supportive of amicus curiae briefs, preferring facts that had bubbled up through the trial record and been put through the rigors of the adversarial process. But both acknowledged the usefulness of amicus briefs, particularly when the record was not well developed.

All three justices agreed that the Court rarely asked outside help, such as a court-appointed expert or a special master, to assist them with highly technical scientific information. They also agreed that, in general, the courts are not as effective at fact finding as Congress or the state legislatures are and thus owe those bodies a certain degree of deference. But Justice Stevens also noted that when inquiries are very focused, as in a trial, judicial fact finding can be superior to a legislature's fact finding, which tends to be more effective in open-ended inquiries. In his view, the adversarial process is an especially effective way of getting at the facts, particularly through cross-examination and other procedures for screening and challenging evidence. Accordingly, Justice

Stevens placed a premium on appellate courts' respect for a lower court's fact finding because trial judges can assess the credibility of witnesses: "I am very big on giving deference to the lower-court judge who has heard the witnesses."[3]

When asked how they would deal with cases in which changing facts and circumstances might affect their interpretation of the Constitution, all three acknowledged that changes in factual circumstances could require a change in the law. Both Justice Breyer and Justice Stevens cited *Brown v. Board of Education* as a case in which changed facts did *not* make a difference because, in their opinion, the facts in *Brown* supported only an overarching normative principle. But Justice Stevens and Justice O'Connor did identify the affirmative action case of *Grutter v. Bollinger* as a case in which the ruling strongly depended on the factual context; Justice Stevens suggested that new facts and research might lead the Court in related or different directions, such as justifying the use of race beyond the realm of higher education. Faigman noted that the remarks confirmed the view that many constitutional cases contain mixed questions of fact and law: "There is an unmistakable empirical component, but the values infused in the determination of the facts may demand a particular result despite changed circumstances. . . . The facts of the matter may become irrelevant if the constitutional value remains."[4]

Constitutional fact finding is a complex endeavor, driven by both facts and values. This chapter examines the process of constitutional fact finding from multiple perspectives. Judicial decision making itself provides one dimension, but the standpoints of advocates and scientists are also critical to an understanding of the overall process. I begin with a discussion of the Supreme Court's decision in *Daubert v. Merrell Dow Pharmaceuticals, Inc.,* a landmark case addressing the admissibility of scientific evidence in the federal courts and the Court's leading attempt to reconcile the world of litigation, with its adversarial process and strict rules of evidence, with the world of science and empirical methodologies. I then explore some of the questions that arise in gatekeeping, judicial notice, the use of expert witnesses and amicus curiae briefs, and the influence of law and advocacy on science itself. To provide additional context for these issues, I examine the University of Michigan affirmative action cases in detail—from initial filings through multiple appeals. The chapter concludes with a review of some policy recommendations that commentators have proposed in response to weaknesses in the constitutional fact-finding process.

## *Daubert* and Scientific Knowledge

The Supreme Court's 1993 decision *Daubert v. Merrell Dow Pharmaceuticals, Inc.* clarified the standards for admitting scientific evidence under the Federal Rules of Evidence as well as case law setting limits on the range of expert witness testimony.[5] The *Daubert* case itself focused on tort litigation against Merrell

Dow, manufacturer and distributor of Bendectin, a drug that had been widely prescribed for pregnant women's morning sickness from the mid-1950s until 1983, when it was removed from the market. When the drug was suspected of causing deformities in newborn children, hundreds of lawsuits were filed against the company. The *Daubert* plaintiffs had sought to introduce expert testimony that would show a connection between Bendectin and birth defects. The trial court, however, refused to admit the proffered evidence under a widely followed rule established in *Frye v. United States*, a 1923 case in which a federal court had held that, in order for expert testimony to be admissible, the expert's knowledge had to be based on information that had attained "general acceptance" within a scientific community. Under the *Frye* rule, general acceptance typically meant that the testimony had to be based on data that had been published in peer-reviewed journals. The proffered testimony in *Daubert* did not meet the baseline standard.

Writing for the Court, Justice Blackmun held that *Frye*'s general acceptance rule was no longer the appropriate standard under the 1975 Federal Rules of Evidence. In doing so, he concluded that the federal rules had superseded the *Frye* rule and created a new phrase—"scientific knowledge"—that had replaced general acceptance. Consequently, the rules also imposed a heavier burden on federal district court judges to assess the reliability of the proffered scientific evidence, a gatekeeping responsibility to inquire into scientific validity before admitting the testimony. Although *reliability* and *validity* can have specific meanings for scientists (*validity* can refer to whether a metric is in fact measuring what it is supposed to be measuring, *reliability* to whether a technique produces consistent results), in the context of the federal evidence rules the terms carry broader, more everyday meanings. Reliability implies trustworthiness, and validity implies a legitimacy that is based on whether the evidence is "good" science. The Court suggested four criteria to evaluate the validity of the scientific evidence: (1) the theory or technique has been tested and is falsifiable; (2) it has been subjected to peer review and publication; (3) standards have been employed for a specific scientific technique, and the technique has a known or potential rate of error; and (4) the theory or technique has general acceptance within a scientific community.[6]

By suggesting a favored but not exhaustive set of criteria by which to evaluate whether an expert's testimony is based on scientific knowledge, Justice Blackmun established preferences for an epistemology rooted in a prominent philosophy of science. He cited the work of philosophers Karl Popper and Carl Hempel for the proposition that scientific theories or techniques should be testable and falsifiable; in other words, it is possible to prove that a scientific theory is wrong or incorrect by additional testing, in contrast to propositions that cannot be tested or refuted—such as faith-based arguments regarding the existence of a supreme being. Quoting Popper, Justice Blackmun noted: "The criterion of the scientific status of a theory is its falsifiability, or refutability, or testability."[7]

Falsifiability is a useful philosophical proposition that helps define a line between science and nonscience, but it has not enjoyed widespread support among either scientists or philosophers of science. As a practical matter, most scientists do not engage in the practice of falsifying theories; instead, they spend most of their time trying to confirm existing and new theories.[8] Chief Justice Rehnquist found the concept of falsifiability to be more slippery than Justice Blackmun did: "I defer to no one in my confidence in federal judges; but I am at a loss to know what is meant when it is said that the scientific status of a theory depends on its 'falsifiability,' and I suspect some of them will be, too."[9]

Critics of *Daubert* have been less discreet, not only because of the Court's reliance on Popper and the falsifiability test but because the Court placed strong dependence and trust in empiricism as a means of acquiring knowledge. Timothy Zick, for example, argues that "what is missing from the *Daubert* discussion and core framework is any mention or recognition of culture, institutions, politics, or other widely recognized mediating factors which complicate claims of scientific objectivity and universality. *Daubert's* conception of science is essentially 'Popperian'—a linear view of the scientific project which vests judicial faith in empirical testing as the principal means to verifiable 'truths.'"[10]

Epistemological questions notwithstanding, *Daubert* vests in federal district court judges significant responsibilities to determine the reliability of scientific evidence, even though most judges are not formally trained in the sciences and can face a daunting task in playing "amateur scientist," as Chief Justice Rehnquist labeled the role in his *Daubert* opinion. Judge Alex Kozinski noted in his opinion in *Daubert*, after the case had been remanded back to the Ninth Circuit: "Though we are largely untrained in science and certainly no match for any of the witnesses whose testimony we are reviewing, it is our responsibility to determine whether those experts' proposed testimony amounts to 'scientific knowledge,' constitutes 'good science' and was 'derived by the scientific method.'"[11] Moreover, when the theories or techniques involved in the litigation are on the leading edge of scientific discovery, "scientists often have vigorous and sincere disagreements as to what research methodology is proper"; the judge must resolve disputes "among respected, well-credentialed scientists about matters squarely within their expertise, in areas where there is no scientific consensus as to what is and what is not 'good science.'"[12] (The Ninth Circuit panel ruled that the plaintiffs' proffered expert testimony in *Daubert* was still inadmissible under the new guidelines.) Federal judges do face significant challenges; but as a result of the gatekeeping responsibilities under *Daubert*, increased attention has been given to judicial training and education, the use of special masters to assist judges, and other structural solutions to augment the judiciary's capacity to assess scientific evidence.

In a later case, the Supreme Court ruled that a judge's gatekeeping responsibilities apply not only to expert testimony based on scientific knowledge but
also to expert testimony based on "skill—or experience-based observation."[13]
For instance, a beekeeper who has spent years observing the bees' patterns of
flight can qualify as an expert witness, even without formal training or education in entomology. The Court adopted a flexible test for the admission of nonscientific expert testimony, requiring "intellectual rigor" but not mandating the
four criteria for scientific reliability that the Court articulated in *Daubert*. The
Federal Rules of Evidence were amended in 2000 to incorporate *Daubert* and
related cases, and the applicable rule now states:

> If scientific, technical, or other specialized knowledge will assist the trier
> of fact to understand the evidence or to determine a fact in issue, a wit-
> ness qualified as an expert by knowledge, skill, experience, training, or
> education, may testify thereto in the form of an opinion or otherwise, if
> (1) the testimony is based upon sufficient facts or data, (2) the testimony
> is the product of reliable principles and methods, and (3) the witness has
> applied the principles and methods reliably to the facts of the case.[14]

What *Daubert* and its progeny have thus generated is a system under which trial
court judges have extensive responsibilities, powers, and discretion to flexibly
assess expert testimony, whether it is based on scientific knowledge or an
expert's skill or experience.

Although the *Daubert* line of cases applies to trial court gatekeeping, it has
several implications for legislative and constitutional fact finding, even if constitutional interpretation occurs largely at the appellate court level or eventually in the Supreme Court. First, trial courts are the first line of the judiciary in
almost all constitutional cases; even if precedent-bound in addressing the legal
issues, they must engage in adjudicative fact finding to establish the context
and record for the constitutional claims. Second, because constitutional cases
can involve "mixed questions of law and fact," distinctions between adjudicative and legislative fact finding can easily blur at the trial court level; expert
witnesses can yield useful facts that are both adjudicative and legislative in nature, and distinctions between the two types of facts may be sorted out later
during the judge's decision making process rather than during the course of the
trial. Third, trial courts can and often do engage in constitutional interpretation
and the development of new constitutional rules if a claim appears to raise
novel questions of law; experts can thus be employed specifically to address
issues of constitutional meaning and value.

Nevertheless, like the federal courts of appeals and the Supreme Court, a
federal trial court engaging in constitutional or legislative fact finding is not
limited to what the parties introduce into the record and can rely on additional

sources, such as amicus curiae briefs, or engage in its own fact finding in order to address broader questions of law. As noted, some members of the Supreme Court (as well as other members of the federal judiciary) may prefer to rely on sources that have gone through the process of reliability determinations, formal testimony, and cross-examination because the evidence will have been subjected to the rigors of the adversarial process before percolating into the appellate courts. Where *Daubert* may be helpful in the interpretive process is in suggesting a set of screens and filters for legislative fact finding when it involves scientific information. If courts choose to engage in additional legislative fact finding beyond what the parties offer into evidence, the *Daubert* criteria provide a potential starting point for evaluating scientific literature available in appellate briefs from the parties, amicus briefs, and the courts' independent research. A *Daubert*-like inquiry into the reliability and validity of studies introduced in amicus briefs or other research would introduce more rigor to the normally open-ended process of legislative fact finding and, if documented in the lower court's opinion, could ultimately provide a more useful record for a higher court taking the case on appeal.

## Judicial Notice: Adjudicative versus Legislative Facts

The primary method allowing courts at all levels to engage in open-ended constitutional or legislative fact finding is known as "judicial notice," the procedure by which a court can recognize facts, usually ones of common knowledge, that it can then take into consideration without requiring evidence to be introduced to establish the facts. In other words, judicial notice allows courts to accept facts as given, thus bypassing the usual evidentiary rules. Judicial notice is essential to the efficiency of trials and hearings because it allows the court to take notice of laws and basic information about the world without requiring the parties to introduce obvious and repetitive evidence as if the court were operating with an absolutely blank slate.

Federal Rule of Evidence 201 governs judicial notice of adjudicative facts and limits judicial notice to a fact that is "not subject to reasonable dispute" either because it is "generally known within the territorial jurisdiction of the trial court" or because it is "capable of accurate and ready determination by resort to sources whose accuracy cannot reasonably be questioned."[15] Indisputability is the key. An example of an adjudicative fact that could be judicially noticed is "The University of Michigan Law School is located in Ann Arbor, Michigan," a fact that none of the parties or the judge would contest. But Rule 201 explicitly excludes legislative fact finding from its coverage because of the basic difference between adjudicative and legislative facts. According to the advisory committee's notes to the rule, "Adjudicative facts are simply the facts of the particular case. Legislative facts, on the other hand, are those which have relevance to legal reasoning and the lawmaking process, whether in the formulation of a legal principle or ruling by a judge or court or in the enactment of a legislative body."[16] Quoting Kenneth Culp Davis, the originator of adjudicative-legislative fact distinction, the notes offer the following justification for excluding legislative fact finding from Rule 201: "Judge-made law would stop growing if judges, in thinking about questions of law and policy, were forbidden to take into account the facts they believe, as distinguished from facts which are 'clearly . . . within the domain of the indisputable.' Facts most needed in thinking about difficult problems of law and policy have a way of being outside the domain of the clearly indisputable."[17] The rule thus reflects a policy determination that judges should not be hamstrung by an evidentiary rule when engaged in constitutional or other legislative finding because the issues at stake may require a broad examination of law and empirical information to assist in developing normative legal rules and principles.

Without a formal rule of evidence limiting legislative fact finding, the courts are left to police themselves. The result has been little case law on legislative fact finding; what does exist imposes practically no limits on the use of scientific evidence as legislative or constitutional facts. Indeed, *Brown v. Board of Education* and *Roe v. Wade* are frequently cited as basic examples of cases involving legitimate uses of legislative facts. And the Supreme Court, with its own use of scientific evidence in its opinions, has not limited constitutional fact finding in any formal way; typically, the justices criticize the basic reasoning of the other justices, not whether a justice can appropriately take judicial notice of a scientific study. For example, in *Roe v. Wade*, Chief Justice Burger did not fully agree with Justice Blackmun's trimestral framework, but he did not question Justice Blackmun's ability to take judicial notice of the data: "I am somewhat troubled that the Court has taken notice of various scientific and medical data in reaching its conclusion; however, I do not believe that the Court has exceeded the scope of judicial notice accepted in other contexts."[18]

But the Supreme Court does occasionally get into debates about lower court findings of fact and whether the Court has properly deferred to those findings or has substituted its own set of facts via judicial notice. For instance, in striking down the Virginia Military Institute's males-only admissions policy in *United States v. Virginia*, Justice Ginsburg gave little weight to some of the lower court findings on gender-based developmental differences and instead found support in research that showed the success of women in military settings. Justice Scalia's dissent focused significant attention on the Court's discounting of the lower court findings: "[The Court] makes evident that the parties to this litigation could have saved themselves a great deal of time, trouble, and expense by omitting a trial. The Court simply dispenses with the evidence submitted at trial—it never says that a single finding of the District Court is clearly erroneous—in favor of the Justices' own view of the world."[19] The "clearly erroneous" standard is the standard that appellate courts normally apply to lower court findings of fact, yielding to the lower court unless it has committed clear error because of its superior ability to assess the credibility of witnesses. But the Court majority was not bound by those factual findings because it was engaging in legislative fact finding to answer the basic constitutional questions in the case. The trial court's findings of fact on gender-based developmental differences were legislative facts since they addressed the general question of whether male-only education had a justifiable basis (compared to how the specific program at VMI operated, a finding of adjudicative fact that enjoyed more deference). Legislative facts can be disputable, and often are; Justice Ginsburg had concluded that one set of legislative facts was more informative and convincing than another set—shaded, of course, by the underlying normative value of gender equality.

## Science and Adversarial Justice

Disputes are endemic to litigation and the adversarialism that animates the American justice system. The adversary system is predicated on the assumption that the clash of interests and the evidence that each party produces out of self-interest will result in an eventual "truth" and thus a correct and just resolution of the dispute—a process that is significantly different from the knowledge-seeking, ostensibly value-neutral mechanisms typically employed in scientific endeavors. The elaborate rules of procedure and evidence, including cross-examination, provide rigor to the adversarial process so that evidence presented by one side is not assumed to be right or true. But with this system of adversarial justice comes the potential for evidence and arguments to be prejudiced and tainted: bias is inherent in the adversarial system; and winning the case is the primary interest of parties and their advocates, not necessarily ensuring that the judge or the jury arrives at the correct "truth."

Scientific evidence and expert witnesses are thus employed largely to serve instrumental ends, advancing the interests of the party that introduces the evidence. This does not necessarily imply that the scientific evidence itself is biased, but it does mean that it will be treated in the context of one side's interests and subjected to the rules of evidence, including the *Daubert* standards and cross-examination. Opposing parties in turn have a responsibility to try to minimize the effectiveness of that scientific evidence, whether by arguing its irrelevancy, undermining or discrediting it through cross-examination, or disputing the evidence with a countervailing body of scientific evidence and expert witnesses. And while scientific evidence plays an informational role for the judge or the jury, it is also a rhetorical tool for the party submitting the evidence. A scientific expert—particularly if characterized as a "leading" or "preeminent" authority in the field—is no ordinary witness. Inherent in the introduction of an expert witness is an *argumentum ab auctoritate*, an appeal to an authority figure who is lionized and treated as oracular, at least from the perspective of the party offering the expert.

The centrality of scientific evidence in many types of litigation has inevitably created regular roles for scientists as expert witnesses and affected the development of scientific investigation in order to generate the information needed to resolve disputes. Some scientists have become repeat players in litigation, lending their names and expertise to favored causes or the highest bidder. Some scientists work only in service to litigators or parties; for example, law firms involved in medical malpractice litigation often have in-house scientists who review and prepare cases. Clearinghouses and referral networks for experts are also commonplace. As Sheila Jasanoff observes, what the judge or the jury sees in practice are "two carefully constructed representations of reality, each resting on a foundation of expert knowledge but each profoundly conditioned by the culture of expert witnessing as it intersects with the interests, ingenuity, and resources of the proffering party."[20]

The pressures of advocacy can also affect scientific discovery itself. It is routine for statistical evidence to be generated in civil rights litigation to address specific questions that the parties must answer in order to advance their case, such as measuring the levels of segregation within a school district or determining whether there are lingering racial disparities in a government contracting market caused by past discrimination. But litigation interests can also drive more general scientific investigations, the kind of research that could spawn information of use to courts engaging in legislative or constitutional fact finding. For example, a large portion of the social science research on the educational benefits of diversity in higher education was generated after 1996, when a federal court struck down the admissions program at the University of Texas School of Law and called into question the constitutionality of race-conscious admissions plans for the first time in a generation. What had been presumed for nearly twenty years, but had not been well researched, was the idea that student-body diversity actually led to cross-racial interaction and improved learning in university settings. Anticipating more litigation, including an inevitable appeal in the Supreme Court, many social scientists began to test and document the hypotheses that most leaders in higher education had already assumed formed the reality on their campuses.[21]

Although scientific research generated in response to an important social problem does not necessarily imply that it is biased, it does engender important questions about the integrity of scientific investigation. How closely together should scientists and advocates work? Will researchers already predisposed to certain results set their initial hypotheses and testing methods to reach those results? Might researchers quell (or be asked to quell) data that do not support a legal claim or defense? If one adheres to a positivist perspective on scientific inquiry, then the demands of advocacy and the adversarial system of justice can be inconsistent with, and even inimical to, scientific investigation, an endeavor predicated on objective methods that attempt to eliminate bias. But even if one adopts the position of a postmodernist, denying the objectivity of any scientific inquiry, there are still important practical reasons for investing in at least the appearance of objectivity: scientific knowledge enjoys a privileged place within the law of evidence and is viewed more credibly in the minds of decision makers precisely because it is defined by its objective methods—as the *Daubert* case reinforces.

## Junk Science

*Daubert*, the rules of evidence, and the adversarial system in general are all designed to serve as filters for scientific knowledge, preventing unsound, untested, or purely suppositional studies—what Peter W. Huber has labeled "junk science"—from entering and contaminating the legal decision-making process.[22] But because legislative fact finding allows judges to go beyond the record and examine additional sources of information, whether they arrive through amicus curiae briefs or are products of the judges' own research, the filtering process can be sidestepped. Judges can certainly apply the *Daubert* standards to scientific studies that are gleaned from outside the evidentiary record, but whether any judges do so in practice is itself an empirical question without a clear answer.

Amicus briefs can be an especially important source of information for judges, who do pay attention to them. In the Supreme Court appeal of the University of Michigan affirmative action cases, for instance, a total of more than one hundred amicus briefs were filed by various interests; the justices relied on several of the briefs during the oral arguments and in their majority and dissenting opinions. Because they summarize and condense literature into a single compilation, amicus briefs can be particularly helpful to courts that cannot devote sufficient resources to engage in extensive research in scientific literature. But science-laden briefs also have the potential to bring in advocacy in the guise of science, so much so that some commentators have likened many Brandeis briefs to disingenuous lobbying efforts.[23] Occasionally, a group of scientists or a scientific association may offer a brief that is nonpartisan, but most briefs stake out positions and support one of the parties. Even if the science itself is not biased, the presentation of the science, as well as any omitted studies, are biased in favor of one side in the litigation over the other. Procedural rules and rules of court allow judges to regulate and limit the submission of amicus curiae briefs, but there are no formal checks on the actual content of the briefs, other than the judges' investigations into the studies contained in them. Judges are essentially left to their own devices.

## A Fact-Finding Example: The University of Michigan Cases

To illustrate how some of these fact finding issues have operated in practice, I will use the following sections to examine the University of Michigan cases—*Grutter v. Bollinger* and *Gratz v. Bollinger*—in some depth. The record in the *Grutter* case is especially rich because it went to a full trial that lasted for more than two weeks and was the subject of a lengthy set of opinions in the U.S. Court of Appeals for the Sixth Circuit before being taken up by the Supreme Court. Expert reports were filed in both cases, and a number of experts testified in the *Grutter* trial. Statistical evidence was generated to determine how the admissions programs operated, and several independent studies were developed during the course of the litigation. In addition, amicus curiae briefs were filed at all court levels, and a record number of amicus briefs were submitted to the Supreme Court.

### *Background:* Bakke *to* Hopwood

Although the Supreme Court's 1978 ruling in *Regents of the University of California v. Bakke* appeared to have settled the question of whether race-conscious affirmative action programs were constitutional, litigation was initiated in the 1990s to challenge the basic ruling in *Bakke*.[24] The Supreme Court had fragmented in the case, with a bare majority ruling that an admissions policy that set aside sixteen out of one hundred seats in the entering class at the University of California, Davis medical school for disadvantaged minority students was illegal; a different majority, however, upheld the use of race in admissions. Justice Lewis F. Powell was a member of both majorities, and his opinion offered an admissions plan that was in operation at Harvard College as a lawful alternative to the Davis medical school plan. Proposing that the promotion of educational diversity was a compelling interest that could justify the modest use of race, Justice Powell suggested that an admissions policy that did not employ quotas or set-asides but used race as a "plus" factor among several others would be constitutional. Selective colleges and universities throughout the country relied on Justice Powell's opinion and his discussion of the Harvard plan to revise their admissions policies.

Despite the ruling in *Bakke*, affirmative action policies continued to generate enormous controversy. A number of Supreme Court decisions during the 1980s and 1990s struck down different affirmative action programs outside of higher education, and affirmative action opponents began litigating cases to try to undo affirmative action programs in higher education as well. At the same time, ballot initiatives were launched to try to undo race-conscious programs at the state and local levels, not only in higher education but in employment and contracting. California's Proposition 209, passed by the voters in 1996, and Washington's Initiative 200, passed by the voters in 1998, were successful campaigns that outlawed affirmative action programs in state and local government.

The case that stunned the higher education community was *Hopwood v. Texas*, a 1996 constitutional challenge to the race-conscious admissions policy at the University of Texas School of Law.[25] Although the policy at the University of Texas was problematic under *Bakke* because it applied a different set of admissions standards to underrepresented minority students, the U.S. Court of Appeals for the Fifth Circuit went much further than striking down the admissions policy pursuant to *Bakke*. The Fifth Circuit ruled that because of the Supreme Court's post-*Bakke* decisions in the affirmative action arena, *Bakke* was no longer good law. Without *Bakke* as a binding precedent, the Fifth Circuit freed itself to develop its own constitutional analysis. The court concluded that promoting educational diversity was not a compelling interest and that remedying past discrimination was the only interest that could justify race-conscious measures. The court then proceeded to strike down the Texas admissions policy. The case was appealed to the Supreme Court; however, the justices declined to review *Hopwood*, which effectively outlawed higher education affirmative action programs in the three states covered by the Fifth Circuit—Texas, Louisiana, and Mississippi.

The *Hopwood* case sent shock waves throughout the world of higher education, and educational leaders across the country began developing strategies to defend against further attacks on their affirmative action policies. One element of the strategy was to build up the research base that would show the educational benefits of diversity that resulted from affirmative action programs.[26] Justice Powell had not relied on social science findings to argue that promoting educational diversity was a compelling interest; the scientific literature in 1978 was minimal, and he had relied largely on the opinions of higher education leaders to justify his ruling in *Bakke*. After *Hopwood,* researchers began convening conferences and forming new partnerships and ventures to compile existing studies and to commission research on the benefits of diversity. For instance, The Civil Rights Project at Harvard University was founded in 1996 in the aftermath of the *Hopwood* case, with a goal of developing a new body of interdisciplinary research on affirmative action and educational inequality.

### Challenging the University of Michigan Policies

The Center for Individual Rights, the nonprofit law firm based in Washington, D.C., that had litigated the *Hopwood* case, initiated litigation against the University of Michigan in two separate cases in late 1997. *Grutter v. Bollinger* challenged the admissions policy at the University of Michigan Law School, while *Gratz v. Bollinger* challenged the undergraduate admissions policy at the university's College of Literature, Science, and the Arts. The law school admissions policy was patterned directly after the Harvard plan described in *Bakke* and employed race as one of several factors in a "whole file review" system that examined grades and standardized test scores, along with various factors in the applicant's background and experience, to create a student body that was both academically well prepared and broadly diverse. In particular, the admissions policy sought to attain a critical mass of underrepresented minority students whose numbers in the student body could meaningfully contribute to diversity—in other words, beyond token numbers. The undergraduate admissions policy in place in 1997, when the *Gratz* lawsuit was filed, was a rolling admissions policy that also examined multiple factors; but it specifically tracked the admissions of different categories of students throughout the admissions season and maintained a set of protected spaces to allow for the late-season admission of certain students, including athletes, foreign applicants, ROTC students, and underrepresented minority students. In 1998, the undergraduate admissions policy was extensively revised: a new system assigned various points based on grades, test scores, socioeconomic status, athletic talent, geographic factors, alumni relationships, personal achievement, leadership and service skills, and outstanding written essays—up to a maximum total of 150 points. Applicants who were members of underrepresented minority groups would receive twenty points automatically (within the 150 maximum). The policy also allowed various categories of students, including underrepresented minorities, to be flagged early in the initial screening process for later review.

The university defended its admissions policies, largely on the basis of the *Bakke* decision as a binding precedent, but also sought to augment the record with evidence demonstrating the educational benefits of diversity. Numerous expert reports were filed in both cases; the largest and most important was a report produced by Patricia Y. Gurin, a psychology professor at the University of Michigan. The Gurin Report relied on three sources of data: (1) national data collected from more than 9,300 students at nearly two hundred colleges and universities; (2) survey data collected over a number of years from more than 1,300 undergraduate students who entered the University of Michigan in 1990; and (3) data drawn from a study of undergraduate students who were enrolled in a class in the Intergroup Relations Conflict and Community Program at the University of Michigan. Gurin's conclusions were consistent across the data sets, showing that student-body diversity influenced both diversity in the classroom and diversity in informal interactions outside the classroom, which in turn led to improvements in active thinking, growth in intellectual engagement and motivation, and growth in intellectual and academic skills.[27]

The plaintiffs adopted a different strategy regarding the educational benefits of diversity and chose not to cross-examine Gurin or turn to experts to disprove those benefits. Instead, they conceded that diversity was a worthy interest—something "good, important, and valuable." But the value of diversity was negated by its being too amorphous and ill-defined to rise to the level of being a compelling interest. The diversity interest was "too limitless, timeless, and scopeless" and "had no logical stopping point."[28] Thus, rather than contest the university on a legislative fact, the plaintiffs argued the legal point directly: despite its apparent value, diversity was by definition not compelling.

In the *Gratz* case, the plaintiffs and the university both filed motions for summary judgment, which is a mechanism that allows the court to bypass a trial because there are no factual issues in dispute and the evidence that has already been submitted is sufficient for the court to make a decision. In December 2000, Judge Patrick Duggan issued his ruling upholding the university's point system policy but striking down the prior policy as too quota-like because of its use of "protected spaces" that saved seats for minority students during the course of the admissions cycle. In upholding the university's interest in promoting diversity, he recognized the scientific evidence on the educational benefits of diversity and cited the Gurin Report along with amicus curiae briefs submitted by the federal government, the Association of American Law Schools and other higher education associations, and the American Council on Education. The judge also discounted an amicus brief filed by the National Association of Scholars, an organization opposed to affirmative action, which contained a detailed critique of the Gurin Report, attacking its statistical methodologies and conclusions. Although coming from an amicus rather than the plaintiffs themselves, the critique was the equivalent of a cross-examination of the Gurin Report.

The *Grutter* case went to a full trial one month after the district court's decision in the *Gratz* case. The same expert reports on the benefits of diversity that had been submitted in the *Gratz* case were offered in the law school case, and additional expert witnesses were admitted for each side to comment on the admissions process from a statistical perspective. The plaintiffs' statistician proposed that, under his statistical analysis, holding grades and test scores constant, minority students had a considerably higher likelihood of being admitted to the law school, which suggested that there might be a hidden quota in place. The university's expert, however, criticized the plaintiffs' expert's methodology as misleading and suggested that the same statistical results would be achieved no matter how much race was used as a factor in admissions; he further testified that a race-blind system would have dramatically negative effects on minority admissions to the school. In addition, students who had been allowed to intervene in the litigation to represent interests distinct from the university also presented expert witnesses focusing on issues of discrimination involving standardized testing, ongoing problems of segregation, racial climates on college campuses, and the career paths and successes of minority graduates of the law school.[29]

Judge Bernard Friedman issued his decision in the *Grutter* case in March 2001, coming to a conclusion opposite to the one that Judge Duggan had reached in *Gratz* on the constitutionality of race-conscious policies.[30] Although Judge Friedman also recognized that student-body diversity was an important and laudable goal and cited the Gurin Report and testimony from legal educa-tors, he adopted parallel reasoning with the Fifth Circuit in the *Hopwood* case, ruling that *Bakke* was no longer good law and that the diversity rationale was not compelling because it did not serve a remedial interest. He found the plaintiffs' statistical expert to be convincing and concluded that the law school had em-ployed the functional equivalent of a quota; based on the statistical evidence, as well as other problems with the plan, it was not narrowly tailored. Judge Fried-man further ruled that the student intervenors' case could not justify the plan either because it relied on a theory of remedying societal discrimination, which had already been ruled by the Supreme Court not to be a compelling interest.

### Sixth Circuit Appeals

Both cases were appealed to the U.S. Court of Appeals for the Sixth Circuit, but the appellate court issued a decision only in the *Grutter* case. Before the Sixth Circuit could issue a decision in the *Gratz* case, the Supreme Court decided to take the *Grutter* appeal and ordered the *Gratz* case to be taken up as well in order to link the two cases for briefing and oral arguments. Although the Sixth Circuit never issued a ruling in *Gratz*, the briefing in the case contained an un-usual dynamic involving the scientific evidence in the case, particularly the Gurin Report. The parties themselves did not spend much time on the scientific evidence and focused largely on the applicability of *Bakke* and other legal argu-ments; different amici curiae, however, offered arguments and counter-arguments on the legitimacy of the scientific evidence. As it had done at the trial court level, the National Association of Scholars submitted a brief to the Sixth Circuit critiquing the Gurin Report. But in response to that brief, another brief was filed on behalf of the Stanford Institute for Higher Education Research (SIHER) in support of the Gurin Report and critiquing the critique; the SIHER brief also criticized the National Association of Scholars' brief for exceeding the appropriate role of an amicus curiae by taking on the role of a party and cross-examining evidence outside of the record.[31] The Sixth Circuit never addressed these arguments in *Gratz*, but a similar set of debates arose among the concur-ring and dissenting judges in the *Grutter* case.

The Sixth Circuit issued its five-to-four-vote decision in the *Grutter* case in May 2002, reversing Judge Friedman and upholding the law school's admissions policy as narrowly tailored to serve the compelling interest in promoting stu-dent-body diversity.[32] In an opinion by Chief Judge Boyce Martin, the Sixth Cir-cuit ruled that *Bakke* was still good law and that Justice Powell's opinion was still controlling in the *Grutter* case. The law school plan closely paralleled the Harvard College plan and was therefore narrowly tailored under the guidelines offered by Justice Powell's opinion. The Sixth Circuit acknowledged the statisti-cal evidence that the plaintiffs had introduced but simply noted that the evi-dence reflected the effectiveness of a race-conscious policy, not the existence of a quota. The majority opinion in the case did not discuss the Gurin Report or the educational benefits of diversity since it ruled that *Bakke* was binding precedent, which was sufficient to answer the compelling interest question. But a dissenting opinion by Judge Danny Boggs launched a scathing attack on the majority opinion and the scientific evidence that supported the educational benefits of diversity. Judge Eric Clay wrote a concurring opinion to reply directly to Judge Boggs's dissent.

Judge Boggs argued in dissent that the majority had fundamentally misinterpreted *Bakke*; he also found the plaintiffs' statistical evidence to be a powerful indicator that race was an overwhelming factor in admissions and led to a de facto quota. Judge Boggs also questioned the educational benefits of diversity and whether they could be achieved by pursuing a critical mass of minority students. In doing so, he concluded that the Gurin Report was "questionable science, was created expressly for litigation, and its conclusions do not even support the Law School's case." He further argued: "The 'study' suffers from profound empirical and methodological defects that lead me to doubt its probative value."[33] Judge Boggs discussed in detail what he considered to be serious flaws in the report, including its inability to indicate how much diversity is required to yield the benefits (in other words, how much critical mass is required); its use of self-reported student data, which Judge Boggs found to be too subjective; and the failure of its statistical regressions to show a direct link between increasing diversity and its benefits. Although he did not cite the National Association of Scholars' amicus brief, his criticisms paralleled many of its criticisms of the Gurin Report.

In response to Judge Boggs, Judge Clay offered an extensive defense of the Gurin Report, quoting it at great length and discussing the strength of its methodologies and its findings, calling it "one of the most broad and extensive series of empirical analyses conducted on college students in relation to diversity."[34] He further stated: "Although the dissent criticizes this study on various points, the fact remains that the study has been hailed on many fronts."[35] Judge Clay then proceeded to discuss how promoting student-body diversity addresses parallel goals of ameliorating racial isolation and promoting educational equality and cited additional studies on the weaknesses of race-neutral admissions policies. In a more direct rebuke of Judge Boggs, he stated: "The dissent's arguments as to why diversity cannot serve as a compelling state interest constitute nothing more than myopic, baseless conclusions that ignore the daily affairs and interactions of society today which very well may be experienced by all."[36]

## The Science of Diversity

As the University of Michigan cases were being litigated and appealed, social scientists were generating new studies on the educational benefits of diversity and the relative ineffectiveness of race-neutral admissions policies. William G.

Bowen, former president of Princeton University, and Derek Bok, former president of Harvard University, published *The Shape of the River*, an expansive study that analyzed data on more than 45,000 students who had attended selective universities between the 1970s and the 1990s and documented the successes that affirmative action had engendered.[37] The Civil Rights Project at Harvard University commissioned several studies on the benefits of diversity and issued two volumes of compilations: *Chilling Admissions: The Affirmative Action Crisis and the Search for Alternatives* and *Diversity Challenged: Evidence on the Impact of Affirmative Action.*[38] As a result of a conference of leading researchers convened at Stanford University in 1999, the volume *Compelling Interest: Examining the Evidence on Racial Dynamics in Colleges and Universities* was published in 2003.[39] Among the most prominent of the new studies, they were eventually cited by the Supreme Court in its *Grutter* opinion.

Studies that could undermine the benefits-of-diversity research and support the plaintiffs' arguments were, however, far more limited. The reports generated by groups such as the National Association of Scholars and the Center for Equal Opportunity, which also participated as an amicus curiae in the Michigan cases, were primarily critiques and responses to the Gurin Report, not research studies generating new findings. "Does Enrollment Diversity Improve University Education?," a study published in 2003 by social scientists Stanley Rothman, Seymour Martin Lipset, and Neil Nevitte, critiqued various diversity research studies for their methodological defects and drew the conclusion from its own research that increasing black student enrollments correlated negatively with the student, faculty, and administrator evaluations of the racial atmosphere on college campuses.[40] In other words, higher percentages of black students appeared to be associated with declines in a positive racial climate, not with more cross-racial interaction or other educational benefits. One weakness with this study, however, was its lack of focus on selective universities; larger minority enrollments were found at nonselective institutions, which suggested that other dynamics such as ongoing racial prejudice could be at work. In any case, Justice Thomas relied on the research by Rothman et al. in his dissenting opinion in *Grutter*.

In addition to studies on the benefits of diverse student bodies, research studies were generated to examine the effectiveness of "percent plans"—admissions policies developed in Texas, California, and Florida to promote diversity through ostensibly race-neutral criteria.[41] A typical plan offered admission to a state university to all students who graduated in an upper percentage—for instance, the top 10 percent—of their graduating high school class. The premise of a percent plan was that students in disadvantaged and high-minority high schools who might not otherwise gain entry through normal admissions channels would gain automatic admission to the system because of their high school achievements. A common criticism of the percent plans, however, was that they were predicated on residential and educational segregation: to pick up more minority students, schools had to be highly segregated; so the percent plans only reinforced the segregation. In addition, the plans would be unworkable for graduate or professional school admissions as well as for private universities and small colleges that could not admit a high volume of students. Several appellate briefs cited the studies on percent plans, as did Justice Ginsburg's dissent in the *Gratz* case. Although the *Grutter* majority did not cite the studies, Justice O'Connor agreed with the underlying criticisms of the percent plans and argued that they were not effective alternatives to the law school's race-conscious policy.

## Supreme Court Appeals

The Supreme Court appeals of the University of Michigan cases drew national and international attention. A record number of amicus curiae briefs were filed in the case, representing higher education, students, corporations, labor unions, the military, state governments, professional associations, and a wide range of public interest organizations. The U.S. government filed briefs supporting the interest in diversity but proposed that race-neutral measures such as percent plans should be used instead of race-conscious measures. Among the briefs containing extensive scientific findings in support of the University of Michigan were those from the American Educational Research Association et al., the American Psychological Association, the American Sociological Association, the National Education Association et al., the National Center for Fair and Open Testing (FairTest), and social scientist Glenn Loury and colleagues. In support of the plaintiffs, briefs with social science critiques were filed by the Center for Equal Opportunity et al. and the National Association of Scholars. As it had done in the lower courts, the National Association of Scholars offered specific criticisms of the Gurin research, while the American Educational Research Association brief in *Grutter* and the American Psychological Association brief defended the Gurin study.

Social science evidence was not a major focus of discussion during the oral arguments in the Michigan cases. However, John Payton, the attorney representing the University of Michigan in the undergraduate case, did spend time addressing the scientific findings from the Gurin study and the statistical evidence on the likely effects of race-neutral policies on the admission of minority students.[42] Questions also arose over the critical mass concept employed at the law school, raising flags about whether critical mass was actually a quota. Justice Scalia posed a series of sharp questions about whether 2 percent, 4 percent, 8 percent, or between 8 percent and 12 percent might constitute a critical mass and ultimately lead down the path into "quota land."[43] Maureen Mahoney, the appellate attorney representing the law school, had no empirical answer because there was no exact answer. "Critical mass" was intentionally imprecise in order to avoid being a quota; instead, it was designed to be a flexible goal that allowed the school to obtain more than token numbers of students, a number sufficiently large enough to make a difference in terms of benefiting from diversity. Whether critical mass was a quota in practice was another question, one that could be answered by looking at the record itself and drawing inferences from the data and the testimony.

As is the case with most Supreme Court cases involving scientific evidence, it is difficult to discern exactly how influential the evidence was in the Court's decision processes. Because the *Grutter* Court employed a more deferential version of strict scrutiny and recognized the academic freedom interests of the University of Michigan, the evidentiary burden on the school was not as elevated as in remedial affirmative action cases, where a "strong basis in evidence" has been required. The Court did cite trial court findings on the benefits of diversity, which were demonstrated by both scientific evidence and the testimony of educational leaders. The *Grutter* Court also quoted the American Educational Research Association brief, writing that "in addition to the expert studies and reports entered into evidence at trial, numerous studies show that student body diversity promotes learning outcomes, and 'better prepares students for an increasingly diverse workforce and society, and better prepares them as professionals.'"[44] And the Court cited Bowen and Bok's *The Shape of the River*, The Civil Rights Project's *Diversity Challenged*, and Stanford University's *Compelling Interest*. How carefully the Court reviewed the studies, which presumably came through amicus brief citations or the Court's own research, is unclear.

The Court also cited the briefs of retired military officers, major corporations, and the Association of American Law Schools in arguing for the benefits of diversity. In doing so, the Court noted that the corporate and military perspectives added a dose of reality—"these benefits are not theoretical [referring to the scientific evidence] but real"—and proceeded to discuss the specific benefits documented by the briefs.[45] The Court's use of "theoretical versus real" might be a reference to academic versus nonacademic evidence, or it might suggest that practical information is just as useful, if not more so, to the Court than scientific information is.

The attacks and defenses involving the scientific evidence were not as sharp as they had been in the Sixth Circuit opinions, with Justice Thomas only offering alternative studies in his dissenting opinion that tended to undermine the benefits arguments, including research on historically black colleges and universities. And Justice Scalia did not confront the scientific evidence directly; he instead chose to employ a more generally dismissive and sarcastic tone:

This is not, of course, an "educational benefit" on which students will be graded on their Law School transcript (Works and Plays Well with Others:

B+) or tested by the bar examiners (Q: Describe in 500 words or less your cross-racial understanding). For it is a lesson of life rather than law—essentially the same lesson taught to (or rather learned by, for it cannot be "taught" in the usual sense) people three feet shorter and twenty years younger than the full-grown adults at the University of Michigan Law School, in institutions ranging from Boy Scout troops to public-school kindergartens. If properly considered an "educational benefit" at all, it is surely not one that is either uniquely relevant to law school or uniquely "teachable" in a formal educational setting.[46]

*Looking Forward*

Whether the Supreme Court will require a substantial body of social science evidence as a predicate for future compelling interest debates is an open question. The deferential strict scrutiny that the Court employed in *Grutter* may or may not be extended to other contexts. Scientific evidence could therefore be even more crucial in defending future compelling interest claims. While the Supreme Court's decision making may be opaque, what the University of Michigan cases do demonstrate is the importance of scientific evidence in civil rights advocacy. There was no shortage of scientific citations in the constellation of witnesses, reports, briefs, and judicial opinions. And when the parties did not engage in debates over the scientific evidence, the amicus curiae briefs did. Some of the appellate-level debate might have been settled in the trial court if the plaintiffs' themselves had chosen to cross-examine the university's experts or challenged the evidence in some other way, but they did not. They might have learned a lesson if they had consulted the record in the *Brown v. Board of Education* cases, where the attorneys learned quickly to attack the scientific evidence after they had initially treated it as irrelevant. There may have been gaps in the research itself; but many of the questions had been considered common sense by educators and researchers until litigation called them into question, and only a few years had elapsed since the gauntlet had been cast down.

Affirmative action remains among the most controversial topics in public discourse: the splits in the trial court decisions and the close votes in the Sixth Circuit and the Supreme Court demonstrate how divisive the issue can be. Science helped inform the debate in the University of Michigan cases, and the ongoing debate fueled the expansion of scientific knowledge about the benefits of diversity in higher education. Yet it is unlikely that the values and positions of anyone involved in the litigation changed significantly because of the science, nor should one expect public attitudes regarding affirmative action to markedly shift anytime soon. Values in this area are as deeply entrenched as in any area of law or public policy.

## Potential Reforms

Reforms in the area of judicial fact finding and the regulation of scientific evidence have been floating in the law reviews and other academic journals for many years, with only a few changes occurring in the rules and policies that govern the fact-finding process. The *Daubert* case was certainly a major shift in the law of evidence, and its implications are still being worked out in the courts. With their increased gatekeeping responsibilities, judges clearly have to be more knowledgeable about science, or at least be willing to get help when they need it. Constitutional and legislative fact finding, however, have been largely immune to reform, and predictably so. By definition, legislative fact finding is supposed to be open-ended so that courts are not overly constrained in their ability to employ facts to make legal rules. But should it be so open-ended? Should structures be developed to improve the filtering and screening processes needed to keep out junk science? Should the sources of constitutional fact finding, such as amicus curiae briefs, be more tightly regulated? A few proposals are worth reviewing.

Many basic recommendations have focused on increasing the capacity of judges to address scientific evidence intelligently. Few would deny that better education and training, even as early as law school, would be important first steps in increasing judicial capacity. The Federal Judicial Center is the primary governmental agency charged with judicial education, and the center offers regular trainings and publications such as the *Reference Manual on Scientific Evidence* to assist federal judges in their gatekeeping responsibilities; more can be done and more can be funded, including developing relationships with academics, scientific associations, and other organizations to help augment judicial capacity.

More controversial proposals have revolved around adding capacity to the courts in the form of court-appointed experts, special masters, technically trained clerks, special panels, and other vehicles to introduce scientific expertise into the formal structure of fact finding and decision making. Some proposals involve the appointment of ad hoc science experts to assist with specific litigation that is especially technical or complicated—in essence, a one-time expert. As with any proposal that involves the entry of a new element into the decision-making equation, objections can be expected from advocates who do not want to lose control of the flow of information to and from the judge. Injecting a new element of expertise into the decision-making process presumes that the new element comes without bias or reflects biases and values identical to the judge's. Experts recruited to help the judge review the evidence after it has been submitted by the parties can be expected to draw less opposition than special masters who have the power to conduct their own fact finding and make recommendations to the judge. Employing a special master might carry greater efficiencies; yet efficiencies, as Jasanoff notes, might "be bought only at the price of privileging one set of biases over another."[47]

One proposal that has arisen in the context of school desegregation litigation has been the creation of special panels of social scientists who are removed from the adversarial process and free to have quasi-academic discussions over scientific issues in a case: "A panel would allow experts to meet in a noncourtroom context and exchange views and data with one another. They would participate in litigation in a way more consistent with their scholarly and academic roles, and should therefore experience fewer of the role and skill problems associated with party witnessing."[48] As one would expect, the results of surveys on this type of proposal have found support among social scientists but opposition among attorneys.[49] Information-control issues are the central concern, and the size of the panel and its composition and balance raise several areas of potential bias against one or more of the parties.

The Federal Rules of Evidence give judges a large amount of power and discretion to appoint one-time experts, but some capacity-building proposals are more permanent and structural. Arthur Selwyn Miller and Jerome A. Barron, for instance, have proposed that a new rule of evidence to complement the existing rule regarding judicial notice of adjudicative facts should be created to govern judicial notice of legislative facts.[50] In arguing that the courts' legislative fact finding should be bound by more limits, they propose mechanisms such as a pre-trial or -oral-argument hearing that would foster the airing and challenging of scientific evidence relevant to a court's legislative or constitutional fact finding.

Another type of proposal involves shifting the responsibility for detailed legislative fact finding from an appellate court back to a trial court in order to evaluate the evidence more thoroughly and circumspectly than the appeals court could accommodate through the usual appellate briefs or its own research. One technique might involve an appeals court's remanding a case back to a trial court when the lower court record does not reflect adequate legislative fact finding.[51] The trial court could engage in additional fact finding subject to the rules of evidence and cross-examination. The case could then be reheard by the appeals court with a full briefing of the legal issues and a more thorough trial record. Although endorsed by a number of academic commentators and employed by the Supreme Court in at least one case, this technique has not taken hold as a common vehicle in the federal courts, perhaps because of its potential awkwardness—shifting much of the power to make law from a higher court to a lower court—or because of the additional time and resources required for cases to travel back and forth between the courts.[52]

A number of commentators have also recommended the creation of a permanent research service for the federal judiciary.[53] Kenneth Culp Davis, for example, has recommended a research service specifically for the Supreme Court, comparable to the Congressional Research Service, that would assist the court with its legislative fact finding: "The sole purpose [of the research service] should be to increase the Court's freedom to obtain whatever research assistance it decides it needs. The Court should have the privilege of asking for research either on a problem about a pending case or about a narrow or broad area of law."[54] Costs become a major factor in these more expansive proposals, and justifications for having a new service would have to be considerable to gain a significant number of staff; however, a proposal such as Davis's, which would limit the research service to just the Supreme Court, might be more workable than one having to provide a service for the full federal judiciary.

Other proposals have focused less on judicial capacity than on changing the rules of evidence or adding additional requirements for the admission of amicus curiae briefs, which are not subject to the same screening mechanisms as evidence introduced at trial. Michael Rustad and Thomas Koenig have, for instance, recommended that amicus curiae briefs containing social science references carry additional disclosure requirements beyond simply indicating which party is being supported and what the basic interests of the amicus curiae happen to be. They suggest adding information such as "the qualifications of the principal investigators, the funding sources for the studies, and possible conflicts-of-interest"; they would also require an amicus curiae to "submit by appendix published and unpublished reports which describe the methodology and underlying data utilized. The Court should be informed if a study was produced for the purpose of litigation rather than for publication in a peer-reviewed professional social science journal."[55] These suggestions are considerably more onerous than the requirements for nonscientific amicus briefs, but some or all of them would provide useful information to the courts by replicating the gatekeeping requirements that trial courts must employ when screening expert witnesses.

John Monahan and Laurens Walker have offered an even more far-reaching proposal, recommending that the courts should treat well-established social science evidence as "social authority" to be accorded the same weight as legal precedent in the scheme of judicial decision making.[56] Under their proposed regime, social science evidence would be best obtained through written briefs from the parties and by independent judicial research. Evidence would be evaluated as the functional equivalent of legal precedent if it "(1) has survived the critical review of the scientific community; (2) has employed valid research methods; (3) is generalizable to the case at issue; and (4) is supported by a body of other research."[57] In keeping with the treatment of social science evidence as equal to legal precedent, appellate courts would not be bound by the empirical conclusions of lower courts; but lower courts would be bound by the empirical conclusions of higher courts. Perhaps because it elevates social science to such a lofty plane in the system of judicial decision making—and places an exceptionally strong trust in the underlying legitimacy of social science—the social authority model has not been embraced by the courts. Nevertheless, the proposal itself illuminates the rhetorical power and resonance that scientific inquiry has come to enjoy in recent years.

Whether the courts will choose to adopt any of these proposals remains to be seen. They are not new ideas. The courts are responsive institutions, not innovative ones, and are slow to regulate themselves. Despite the fast-paced growth of science and technology, the judiciary's inertia may prevent any immediate changes in the law or the rules of evidence. Because constitutional and legislative fact finding are inherently broad and open-ended processes that mix facts with law and theories with social realities, the courts may have enough invested in the status quo to keep it that way.

# 7

# Directions and Conclusions

$A$s the preceding chapters have demonstrated, scientific evidence has enjoyed an influential but often checkered history in equal protection litigation. Even before the ratification of the Fourteenth Amendment, the courts turned to contemporaneous science to reinforce constitutional theories and values. The typical result, of course, was that science and constitutional interpretation aligned perfectly to support many forms of subordination, whether they involved race, ethnicity, citizenship status, or gender. Notwithstanding the enactment of Reconstruction-era legislation and the addition of the Thirteenth, Fourteenth, and Fifteenth Amendments to the federal Constitution, dominant ideologies of social inequality—scientific racism and social Darwinism, in particular— pervaded scientific theories and judicial interpretations of the law and continued to do so well into the twentieth century.

If *Brown v. Board of Education* marked a turning point for American society's conception of equality under the law, it also signaled a sea change in the role of scientific evidence in civil rights advocacy and judicial decision making. As we have seen in many of the Supreme Court's equal protection cases since *Brown*, the results of scientific research appear in most legal briefs and arguments; even when the Court omits or discounts scientific findings, its underlying values are often strongly influenced by science, whether in the elimination of antimiscegenation laws and the last vestiges of Jim Crow in *Loving v. Virginia* or the evolution and expansion of gay and lesbian rights in *Romer v. Evans*.

In turn, scientific inquiry has been affected by developments in constitutional law. At times, judicial decisions have directly influenced the path of scientific inquiry, as when 1990s legal challenges to race-conscious affirmative action in higher education catalyzed the production of scientific analyses on the benefits and burdens of educational diversity. At other times, science has been influenced less directly by judicial decisions and more by broader societal norms and values that have also affected advocates and members of the judiciary. Scientific racism and eugenics, for instance, enjoyed prominence within scientific circles for many years; in time, human rights norms and growing egalitarianism helped push much of that research to the periphery of mainstream science. Arguments for biological determinism have not disappeared entirely: consider, for example, the attention and controversy generated by the publication of Richard J. Herrnstein and Charles Murray's book on racial and class-based differences in IQ scoring, *The Bell Curve*, in the mid-1990s. But the landscape of the biological and social sciences in the late twentieth and early twenty-first centuries, even when covered by the mantle of value-neutral empiricism, is dominated by research that shuns the overt racism and sexism of past decades.

We can therefore expect that contemporary debates on the constitutionality of public policies such as race-conscious affirmative action programs outside of higher education admissions, same-sex public schools and classrooms, and state and local laws that affect gays and lesbians will likely be informed by recent scientific findings addressing the benefits and harms of these policies. And if the base of knowledge in any of these areas is equivocal or underdeveloped, we can also expect the legal controversies to spur new lines of scientific inquiry and research.

The interrelationships of law, advocacy, scientific research, societal values, and dominant ideologies will no doubt continue as science and technology progress and the courts address new problems of discrimination and inequality. In this concluding chapter, I briefly explore a few areas in which scientific evidence and civil rights litigation may intersect to generate new developments in constitutional law. The chapter discusses examples of recent scientific research that may influence equal protection doctrine, including the treatment of new group classifications and the requirement of proving discriminatory intent. I also consider more general trends in constitutional jurisprudence, where there may be an increasing reliance on scientific and other empirical evidence to justify civil rights policymaking and the enforcement of equal protection norms.

## Genetics and Emerging Classifications

Unlike legislative bodies, the courts are not inclined to generate new civil rights protections when novel or emergent problems of discrimination arise. Indeed, the courts recognize their more reactive role in the constitutional design, and they typically defer to the legislative or executive branches as the more appropriate forums for developing new theories and practices to address discrimination. Many of the Supreme Court's equal protection decisions thus reflect the model inherent in footnote 4 of the *Carolene Products* case and espoused by process theorists such as John Hart Ely: heightened scrutiny should be reserved for those rare circumstances in which significant defects arise in normal political channels. But if Congress or the state legislatures are not particularly interested in addressing civil rights problems, whether because of indifference or even hostility toward particular groups, how should the courts respond? In particular, as scientific advancements and revisions to scientific theories portend new types of classifications and potential forms of discrimination, what are the appropriate judicial responses?

One trend in contemporary science is a movement away from the study of race as a purely biological category. For instance, the American Anthropological Association, the leading professional association for the discipline, issued a statement in 1998 suggesting that race may no longer be a valid basis for scientific inquiry. The introduction to the statement reads in part:

> With the vast expansion of scientific knowledge in this century . . . it has become clear that human populations are not unambiguous, clearly demarcated, biologically distinct groups. Evidence from the analysis of genetics (e.g., DNA) indicates that most physical variation, about 94%, lies *within* so-called racial groups. Conventional geographic "racial" groupings differ from one another only in about 6% of their genes. This means that there is greater variation within "racial" groups than between them. In neighboring populations there is much overlapping of genes and their phenotypic (physical) expressions. . . . The continued sharing of genetic materials has maintained all of humankind as a single species.[1]

The Supreme Court has recognized that race, while rooted in perceptions of biological difference, is largely a creation of social and political forces. The Court's 1987 opinion in *Saint Francis College v. Al-Khazraji*, in which it approved a race discrimination claim under a federal antidiscrimination statute by an Arab American, contains references to scientific literature reaching many of the same conclusions contained in the American Anthropological Association statement. At the same time, the Court recognized that, while racial and ethnic categories may be highly fluid, discrimination can still be a significant problem, regardless of what the latest science may say. Stereotypes persist; and racial profiling, whether it involves traffic stops, airport searches, or differential medical treatment, has been well documented in recent years. [2]

Advances in genetics, such as the mapping of the human genome, suggest that traditional conceptions of race provide imprecise categories to measure group differences. Nevertheless, new metrics of group classifications are also emerging that may form the basis for discrimination and group subordination. Some of these classifications may align with traditional notions of race and ancestry; others may not. One recently documented problem has been the use of genetic information as a predictive tool in medical diagnosis and health care treatment. For example, a currently healthy individual, after undergoing genetic testing, may be found to have a genetic predisposition toward a heart disorder or a particular disease; as a consequence the individual may be denied health insurance because the carrier considers the genetic predisposition to be a pre-existing medical condition. Additional forms of discrimination might come in the form of unequal access to life and disability insurance or employment or in judicial processes such as adoption or child custody decisions. Both the federal government and numerous state governments have begun to recognize the emerging problem of genetic discrimination; for instance, President Bill Clinton issued an executive order in 2000 that prohibits genetic discrimination in federal government employment.[3] But coverage is still incomplete; even with the passage of legislation, cases of discrimination pose a persistent problem.

Suppose that a county government decided to employ a public health program that provided genetic testing for its employees in order to test for various predispositions for diseases, including hypothetical disease XYZ, which affects an identifiable group of individuals, a large majority of whom, but not all, are Asian American. If the county then decided to impose a regime of higher premiums and co-payments from individuals who received government-sponsored medical insurance and were identified among those having genetic predispositions toward diseases, including disease XYZ, how might the equal protection clause protect these individuals from discrimination? (Contrast a policy that required all Asian American employees, but no other groups, to be screened and pay additional costs because of a statistically higher predisposition toward the disease. Such a policy would likely trigger equal protection concerns.) Although there might be some alignment between race and predisposition for disease XYZ, the Supreme Court's decisions regarding disparate impact would likely preclude an equal protection claim solely on the basis of race unless there was also evidence of racial animus on the part of the government. An ancestry claim might gain more traction, particularly if the classification were explicitly based on ancestral traits; but the government's reliance on specific health status and test results to define the class, rather than ancestral characteristics alone, might undermine that line of argument.

Might the courts consider heightened scrutiny for a distinct group composed of individuals with genetic predispositions to a disease? Perhaps, but the Supreme Court has been reluctant to extend either suspect or quasi-suspect classification status to identifiable groups in the past. Therefore, a newly emerging group classification, without a history of past discrimination or evidence of political powerlessness, might not fare well under a heightened scrutiny theory. Under a rational basis test, the lowest level of scrutiny, plaintiffs might have a stronger likelihood of success, although a court might conclude that the imposition of higher premiums or co-payments is rationally related to a legitimate interest in government's spreading the costs of disease prevention and treatment. Under any circumstance, scientific findings would likely play a central role in both the plaintiffs' case and the government's case. Civil rights statutes, not the equal protection clause, have become stronger vehicles for addressing discrimination in recent years; legislation and administrative enforcement rather than constitutional litigation might be the preferred method for addressing the problems developed in this hypothetical but potentially real-life scenario.

## Cognitive Science and the Intent Doctrine

Another area in which recent scientific developments may alter the terrain of equal protection litigation is in the court-imposed mandate of discriminatory intent. Embodied by the Supreme Court's 1976 decision in *Washington v. Davis*, the intent doctrine requires that a public policy be at least partly motivated by the intent to discriminate against a group in order to trigger an equal protection violation. As currently structured, the intent doctrine precludes the redress of legal claims in which there are clear adverse effects on a group but also little or no evidence of discriminatory motives; the doctrine therefore focuses less on addressing the actual harms that a group may have suffered than on rooting out bad intentions. Unlike federal civil rights statutes such as Title VII of the Civil Rights Act of 1964 or the Voting Rights Act of 1965, the equal protection clause does not offer a general theory of disparate impact for plaintiffs to litigate claims against governmental entities.

The intent doctrine is animated largely by an interest in pointing the finger at a bad actor (or set of actors) whose motivations, attitudes, and actions are deemed wrongful and invidious. Yet a growing body of research in social psychology, cognitive science, and neuroscience has demonstrated that biases, whether based on race, gender, age, sexual orientation, or other group characteristics, can operate outside the realm of consciousness, leading individuals to have automatic and unintended preferences for members of one group over another.[4] Writing in 1987 in the context of addressing racial discrimination, law professor Charles R. Lawrence described the problem as "reckoning with unconscious racism."[5]

Unlike much of the psychological research on discrimination before the 1970s, which focused on the nature of prejudicial attitudes and the underlying motivations of discriminatory behavior, more recently developed theories in cognitive science have focused on mental processes that, through the normal course of information processing, can lead to biases and discriminatory acts. Within the field of cognitive science, it has been well established in recent years that categorization is an essential mechanism by which individuals process the large volume of information taken in by the senses and provide order to the world around them. Cognitive structures, often called schemas, represent knowledge about concepts or stimuli, including attributes and relations among those attributes. A central premise of cognition theory, as law professor Linda Hamilton Krieger has noted, is "that cognitive structures and processes involved in categorization and information processing can in and of themselves result in stereotyping and other forms of biased intergroup judgment previously attributed to motivational processes."[6] Stereotyping, including racial or gender stereotyping, can thus be a normal part of the processing of information by the human mind, often operating on a subconscious level and outside the realm of intentionality and conscious motivation.

More specific to problems of unlawful stereotyping and bias, recent studies suggest that *explicit* attitudes toward group-related biases such as racism and sexism—measurable by surveys and self-reporting—have decreased over time; however, measures of *implicit* attitudes reveal that biases remain widespread. One prominent metric of implicit bias is the Implicit Association Test (IAT), which evaluates bias by measuring the speed (a subject's reaction time in milliseconds) with which a test taker associates group status—such as white versus black, male versus female, or young versus old—with a particular description or characteristic that can be categorized as good or bad.[7] Faster reaction times and associations between group membership and a characteristic (for example, white equals good or black equals bad) can reveal a test taker's implicit biases, which may in fact differ significantly from his or her explicit attitudes. Related studies looking at brain activity using magnetic resonance imaging have found that brain areas which involve emotional responses and the perception of novel or threatening stimuli were activated by subliminal images of outgroup members (for example, a white subject viewing a photo of a black person); the activation of the brain also correlated with scores on the IAT and did not correlate with expressed attitudes, suggesting the neurological bases for implicit attitudes and biases.[8]

Social psychologist Nilanjana Dasgupta summarized the implicit attitudes literature in 2004: "By now almost a hundred studies have documented people's tendency to automatically associate positive characteristics with their ingroups more easily than outgroups (i.e., ingroup favoritism) as well as their tendency to associate negative characteristics with outgroups more readily than ingroups (i.e., outgroup derogation)."[9] She further noted that, "in the domain of race, White Americans, on average, show strong implicit preference for their own group and relative bias against African Americans. . . . Similar results have been obtained in terms of White Americans' implicit attitudes toward other ethnic minority groups such as Latinos, Asians, and non-Americans."[10]

Moreover, studies have shown parallel attitudes and biases against the elderly and against lesbians and gay men; there is also ample evidence for "the pervasiveness of stereotypic beliefs about outgroups especially when those outgroups are racial minorities, the elderly, and women."[11] And as law professor

Jerry Kang has proposed, there is "overwhelming evidence that implicit bias measures are dissociated from explicit bias measures. Put another way, on a survey I may honestly self-report positive attitudes toward some social category, such as Latinos. After all, some of my best friends are Latino. However, implicit bias tests may show that I hold negative attitudes toward that very group. This is dissociation—a discrepancy between our explicit and implicit meanings."[12]

Recent scientific literature thus suggests that the intent doctrine may be predicated on incomplete or inaccurate assumptions about the nature of discrimination. The dominant psychological literature on discrimination before *Washington v. Davis* implicated prejudicial attitudes and intentional manifestations of prejudice through discriminatory acts; more recent literature on social cognition suggests, however, that intentionality is not a necessary precondition for bias. By mandating that plaintiffs demonstrate discriminatory intent in all cases, the current doctrinal requirements are inadequate in addressing public policies that may be motivated by the best of intentions but are nonetheless stereotypical and biased against particular groups just as much as policies that are invidiously motivated. Justice Ginsburg, in her concurring opinion in *Grutter v. Bollinger,* recognized that "it is well documented that conscious and unconscious race bias, even rank discrimination based on race, remain alive in our land, impeding realization of our highest values and ideals."[13]

It is unlikely that the Supreme Court will revisit or overrule the *Washington v. Davis* decision in the immediate future. The Court remains conservative in the area of equal protection; even with compelling research findings on implicit biases, it may still be concerned about limiting the volume of cases that might be filed against state and local governments under a disparate impact standard. Nevertheless, recent psychological literature and the implicit bias testing methodologies might be useful in detecting and assessing discriminatory intentions, particularly when individual actors or small numbers of policymakers are involved, as in prosecutorial action or jury selection. Metrics such as the IAT might be invoked to illuminate implicit biases that run counter to express statements of intent and motive. Evaluating the collective intentions of a larger governmental body such as a state legislature might prove more unwieldy, but the scientific literature could still prove useful in developing plaintiffs' arguments on intent or in constructing rebuttals to the government's arguments of nondiscriminatory motivations. At the very least, the cognitive research findings serve as a strong defense for the retention and expansion of the disparate impact theory via civil rights statutes.

## Empirical Jurisprudence

Although the Supreme Court's use of scientific research in constitutional fact finding continues to be sporadic, the invocation of scientific evidence can still generate significant heat and controversy among the justices. In *Roper v. Simmons*, for instance, the Court ruled in 2005 that the Eighth Amendment's ban on cruel and unusual punishment prohibits state implementation of a juvenile death penalty. Concluding that evolving standards of decency had shifted significantly since the Court's 1989 decision allowing the death penalty for individuals who were sixteen or seventeen years old at the time they committed crimes, Justice Kennedy turned to changes in state death penalty laws and recent international developments as well as to social science findings on juvenile crime and juvenile psychological development. Citing several research studies, he concluded that juveniles were not among the worst offenders in the criminal justice system for three reasons:

> First, as any parent knows and as the scientific and sociological studies respondent and his *amici* cite tend to confirm, "[a] lack of maturity and an underdeveloped sense of responsibility are found in youth more often than in adults and are more understandable among the young. These qualities often result in impetuous and ill-considered actions and decisions." . . . The second area of difference is that juveniles are more vulnerable or susceptible to negative influences and outside pressures, including peer pressure. This is explained in part by the prevailing circumstance that juveniles have less control, or less experience with control, over their own environment. . . . The third broad difference is that the character of a juvenile is not as well formed as that of an adult.[14]

Writing in dissent, Justice Scalia upbraided the *Roper* majority not only for its interpretation of the changing standards among the states and its reliance on foreign law but for its use of social science findings:

> Today's opinion provides a perfect example of why judges are ill equipped to make the type of legislative judgments the Court insists on making here. To support its opinion that States should be prohibited from imposing the death penalty on anyone who committed murder before age 18, the Court looks to scientific and sociological studies, picking and choosing those that support its position. It never explains why those particular studies are methodologically sound; none was ever entered into evidence or tested in an adversarial proceeding. . . . [A]ll the Court has done today, to borrow from another context, is to look over the heads of the crowd and pick out its friends.

After suggesting some methodological inconsistencies between the Court's cited studies and other scientific studies, Justice Scalia added: "Given the nuances of scientific methodology and conflicting views, courts—which can only consider the limited evidence on the record before them—are ill equipped to determine which view of science is the right one."[15] Although Justice Scalia incorrectly proposed that the Court could only consider scientific evidence in the record (a limitation that applies to adjudicative fact finding but not to legislative or constitutional fact finding), his dissent echoed the longstanding concerns expressed by judges and commentators that scientific evidence can be inconclusive or biased and that legislatures rather than courts are better equipped to assess empirical findings.

Whether cases such as *Roper v. Simmons* are signaling a growing judicial reliance on science in constitutional fact finding remains to be seen. Law professor Timothy Zick has argued that the Supreme Court is increasingly (and perilously) turning to empiricism in its constitutional decision making, so much so that the Court's jurisprudence may come to resemble the formalism and scientific jurisprudence that characterized the decisions of the late nineteenth century and the *Lochner* era. According to Zick, "constitutional empiricism is, in part, an extension of the balancing construct, an effort to measure state interests prior to placing them on the scale. This is manifested in the empirical testing of legislative predicates—suspected harms, predictions, theories, and causal claims." Moreover, he contends that, "beyond balancing, the courts, in the same search for objectivity and determinacy, have increasingly turned to calculation, falsification, formulas, equations, and ratios in an effort to interpret the meaning of various constitutional guarantees."[16] And with jurists such as Judge Richard Posner of the U.S. Court of Appeals proposing that "it is the lack of an empirical footing that is and always has been the Achilles heel of constitutional law, not the lack of a good constitutional theory," there may be a resurgence in the scientism that the courts first visited decades ago but have largely abandoned in contemporary jurisprudence.[17]

In the area of equal protection law, the Supreme Court does not appear to be invoking scientific evidence or scientific reasoning in a systematic way, and its constitutional fact finding will likely turn to science on occasion to inform opinions and undergird rhetorical arguments, just as it has in the past. What may be a significant trend is the Court's imposition of heavier evidentiary burdens on the government to justify civil rights laws and public policies such as affirmative action plans and legislative districting plans that contain majority-minority electoral districts. For instance, the Court's "strong basis in evidence" requirement for remedial affirmative action policies requires governmental entities to provide a significant volume of evidence, including statistical disparity studies and economic analyses, in order to demonstrate a compelling interest and comply with strict scrutiny.

The Court has also elevated governmental burdens in the area of congressional civil rights enforcement, where it has begun requiring a significant amount of evidence and fact finding from Congress to justify legislation enacted pursuant to section 5 of the Fourteenth Amendment, which empowers Congress to enforce that amendment by appropriate legislation. Beginning in the late

1990s, the Supreme Court began issuing decisions that curtailed Congress's power to authorize plaintiffs to sue states for violations of civil rights laws such as the Age Discrimination in Employment Act and the Americans with Disabilities Act. In *City of Boerne v. Flores*, the Court distinguished legislation that is "remedial" (falling within the powers of Congress under section 5 of the Fourteenth Amendment) and legislation that makes a "substantive change" (exceeding congressional powers).[18] The Court wrote: "Congress does not enforce a constitutional right by changing what the right is. It has been given the power 'to enforce,' not the power to determine what constitutes a constitutional violation."[19] The Court further indicated that "there must be a congruence and proportionality between the injury to be prevented or remedied and the means adopted to that end. Lacking such a connection, legislation may become substantive in operation and effect."[20] The Court's "congruency and proportionality" test in *Boerne* was later coupled with a significant evidentiary standard in *Board of Trustees v. Garrett* to require that Congress thoroughly document state discrimination against a protected group in order to justify an exercise of its power under section 5.[21] Scientific evidence, in conjunction with historical, anecdotal, and documentary evidence, is likely to be essential in order for Congress to establish an appropriate and sufficient predicate for new civil rights legislation.

Although the Court has more recently tempered the *Garrett* evidentiary requirements when legislation involves classifications or interests that have triggered heightened review in equal protection litigation (categories such as race or gender or fundamental interests such as accessing the courts are already well established), it is still likely to pay close attention to congressional fact finding and Congress's reliance on scientific evidence.[22] Whether the Court will find congressional fact finding to be sufficient to satisfy the Constitution is a question that is likely to occupy the dockets of the federal courts for years to come.

THROUGHOUT THIS ANALYSIS of scientific evidence and constitutional interpretation, I have drawn links not only between science and law but between facts and values and ideologies and inequalities. The world of science and the world of constitutional law have each advanced in great measure since the eras of scientific racism and social Darwinism and since the days of *Dred Scott* and *Plessy v. Ferguson*. But those worlds remain inseparable. Contemporaneous values continue to drive both scientific inquiry and constitutional adjudication.

When the Supreme Court has invoked scientific evidence in recent years, it has usually done so with a genuine belief that science can help the Court grapple with some of the difficult moral and social questions that it often encounters in constitutional litigation. Science cannot replace the interpretative judgments that the Court must issue, nor can the Court readily ignore the facts in order to conform to an overriding ideology, at least not as easily as it has done in the past. Without question, science, like law, can be bound by ideologies; but science and law can also move forward in each other's service, as cases such as *Brown v. Board of Education* have demonstrated.

One could advocate for an overarching theory of fact finding that would rein in the courts' occasional ventures into supposition and their disregard for the latest scientific data. But that would probably be an exercise in futility, at least when it comes to the law of equal protection. Few areas of constitutional law are as value-laden as the Supreme Court's equal protection jurisprudence. When push comes to shove, constitutional theories and judicial values can trump the factual and scientific evidence, and perhaps that is what one should expect. Constitutional interpretation is, at bottom, an art and not a science.

# CASES DISCUSSED IN THE TEXT

*Adarand Constructors, Inc., v. Peña*, 515 U.S. 200 (1995).

*Adkins v. Children's Hospital*, 261 U.S. 525 (1923).

*Ambach v. Norwich*, 441 U.S. 68 (1979).

*Ballew v. Georgia*, 435 U.S. 223 (1978).

*Batson v. Kentucky*, 476 U.S. 79 (1986).

*Belton v. Gebhart*, 32 Del. Ch. 343, 87 A.2d 862 (Del. Ch. 1952).

*Berea College v. Kentucky*, 211 U.S. 45 (1908).

*Board of Education v. Dowell*, 498 U.S. 237 (1991).

*Board of Trustees v. Garrett*, 531 U.S. 356 (2000).

*Boiling v. Sharpe*, 347 U.S. 497 (1954).

*Bowers v. Hardwick*, 478 U.S. 186 (1986).

*Boy Scouts of America v. Dale*, 530 U.S. 640 (2000).

*Bradwell v. Illinois*, 83 U.S. 130 (1872).

*Briggs v. Elliott*, 103 F. Supp. 920 (D. S.C. 1952).

*Brown v. Board of Education*, 347 U.S. 483 (1954), 349 U.S. 294 (1955).

*Buck v. Bell*, 274 U.S. 200 (1927).

*Castaneda v. Partida*, 430 U.S. 482 (1977).

*Chae Chan Ping v. United States* (The Chinese Exclusion Case), 130 U.S. 581 (1889).

*City of Boerne v. Flores*, 512 U.S. 507 (1997).

*City of Cleburne v. Cleburne Living Center*, 473 U.S. 432 (1985).

*City of Richmond v. J. A. Croson Co.*, 488 U.S. 469 (1989).

*Concrete Works of Colorado v. City and County of Denver*, 321 F.3d 950 (10th Cir. 2003).

*Craig v. Boren*, 429 U.S. 190 (1976).

*Daubert v. Merrell Dow Pharmaceuticals, Inc.*, 509 U.S. 579 (1993).

*Davis v. County School Board*, 103 F. Supp. 337 (D. Va. 1952).

*Frye v. United States*, 293 F. 1013 (D.C. Cir. 1923).

*Frontiero v. Richardson*, 411 U.S. 677 (1973).

*Geduldig v. Aiello*, 417 U.S. 484 (1974).

*Goodridge v. Department of Public Health*, 440 Mass. 309, 798 N.E.2d 941 (2003).

*Gratz v. Bollinger*, 539 U.S. 244 (2003).

*Strauder v. West Virginia*, 100 U.S. 303 (1880).

*Sugarman v. Dougall*, 413 U.S. 634 (1973).

*Swann v. Charlotte-Mecklenburg Board of Education*, 402 U.S. 1 (1971).

*Sweatt v. Painter*, 339 U.S. 629 (1950).

*Takahashi v. Fish and Game Commission*, 334 U.S. 410 (1948).

*United States v. Carolene Products*, 304 U.S. 144 (1938).

*United States v. Thind*, 261 U.S. 204 (1923).

*United States v. Virginia*, 518 U.S. 515 (1996).

*Washington v. Davis*, 426 U.S. 229 (1976).

*Williams v. Florida*, 399 U.S. 78 (1970).

*Wittmer v. Peters*, 87 F.3d 916 (7th Cir. 1996).

*Yick Wo v. Hopkins*, 118 U.S. 356 (1882).

# NOTES

## CHAPTER 1    INTRODUCTION

1. 347 U.S. 483, 494 (1954).
2. 539 U.S. 306, 308 (2003).
3. Ibid., 330.
4. Ibid., 364, 373 (Thomas, J., dissenting).
5. Ibid., 347 (Scalia, J., dissenting).
6. Kenneth Culp Davis, "An Approach to Problems of Evidence in the Administrative Process," *Harvard Law Review* 55 (1942): 402–10.
7. Fed. R. Civ. P. 52(a) ("Findings of fact shall not be set aside unless clearly erroneous, and due regard shall be given to the opportunity of the trial court to judge of the credibility of the witnesses.").
8. 481 U.S. 279, 287 (1987).
9. Ibid., 312.
10. Ibid., 314–15.
11. David L. Faigman, "Normative Constitutional Fact-Finding": Exploring the Empirical Component of Constitutional Interpretation," *University of Pennsylvania Law Review* 139 (1991): 610.
12. Scott Brewer, "Scientific Expert Testimony and Intellectual Due Process," *Yale Law Journal* 107 (1998): 1557.
13. Dean M. Hashimoto, "Science As Mythology in Constitutional Law," *Oregon Law Review* 76 (1997): 111.
14. 260 U.S. 178, 198 (1922).
15. A recent critique is Sanjay Mody, "*Brown* Footnote Eleven in Historical Context: Social Science and the Supreme Court's Quest for Legitimacy," *Stanford Law Review* 54 (2002): 793, 809–14.
16. See Kenneth L. Karst, *Belonging to America: Equal Citizenship and the Constitution* (New Haven: Yale University Press, 1989).
17. Leon Friedman, ed., *Brown v. Board: The Landmark Oral Argument before the Supreme Court* (New York: New Press, 2004), 65.
18. Timothy Zick, "Constitutional Empiricism: Quasi-Neutral Principles and Constitutional Truths," *North Carolina Law Review* 82 (2003): 1.
19. Richard A. Posner, "Against Constitutional Theory," *New York University Law Review* 73 (1998): 3.
20. Deborah Jones Merritt, "Constitutional Fact and Theory: A Response to Chief Judge Posner," *Michigan Law Review* 97 (1999): 1293.
21. 410 U.S. 113 (1973).

22. *Akron v. Akron Center for Reproductive Health,* 462 U.S. 416, 458 (1983) (O'Connor, J., dissenting).
23. 505 U.S. 833 (1992).
24. Commenting on the challenges that federal judges would face as gatekeepers, Chief Justice William H. Rehnquist doubted that gatekeeping responsibilities actually "imposes on them either the obligation or the authority to become amateur scientists in order to perform that role." *Daubert v. Merrell Dow Pharmaceuticals, Inc.,* 509 U.S. 579, 600–01 (1993) (Rehnquist, C.J., dissenting in part and concurring in part).
25. 509 U.S. 579, 592–93 (1993).
26. John C. Jeffries, Jr., *Justice Lewis F. Powell, Jr.* (New York: Fordham University Press, 2001), 439.
27. The U.S. Court of Appeals for the Fifth Circuit struck down the University of Texas School of Law's admissions plan in *Hopwood v. Texas,* 78 F.3d 932 (5th Cir.), *cert. denied,* 518 U.S. 1033 (1996).
28. *International Brotherhood of Teamsters v. United States,* 431 U.S. 324 (1977); *Hazelwood School District v. United States,* 433 U.S. 299 (1977); *Castaneda v. Partida,* 430 U.S. 482 (1977).
29. 430 U.S. 482, 496, note 17 (1977).
30. 435 U.S. 223 (1976).
31. Ibid., 239.
32. Peter W. Sperlich, "Trial by Jury: It May Have a Future," *Supreme Court Review* (1978): 191.
33. 435 U.S. at 246 (Powell, J., concurring).
34. Ibid.
35. 163 U.S. 537, 551 (1896).

## CHAPTER 2   SCIENCE AND LAW, IDEOLOGY AND INEQUALITY

1. Oliver Wendell Holmes, Jr., "The Path of the Law," *Harvard Law Review* 10 (1897): 469.
2. Earl Warren, "Science and the Law: Change and the Constitution," *Journal of Public Law* 12, no. 1 (1963): 6.
3. Ibid., 5, 4.
4. David L. Faigman, *Laboratory of Justice: The Supreme Court's 200-Year Struggle to Integrate Science and the Law* (New York: Holt, 2004), 364.
5. Thomas Jefferson, *Notes on the State of Virginia: With Related Documents,* ed. David Waldstreicher (New York: Palgrave, 2002), 139–40.
6. 60 U.S. (19 How.) 393, 404–5 (1857).
7. Ibid., 407.
8. Ibid., 409.
9. Christopher Columbus Langdell, *A Selection of Cases on the Law of Contracts: With References and Citations,* 2d ed. (Boston: Little, Brown, 1871).
10. Paul L. Rosen, *The Supreme Court and Social Science* (Urbana: University of Illinois Press, 1972), 24–25.
11. Mark De Wolfe Howe, ed. *Holmes-Pollock Letters: The Correspondence of Mr. Justice Holmes and Sir Frederick Pollock, 1874–1932* (Cambridge, Mass.: Harvard University Press, 1941), 58.
12. Herbert Spencer, *The Man Versus the State* (New York: Appleton, 1892), 202.
13. 198 U.S. 45 (1905).
14. Ibid., 61.
15. Ibid., 75 (Holmes, J., dissenting).

16. 163 U.S. 537, 551 (1896).
17. Ibid., 551–52.
18. Ibid., 543.
19. Ibid., 551.
20. Ibid., 551.
21. Ibid., 552.
22. Ibid., 559 (Harlan, J., dissenting).
23. Ibid., 562.
24. Ibid., 559.
25. Ibid., 561.
26. Rosen, *Supreme Court and Social Science,* 37–38.
27. Roscoe Pound, "Law in Books and Law in Action," *American Law Review* 44 (1910): 35–36.
28. Oliver Wendell Holmes, Jr., *The Common Law* (Boston: Little, Brown, 1881), 1.
29. Karl N. Llewellyn, "A Realistic Jurisprudence—The Next Step," *Columbia Law Review* 30 (1930): 465.
30. 208 U.S. 412, 422 (1908).
31. Ibid., 419.
32. Philip B. Kurland and Gerhard Casper, *Landmark Briefs and Arguments of the Supreme Court of the United States: Constitutional Law* (Washington, D.C.: University Publications of America, 1975), 16:75.
33. 208 U.S. 412, 420 (1908).
34. Ibid., 421.
35. Ibid.
36. 261 U.S. 525, 559–60 (1923).
37. 211 U.S. 45, 59 (1908).
38. See Herbert Hovenkamp, "Social Science and Segregation before Brown," *Duke Law Journal* (1985): 624.
39. Brief for Defendant in Error 40, *Berea College v. Kentucky*, 211 U.S. 45 (1908).
40. Ibid., 40.
41. Hovenkamp, "Social Science and Segregation," 634.
42. Ian F. Haney López, *White by Law: The Legal Construction of Race* (New York: New York University Press, 1996).
43. 260 U.S. 178 (1922).
44. 261 U.S. 204 (1923).
45. 260 U.S. 178, 197 (1922).
46. Ibid., 198.
47. Ibid.
48. 261 U.S. 204, 210 (1923).
49. Ibid., 212.
50. Ibid., 211.
51. Ibid., 209.
52. Ibid., 215.
53. 130 U.S. 581 (1889).
54. 274 U.S. 200 (1927).
55. Mary L. Dudziak, "Oliver Wendell Holmes As a Eugenic Reformer: Rhetoric in the Writing of Constitutional Law," *Iowa Law Review* 71 (1986): 842–44.
56. 274 U.S. 200, 274 (1927) (citations omitted).
57. 316 U.S. 535 (1942).

58. Ibid., 542.
59. 320 U.S. 81 (1943).
60.  323 U.S. 214 (1944).
61. 320 U.S. 81, 99 (1943).
62. Ibid., 100.
63. Peter Irons, *Justice at War: The Story of the Japanese American Internment Cases* (New York: Oxford University Press, 1983), 192–93.
64. Kurland and Casper, *Landmark Briefs*, 40:488–89.
65. 323 U.S. 216.
66. Ibid., 218–19.
67. Ibid., 219.
68. Ibid., 233 (Murphy, J., dissenting).
69. Ibid., 237, note 4.
70. Ibid., 239–40.
71. A thorough discussion can be found in Eric Yamamoto et al., *Race, Rights and Reparation: Law and the Japanese American Internment* (Gaithersburg, Md.: Aspen Law and Business, 2001).

CHAPTER 3   DESEGREGATION AND "MODERN AUTHORITY"

1. Richard Kluger, *Simple Justice: The History of Brown v. Board of Education and Black America's Struggle for Equality* (New York: Vintage, 1977), 706.
2. 275 U.S. 78 (1927).
3. Ibid., 86.
4. Ibid., 87.
5. 321 U.S. 649 (1944).
6. 334 U.S. 1 (1948).
7. Kluger, *Simple Justice,* 267–68.
8. Testimony of Dr. Robert Redfield, *Sweatt v. Painter,* available at *http://www.law.du.edu/russell/lh/sweatt/docs/svptrtoc.htm.*
9. 339 U.S. 629, 634 (1950).
10. 339 U.S. 637, 641 (1950).
11. John P. Jackson, Jr., *Social Scientists for Social Justice: Making the Case against Segregation* (New York: New York University Press), 17–42.
12. Ibid., 18.
13. Gunnar Myrdal, *An American Dilemma: The Negro Problem and Modern Democracy* (New York: Harper, 1944).
14. Ibid., 1021.
15. Jackson, *Social Scientists for Social Justice,* 136–38.
16. Kluger, *Simple Justice,* 321 (quoting William Coleman).
17. The states with segregated systems were Alabama, Arkansas, Delaware, Florida, Georgia, Kentucky, Louisiana, Maryland, Mississippi, Missouri, Oklahoma, North Carolina, South Carolina, Texas, Tennessee, Virginia, and West Virginia. The four states permitting local segregation were Arizona, Kansas, New Mexico, and Wyoming. Sixteen states prohibited segregation, and eleven had no specific legislation on the matter.
18. 103 F. Supp. 337, 340 (D. Va. 1952).
19. 98 F. Supp. 797 (D. Kan. 1951).
20. 103 F. Supp. 920 (D. S.C. 1952).
21. 32 Del. Ch. 343, 348–49, 87 A.2d 862, 865 (Del. Ch. 1952).

22. Kurland and Casper, *Landmark Briefs,* 49:43.

23. Ibid., 49:45.

24. Ibid., 49:49–53.

25. Ibid., 49:52.

26. Ibid., 49:54.

27. Ibid., 49:55–59.

28. Brief of Appellees, Briggs v. Elliott, 34.

29. Kluger, *Simple Justice,* 545.

30. Leon Friedman, *Brown v. Board: The Landmark Oral Argument before the Supreme Court* (New York: New Press, 2004), 13.

31. Ibid., 37.

32. Ibid., 59.

33. Ibid., 63–64.

34. Ibid., 172

35. Ibid., 172–73.

36. 347 U.S. 483, 490 (1954).

37. Ibid., 492–93.

38. Ibid., 493.

39. Ibid.

40. Ibid., 494.

41. Ibid., 494 and note 11.

42. Ibid., 494–95.

43. 347 U.S. 497 (1954).

44. Ibid., 499.

45. Ibid.

46. Ibid., 500

47. Ibid.

48. Kluger, *Simple Justice,* 710–11.

49. Ibid., 711.

50. Ibid.

51. Ibid.

52. Edmund Cahn, "Jurisprudence," *New York University Law Review* 30 (1955): 163.

53. Ibid., 161.

54. Ibid., 167

55. Ibid.

56. Rosen, *Supreme Court,* 200–201.

57. Harry S. Ashmore, *The Negro and the Schools* (Chapel Hill: University of North Carolina Press, 1954), 82.

58. Ibid., 80.

59. Ibid., 81–82.

60. Kurland and Casper, *Landmark Briefs,* 49A:1166–67.

61. 349 U.S. 294, 301 (1955).

62. Kluger, *Simple Justice,* 739.

63. 252 F.2d 122 (5th Cir.), *aff'd,* 358 U.S. 913 (1958).

64. *Lee v. Washington,* 390 U.S. 333 (1968) (prisons); *Johnson v. Virginia,* 373 U.S. 61 (1963) (courtrooms); *Turner v. Memphis,* 369 U.S. 350 (1962); *State Athletic Commission v. Dorsey,* 359 U.S. 533 (1959); *New Orleans City Park Improvement Association v. Detiege,* 358 U.S. 54 (1958); *Gayle v. Browder,* 352 U.S. 903 (1956) (buses); *Holmes v. Atlanta,* 350 U.S. 879 (1955) (golf courses); *Mayor of Baltimore v. Dawson,* 350 U.S. 877 (1955) (beaches).

65. 220 F. Supp. 667 (S.D. Georgia 1963), 684

66. Ibid., 676.

67. Ibid., 678.

68. Ibid.

69. 333 F.2d 55, 61 (5th Cir. 1964).

70. Ibid.

71. 388 U.S. 1, 11 (1967).

72. Ibid., 8.

73. Kurland and Casper, *Landmark Briefs,* 64:942.

74. Ibid., 990.

75. Ibid., 988.

76. Ibid., 1003.

77. Ibid., 958.

78. 388 U.S. 1, 12 (1967).

79. Brewer, "Scientific Expert Testimony," 1553.

80. Mody, "Brown Footnote Eleven," 828.

81. 100 U.S. 303, 307–8 (1880).

### CHAPTER 4   SCIENCE AND EQUAL PROTECTION

1. 347 U.S. 475, 478 (1954).

2. Richard H. Fallon, Jr., "A Constructivist Coherence Theory of Constitutional Interpretation," *Harvard Law Review* 100 (1987): 1194–1209.

3. 539 U.S. 558, 578 (2003).

4. 125 S. Ct. 1183 (2005) (overruling *Stanford v. Kentucky,* 492 U.S. 361 (1989)).

5. Ibid., 1195–97.

6. John Hart Ely, *Democracy and Distrust: A Theory of Judicial Review* (Cambridge, Mass.: Harvard University Press, 1980).

7. Kenneth L. Karst, "Foreword: Equal Citizenship under the Fourteenth Amendment," *Harvard Law Review* 91 (1977): 6.

8. T. Alexander Aleinikoff, "Constitutional Law in the Age of Balancing," *Yale Law Journal* 96 (1987): 945.

9. Jeffrey A. Segal and Harold J. Spaeth, *The Supreme Court and the Attitudinal Model Revisited* (New York: Cambridge University Press, 1993).

10. 539 U.S. 558, 575 (2003).

11. Ibid., 602 (Scalia, J., dissenting).

12. Merritt, "Constitutional Fact and Theory," 1294–95.

13. Hashimoto, "Science As Mythology," 150.

14. Ibid.

15. 304 U.S. 144, 152, note 4 (1938).

16. Laurence H. Tribe, *American Constitutional Law,* 2d ed. (Mineola, N.Y.: Foundation Press, 1988), 1453–54.

17. 323 U.S. 214 (1944).

18. *Federal Communications Commission v. Beach Communications, Inc.,* 508 U.S. 307, 315 (1993).

19. Gerald Gunther, "Foreword: In Search of Evolving Doctrine on a Changing Court: A Model for a Newer Equal Protection," *Harvard Law Review* 86 (1972): 8.

20. *City of Cleburne v. Cleburne Living Center,* 473 U.S. 432 (1985).

21. *Grutter v. Bollinger*, 539 U.S. 306 (2003).

22. *United States v. Virginia*, 518 U.S. 515 (1996).

23. 26 U.S. 229 (1976).

24. *Arlington Heights v. Metropolitan Housing Corporation*, 429 U.S. 252 (1977).

25. Ibid., 248.

26. Tribe, *American Constitutional Law*, 2d ed., 1516–19.

27. 125 S. Ct. 1141 (2005). The Supreme Court only clarified the applicable standard in *Johnson* and did not evaluate the policy under strict scrutiny; instead, it remanded the case to the lower courts to gather additional evidence and conduct the strict scrutiny analysis.

28. *Adarand Constructors v. Peña*, 515 U.S. 200, 224 (1995).

29. 411 U.S. 1 (1973).

30. 481 U.S. 604 (1987).

31. Ibid., 610, note 4.

32. Ibid., 613.

33. 347 U.S. 475 (1954).

34. Brief for Petitioner, 39.

35. 347 U.S. 475, 478 (1954).

36. Ibid., 479.

37. Ibid., 482.

38. 500 U.S. 352 (1991).

39. Ibid., 370.

40. Ibid., 371–72.

41. 442 U.S. 256 (1979).

42. Ibid., 279.

43. 417 U.S. 484 (1974).

44. Ibid., 494, note 20.

45. Ibid., 501 (Brennan, J., dissenting).

46. *Lyng v. Castillo*, 477 U.S. 635, 638 (1986).

47. 334 U.S. 410, 420 (1948).

48. 403 U.S. 365, 372 (1971).

49. *Sugarman v. Dougall*, 413 U.S. 634 (1973) (civil service); In re Griffiths, 413 U.S. 717 (1973) (law); *Examining Board v. Flores de Otero*, 426 U.S. 572 (1976) (civil engineering); *Nyquist v. Mauclet*, 432 U.S. 1 (1977) (financial aid); *Bernal v. Fainter*, 467 U.S. 216 (1984) (notaries public).

50. 457 U.S. 202 (1982).

51. Ibid., 218.

52. Ibid., 218–19.

53. Ibid., 222.

54. Ibid., 223–24.

55. Ibid., 228.

56. Ibid., 230.

57. 427 U.S. 307, 313 (1976).

58. Ibid., 323–24 (Marshall, J., dissenting).

59. 473 U.S. 432 (1985).

60. Ibid., 450.

61. Ibid., 473.

## CHAPTER 5   PROVING DISCRIMINATION

1.  118 U.S. 356 (1882).

2.  I use the following formula:

$$\text{Maximum percentage deviation} = \frac{110{,}000 - 100{,}000}{100{,}000} + \left| \frac{90{,}000 - 100{,}000}{100{,}000} \right| = 0.1 + 0.1 = 0.2 = 20\%$$

3.  410 U.S. 315, 329 (1973).

4.  Ibid., 323.

5.  *Karcher v. Daggett*, 462 U.S. 725 (1983).

6.  *Brown v. Thompson*, 462 U.S. 835 (1983).

7.  364 U.S. 339 (1960).

8.  Ibid., 341.

9.  442 U.S. 256 (1979).

10. 430 U.S. 482 (1977).

11. *Whitus v. Georgia*, 385 U.S. 545 (1967).

12. *Hazelwood School District v. United States*, 433 U.S. 299 (1977).

13. 430 U.S. 482, 503 (1977).

14. Ibid.

15. 476 U.S. 79 (1986).

16. *Swain v. Alabama*, 380 U.S. 202, 223 (1965).

17. 481 U.S. 279 (1987).

18. David C. Baldus, George Woodworth, and Charles A. Pulaski, Jr., *Equal Justice and the Death Penalty: A Legal and Empirical Analysis* (Boston: Northeastern University Press, 1990), 370–75.

19. 481 U.S. 279, 339 (1987).

20. Ibid., 367 (Stevens, J., dissenting).

21. For an overview of commonly used statistical techniques in school desegregation cases, see Ramona L. Paetzold and Steven Willborn, *The Statistics of Discrimination: Using Statistical Evidence in Discrimination Cases* (St. Paul, Minn.: West Group, 2002), chap. 9.

22. Erika Frankenberg, Chungmei Lee, and Gary Orfield, *A Multiracial Society with Segregated Schools: Are We Losing the Dream?* (Cambridge, Mass.: Harvard University, The Civil Rights Project, 2003).

23. *Goss v. Board of Education*, 373 U.S. 683 (1963).

24. *Griffin v. County School Board*, 377 U.S. 218 (1964).

25. 391 U.S. 430 (1968).

26. 413 U.S. 189 (1973).

27. 402 U.S. 1 (1971).

28. *Milliken v. Bradley*, 418 U.S. 717 (1974); *Missouri v. Jenkins*, 515 U.S. 70 (1995).

29. 498 U.S. 237 (1991).

30. *Freeman v. Pitts*, 503 U.S. 467 (1992).

31. *Parents Involved in Community Schools v. Seattle School District No. 1*, 377 F.3d 949 (9th Cir. 2004); *Eisenberg v. Montgomery County Public Schools*, 197 F.3d 123 (4th Cir.), *cert. denied*, 529 U.S. 1019 (1999); *Tuttle v. Arlington County School Bd.*, 195 F.3d 698 (4th Cir. 1999), *cert. dismissed*, 529 U.S. 1050 (2000); *Wessman v. Gittens*, 160 F.3d 790 (1st Cir. 1998).

32. Vote dilution can also occur when a particular election system, such as an at-large system, functions to prevent minorities from electing their chosen candidates. If a sizable but not overly large minority population is geographically concentrated in one part of a city, it might be able to elect a candidate if there were district-based elec-

tions; but a system in which city council members are elected at large may prevent the minority population from gaining enough votes to elect a candidate.

33. *Mobile v. Bolden,* 446 U.S. 55 (1980).

34. Paetzold and Willborn, *Statistics of Discrimination,* chap. 10.

35. *Thornburg v. Gingles,* 478 U.S. 30 (1986).

36. 509 U.S. 630, 635 (1993).

37. Ibid., 644.

38. Ibid., 647.

39. Richard H. Pildes and Richard G. Niemi, "Expressive Harms, 'Bizarre Districts,' and Voting Rights: Evaluating Election-District Appearances after *Shaw v. Reno,*" *Michigan Law Review* 92 (1993): 483.

40. *Miller v. Johnson,* 515 U.S. 900 (1995).

41. 515 U.S. 200 (1995).

42. 488 U.S. 469 (1989).

43. 321 F.3d 950 (10th Cir.), *cert. denied,* 124 S. Ct. 556 (2003).

44. 539 U.S. 306, 328 (2003).

45. 539 U.S. 244 (2003).

46. *Hunter v. Regents of the University of California,* 190 F.3d 1061 (9th Cir. 2000).

47. *Parents Involved in Community Schools v. Seattle School District No. 1,* 377 F.3d 949 (9th Cir. 2004); *Comfort v. Lynn School Committee,* 413 F. 3d 1 (1st Cir. 2005); see also *Brewer v. West Irondequoit Central School District,* 212 F.3d 738 (2d Cir. 2000) (pre-*Grutter* case upholding interest in reducing racial isolation).

48. 87 F.3d 916 (7th Cir. 1996).

49. Ibid., 920.

50. Ibid.

51. Ibid., 920–21.

52. *Michael M. v. Superior Court,* 450 U.S. 464 (1981) (upholding statutory rape law applied only to male defendants because of interest in preventing unwanted teenage pregnancies); *Nguyen v. Immigration and Naturalization Service,* 533 U.S. 53 (2001) (upholding federal immigration law requiring the father of an out-of-wedlock child to provide additional proof of parenthood not required of the child's mother).

53. 83 U.S. 130 (1872).

54. Ibid., 141 (Bradley, J., concurring).

55. 411 U.S. 677 (1973).

56. Ibid., 686.

57. 429 U.S. 190 (1976)

58. Ibid., 197.

59. Ibid., 201.

60. Ibid., 208.

61. Ibid., 204.

62. 453 U.S. 57 (1981).

63. Ibid., 86.

64. 458 U.S. 718 (1982).

65. Ibid. 738–39 (Powell, J., dissenting).

66. 511 U.S. 127 (1994).

67. Ibid., 138, note 9.

68. 518 U.S. 515 (1996).

69. Ibid., 558.

70. Ibid., 576 (Scalia, J., dissenting).

71. Ibid., 577.
72. 539 U.S. 306, 347 (2003) (Scalia, J., dissenting).
73. 450 U.S. 464 (1981).
74. 533 U.S. 53 (2001).
75. 509 U.S. 312 (1993).
76. Ibid., 320.
77. Ibid., 326–27.
78. Ibid., 345–46 (Souter, J., dissenting).
79. Ibid., 321 (quoting *Metropolis Theatre Co. v. Chicago*, 228 U.S. 61, 69–70 [1913]).
80. *Sugarman v. Dougall*, 413 U.S. 634 (1973).
81. *Cabell v. Chavez-Salido*, 454 U.S. 432 (1982) (probation officers); *Foley v. Connelie*, 435 U.S. 291 (1978) (state police officers).
82. 441 U.S. 68 (1979).
83. Ibid., 77–78.
84. Ibid., 79, note 9.
85. Ibid., 87.
86. 440 Mass. 309, 798 N.E.2d 941 (2003).
87. 530 U.S. 640 (2000).
88. 517 U.S. 620 (1996).
89. Ibid., 632.
90. Rosemary J. Erickson and Rita J. Simon, *The Use of Social Science Data in Supreme Court Decisions* (Urbana: University of Illinois Press, 1998), 149–55.

## CHAPTER 6   SCIENCE, ADVOCACY, AND FACT FINDING

1. Faigman, *Laboratory of Justice*, 358.
2. Ibid., 359.
3. Ibid., 361.
4. Ibid., 363.
5. 509 U.S. 579 (1993).
6. Ibid., 593–95.
7. Ibid., 593.
8. Kenneth R. Foster and Peter W. Huber, *Judging Science: Scientific Knowledge and the Federal Courts* (Cambridge, Mass.: MIT Press, 1999), 48–52.
9. Ibid., 600 (Rehnquist, C.J., concurring in part and dissenting in part).
10. Zick, "Constitutional Empiricism," 182.
11. 43 F.3d. 1311, 1315–16 (9th Cir. 1995).
12. Ibid.
13. *Kumho Tire Company v. Carmichael*, 526 U.S. 137 (1999). A Supreme Court case decided between *Daubert* and *Kumho* clarified the appropriate standard that appeals courts must use in assessing a trial court's determination of whether expert testimony should be admitted—an "abuse of discretion" standard that presumes that the lower court has gotten things right and the appeals court must defer unless the judge has obviously applied the wrong law or has made clearly erroneous findings of fact. *General Electric Company v. Joiner*, 522 U.S. 136 (1997).
14. Federal Rule of Evidence 702.
15. Federal Rule of Evidence 201(a).
16. Ibid. (advisory committee notes)
17. Ibid.

18. 410 U.S. 113, 208 (1973) (Burger, C. J., concurring).

19. Ibid., 803–4 (Boggs, J., dissenting).

20. Sheila Jasanoff, *Science at the Bar: Law, Science, and Technology in America* (Cambridge, Mass.: Harvard University Press), 45.

21. Jonathan R. Alger and Marvin Krislov, "You've Got to Have Friends: Lessons Learned from the Role of Amici in the University of Michigan Cases," *Journal of College and University Law* 30 (2004): 510–15.

22. Peter W. Huber, *Galileo's Revenge: Junk Science in the Courtroom* (New York: Basic Books, 1993).

23. Michael Rustad and Thomas Koenig, "The Supreme Court and Junk Social Science: Selective Distortion in Amicus Briefs," *North Carolina Law Review* 72 (1993): 91.

24. 438 U.S. 265 (1978).

25. 78 F.3d 932 (5th Cir. 1996).

26. Jonathan R. Alger, "Unfinished Homework for Universities: Making the Case for Affirmative Action," *Washington University Journal of Urban and Contemporary Law* 54 (1998): 73.

27. Expert Report of Patricia Y. Gurin, Gratz v. Bollinger, No. 97–75231 (E.D. Mich.) & Grutter v. Bollinger, No. 97–75928 (E.D. Mich.); Patricia Y. Gurin, "The Compelling Need for Diversity in Higher Education," *Michigan Journal of Race and Law* 5 (1999): 363.

28. 122 F. Supp. 811, 823 (E.D. Mich. 2000).

29. Students were also allowed to intervene in the undergraduate case, but they lost at each stage and were not able to present their full case in a trial.

30. 137 F. Supp. 821 (E.D. Mich. 2001).

31. As of September 2005, the briefs were available at *http://www.nas.org/reports/gratz_appeal1/gratz_appeal1.pdf* and *http://siher.stanford.edu/documents/pdfs/legalbriefSIHER.pdf.*

32. 288 F.3d 732 (6th Cir. 2002).

33. Ibid., 803–4 (Boggs, J., dissenting).

34. Ibid., 762 (Clay, J., concurring).

35. Ibid., 759.

36. Ibid., 765.

37. William G. Bowen and Derek Bok, *The Shape of the River: Long-Term Consequences of Considering Race in College and University Admissions* (Princeton, N.J.: Princeton University Press, 2000).

38. Gary Orfield and Edward Miller, eds., *Chilling Admissions: The Affirmative Action Crisis and the Search for Alternatives* (Cambridge, Mass.: Harvard Educational Publishing Group, 1998); Gary Orfield with Michal Kurlaender, eds., *Diversity Challenged: Evidence on the Impact of Affirmative Action* (Cambridge, Mass.: Harvard Educational Publishing Group, 2001).

39. Mitchell Chang, Daria Witt, James Jones, and Kenji Hakuta, eds., *Compelling Interest: Examining the Evidence on Racial Dynamics in Colleges and Universities* (Stanford, Calif.: Stanford University Press, 2003).

40. Stanley Rothman, Seymour Martin Lipset, and Neil Nevitte, "Does Enrollment Diversity Improve University Education?" *International Journal of Public Opinion Research* 15 (2003): 8–26.

41. Catherine L. Horn and Stella M. Flores, *Percent Plans in College Admissions: A Comparative Analysis of Three States' Experiences* (Cambridge, Mass.: Harvard University, Civil Rights Project, 2003); Patricia Marin and Edgar K. Lee, *Appearance and Reality in the Sunshine State: The Talented 20 Program in Florida* (Cambridge, Mass.: Harvard University, Civil Rights Project, 2003); Marta Tienda et al., "Closing the Gap? Admissions and

Enrollments at the Texas Public Flagships before and after Affirmative Action," unpublished paper (2003), but as of September 2005 available at *http://www.texastop10. princeton.edu.*

42. Gerhard Casper and Kathleen M. Sullivan, *Landmark Briefs and Arguments of the Supreme Court of the United States: Constitutional Law* (Bethesda, Md.: LexisNexis Academic and Library Solutions, 2004), 321:1211.

43. Ibid., 1181–82.

44. 539 U.S. 306, 330 (2003).

45. Ibid., 331.

46. Ibid., 347 (Scalia, J., dissenting).

47. Jasanoff, *Science before the Bar,* 66.

48. Mark A. Chesler, Joseph Sanders, and Debra S. Kalmuss, *Social Science in Court: Mobilizing Experts in the School Desegregation Cases* (Madison: University of Wisconsin Press, 1988), 181.

49. Ibid., 182–83.

50. Arthur Selwyn Miller and Jerome A. Barron, "The Supreme Court, the Adversary System, and the Flow of Information to the Justices: A Preliminary Inquiry," *Virginia Law Review* 61 (1975): 1236–40.

51. Kenneth L. Karst, "Legislative Facts in Constitutional Litigation," *Supreme Court Review* (1960): 98; Miller and Barron, "Supreme Court, Adversary System, and Flow of Information," 1233–36.

52. Kenneth Culp Davis, "Judicial, Legislative, and Administrative Lawmaking: A Proposed Research Service for the Supreme Court," *Minnesota Law Review* 72 (1986): 9 (citing *Borden's Farm Products Co. v. Baldwin*, 293 U.S. 194, 210 (1934)).

53. Rustad and Koenig, "Supreme Court and Junk Social Science," 161; Davis, "Judicial, Legislative, and Administrative Lawmaking," 1.

54. Davis, "Judicial, Legislative, and Administrative Lawmaking," 17.

55. Rustad and Koenig, "Supreme Court and Junk Social Science," 157–58.

56. John Monahan and Laurens Walker, "Social Authority: Obtaining, Evaluating, and Establishing Social Science in Law," *University of Pennsylvania Law Review* 134 (1986): 477.

57. Ibid., 499.

## CHAPTER 7 DIRECTIONS AND CONCLUSIONS

1. American Anthropological Association, "Statement on Race" (May 17, 1998). The statement is available at *http://www.aaanet.org/stmts/racepp.htm.*

2. Troy Duster, "Buried Alive: The Concept of Race in Science," in *Genetic Nature/Culture,* ed. Alan H. Goodman, Deborah Heath, and M. Susan Lindee (Berkeley: University of California Press, 2003), 258–77.

3. Executive order 13145 (2000).

4. For recent summaries of the large scientific literature on implicit attitudes and biases, see Nilanjana Dasgupta, "Implicit Ingroup Favoritism, Outgroup Favoritism, and Their Behavioral Manifestations," *Social Justice Research* 17 (2004): 143; and Jerry Kang, "Trojan Horses of Race," *Harvard Law Review* 118 (2005): 1489.

5. Charles R. Lawrence, "The Id, the Ego, and Equal Protection: Reckoning with Unconscious Racism," *Stanford Law Review* 39 (1987): 317.

6. Linda Hamilton Krieger, "The Content of Our Categories: A Cognitive Bias Approach to Discrimination and Equal Employment Opportunity," *Stanford Law Review* 47 (1995): 1188.

7. The IAT can be administered via the Internet and is available at *https://implicit.harvard. edu/implicit/*. The website also contains citations and summaries of the large body of psychological literature addressing implicit bias through testing with the IAT.

8. Kang, "Trojan Horses," 1510–11.

9. Dasgupta, "Implicit Ingroup Favoritism," 146.

10. Ibid., 147 (citations omitted).

11. Ibid., 147–48 (citations omitted).

12. Kang, "Trojan Horses," 1512–13.

13. 539 U.S. 306, 345 (2003).

14. 125 S. Ct. 1183, 1195 (2005) (citations omitted).

15. Ibid., 1222–23 (Scalia, J., dissenting).

16. Zick, "Constitutional Empiricism," 179.

17. Posner, "Against Constitutional Theory," 21.

18. 512 U.S. 507 (1997).

19. Ibid., 519.

20. Ibid., 520.

21. 531 U.S. 356 (2000).

22. *Tennessee v. Lane*, 541 U.S. 509 (2004) (upholding legislation guaranteeing access to the courts); *Nevada Department of Human Services v. Hibbs*, 538 U.S. 721 (2003) (upholding gender-related anti-discrimination legislation).

# BIBLIOGRAPHY

Acker, James R. "The Supreme Court's Use of Social Science Research Evidence in Criminal Cases." Unpublished Ph.D. dissertation. State University of New York, Albany, 1987.

Aleinikoff, T. Alexander. "Constitutional Law in the Age of Balancing." *Yale Law Journal* 96 (1987): 943–1005.

Alger, Jonathan R. "Homework for Universities: Making the Case for Affirmative Action." *Washington University Journal of Urban and Contemporary Law* 54 (1998): 73–91.

Alger, Jonathan R., and Marvin Krislov. "You've Got to Have Friends: Lessons Learned from the Role of Amici in the University of Michigan Cases." *Journal of College and University Law* 30 (2004): 503–29.

American Anthropological Association. "Statement on Race," 1998. Available at *http:// www.aaanet.org/stmts/racepp.htm.*

Ashmore, Harry S. *The Negro and the Schools.* Chapel Hill: University of North Carolina Press, 1954.

Ayres, Ian. *Pervasive Prejudice: Unconventional Evidence of Race and Gender Discrimination.* Chicago: University of Chicago Press, 2001.

Baldus, David C., George Woodworth, and Charles A. Pulaski, Jr. *Equal Justice and the Death Penalty: A Legal and Empirical Analysis.* Boston: Northeastern University Press, 1990.

Balkin, Jack M. ed. *What Brown v. Board of Education Should Have Said: The Nation's Top Legal Experts Rewrite America's Landmark Civil Rights Decision.* New York: New York University Press, 2002.

Bell, Derrick. *Race, Racism and American Law.* 4th ed. New York: Aspen Law and Business, 2000.

Bowen, William G., and Derek Bok. *The Shape of the River: Long-Term Consequences of Considering Race in College and University Admissions.* Princeton, N.J.: Princeton University Press, 2000.

Brewer, Scott. "Scientific Expert Testimony and Intellectual Due Process." *Yale Law Journal* 107 (1998): 1535–1681.

Cahn, Edmund. "Jurisprudence." *New York University Law Review* 30 (1955): 150–70.

Carnegie Commission on Science, Technology, and Government. *Science and Technology in Judicial Decision Making: Creating Opportunities and Meeting Challenges.* New York: Carnegie Commission on Science, Technology, and Government, 1993.

Casper, Gerhard, and Kathleen M. Sullivan. *Landmark Briefs and Arguments of the Supreme Court of the United States: Constitutional Law.* Vol. 321. Bethesda, Md.: LexisNexis Academic and Library Solutions, 2004.

Chang, Mitchell, Daria Witt, James Jones, and Kenji Hakuta, eds. *Compelling Interest: Examining the Evidence on Racial Dynamics in Colleges and Universities.* Stanford, Calif.: Stanford University Press, 2003.

Chemerinsky, Erwin. *Constitutional Law: Principles and Policies*. 2d ed. New York: Aspen Law and Business, 2002.

Chesler, Mark A., Joseph Sanders, and Debra S. Kalmuss. *Social Science in Court: Mobilizing Experts in the School Desegregation Cases*. Madison: University of Wisconsin Press, 1988.

Dasgupta, Nilanjana. "Implicit Ingroup Favoritism, Outgroup Favoritism, and Their Behavioral Manifestations." *Social Justice Research* 17 (2004): 143–69.

Davis, Kenneth Culp. "An Approach to Problems of Evidence in the Administrative Process." *Harvard Law Review* 55 (1942): 364–425.

———. "Judicial, Legislative, and Administrative Lawmaking: A Proposed Research Service for the Supreme Court." *Minnesota Law Review* 72 (1986): 1–18.

Dudziak, Mary L. "Oliver Wendell Holmes As a Eugenic Reformer: Rhetoric in the Writing of Constitutional Law." *Iowa Law Review* 71 (1986): 833–67.

Duster, Troy. Buried Alive: The Concept of Race in Science. In *Genetic Nature/Culture: Anthropology and Science beyond the Two-Culture Divide*, edited by Alan H. Goodman, Deborah Heath, and M. Susan Lindee, 258–77. Berkeley: University of California Press, 2003.

Ely, John Hart. *Democracy and Distrust: A Theory of Judicial Review*. Cambridge, Mass.: Harvard University Press, 1980.

Erickson, Rosemary J., and Rita J. Simon. *The Use of Social Science Data in Supreme Court Decisions*. Urbana: University of Illinois Press, 1998.

Faigman, David L. *Laboratory of Justice: The Supreme Court's 200-Year Struggle to Integrate Science and the Law*. New York: Holt, 2004.

———. *Legal Alchemy: The Use and Misuse of Science in the Law*. New York: Freeman, 1999.

———. "'Normative Constitutional Fact-Finding': Exploring the Empirical Component of Constitutional Interpretation." *University of Pennsylvania Law Review* 139 (1991): 541–613.

Faigman, David L., David H. Kaye, Michael J. Saks, and Joseph Sanders. *Science in the Law: Social and Behavioral Science Issues*. St. Paul, Minn.: West Group, 2002.

———. *Science in the Law: Standards, Statistics and Research Issues*. St. Paul, Minn.: West Group, 2002.

Fallon, Richard H., Jr. "A Constructivist Coherence Theory of Constitutional Interpretation." *Harvard Law Review* 100 (1987): 1189–286.

Federal Judicial Center. *Reference Manual on Scientific Evidence*. 2d ed. Washington, D.C.: Federal Judicial Center, 2000.

Feldman, Stephen M. *American Legal Thought from Premodernism to Postmodernism: An Intellectual Voyage*. New York: Oxford University Press, 2000.

Finkelstein, Michael O., and Bruce Levin. *Statistics for Lawyers*. New York: Springer-Verlag, 1990.

Foster, Kenneth R., and Peter W. Huber. *Judging Science: Scientific Knowledge and the Federal Courts*. Cambridge, Mass.: MIT Press, 1999.

Fradella, Henry F. "A Content Analysis of Federal Judicial Views of the Social Science 'Researcher's Black Arts.'" *Rutgers Law Journal* 35 (2003): 103–70.

Frankenberg, Erika, Chungmei Lee, and Gary Orfield. *A Multiracial Society with Segregated Schools: Are We Losing the Dream?* Cambridge, Mass.: Harvard University, Civil Rights Project, 2003.

Friedman, Leon, ed. *Brown v. Board: The Landmark Oral Argument before the Supreme Court*. New York: New Press, 2004.

Goldberg, Steven. *Culture Clash: Law and Science in America*. New York: New York University Press, 1994.

Gunther, Gerald. "Foreword: In Search of Evolving Doctrine on a Changing Court: A Model for a Newer Equal Protection." *Harvard Law Review* 86 (1972): 1.

Gurin, Patricia Y. "The Compelling Need for Diversity in Higher Education." *Michigan Journal of Race and Law* 5 (1999): 363–425.

Haney López, Ian F. "Institutional Racism: Judicial Conduct and a New Theory of Racial Discrimination." *Yale Law Journal* 109 (2000): 1717–1884.

———. *White by Law: The Legal Construction of Race.* New York: New York University Press, 1996.

Hasen, Richard L. *The Supreme Court and Election Law: Judging Equality from Baker v. Carr to Bush v. Gore.* New York: New York University Press, 2003.

Hashimoto, Dean M. "Science As Mythology in Constitutional Law." *Oregon Law Review* 76 (1997): 111–52.

Holmes, Oliver Wendell. *The Common Law.* Boston: Little, Brown, 1881.

———. "The Path of the Law." *Harvard Law Review* 10 (1897): 457–78.

Horn, Catherine L., and Stella M. Flores. *Percent Plans in College Admissions: A Comparative Analysis of Three States' Experiences.* Cambridge, Mass.: Harvard University, Civil Rights Project, 2003.

Hovenkamp, Herbert. "Social Science and Segregation before *Brown*." *Duke Law Journal* (1985): 624–72.

Howe, Mark De Wolfe, ed. *Holmes-Pollock Letters: The Correspondence of Mr. Justice Holmes and Sir Frederick Pollock, 1874–1932.* Cambridge, Mass.: Harvard University Press, 1941.

Huber, Peter W. *Galileo's Revenge: Junk Science in the Courtroom.* New York: Basic Books, 1993.

Irons, Peter. *Justice at War: The Story of the Japanese American Internment Cases.* New York: Oxford University Press, 1983.

Jackson, John P., Jr. *Social Scientists for Social Justice: Making the Case against Segregation.* New York: New York University Press, 2001.

Jasanoff, Sheila. *Science at the Bar: Law, Science, and Technology in America.* Cambridge, Mass.: Harvard University Press, 1995.

Jefferson, Thomas. *Notes on the State of Virginia: With Related Documents*, edited by David Waldstreicher. New York: Palgrave, 2002.

Jeffries, John C. *Justice Lewis F. Powell, Jr.* New York: Fordham University Press, 2001.

Jolls, Christine. "Antidiscrimination and Accommodation." *Harvard Law Review* 115 (2001): 642–99.

Kadane, Joseph B., and Caroline Mitchell. "Statistics in Proof of Employment Discrimination Cases." In *Legacies of the 1964 Civil Rights Act*, edited by Bernard Grofman, 241–62. Charlottesville: University Press of Virginia, 2000.

Kang, Jerry, "Trojan Horses of Race." *Harvard Law Review* 118 (2005): 1489–1593.

Karst, Kenneth L. *Belonging to America: Equal Citizenship and the Constitution.* New Haven, Conn.: Yale University Press, 1989.

———. "Foreword: Equal Citizenship under the Fourteenth Amendment." *Harvard Law Review* 91 (1977): 1–68.

———. "Legislative Facts in Constitutional Litigation." *Supreme Court Review* (1960): 75–112.

Kaye, David. "And Then There Were Twelve: Statistical Reasoning, the Supreme Court, and the Size of the Jury." *California Law Review* 68 (1980): 1004.

Kluger, Richard. *Simple Justice: The History of Brown v. Board of Education and Black America's Struggle for Equality.* New York: Vintage, 1977.

Krieger, Linda Hamilton. "The Content of Our Categories: A Cognitive Bias Approach to Discrimination and Equal Employment Opportunity." *Stanford Law Review* 47 (1995): 1161–1248.

Kurland, Philip B., and Gerhard Casper. *Landmark Briefs and Arguments of the Supreme Court of the United States: Constitutional Law*. Vols. 16, 40, 49, 49A, and 64. Washington, D.C.: University Publications of America, 1975.

Langdell, Christopher Columbus. *A Selection of Cases on the Law of Contracts: With References and Citations*. 2d ed. Boston: Little, Brown, 1871.

Lawrence, Charles R. "The Id, the Ego, and Equal Protection: Reckoning with Unconscious Racism." *Stanford Law Review* 39 (1987): 317–88.

Lempert, Richard. "Befuddled Judges: Statistical Evidence in Title VII Cases." In *Legacies of the 1964 Civil Rights Act*, edited by Bernard Grofman, 263–81. Charlottesville: University Press of Virginia, 2000.

Llewellyn, Karl N. "A Realistic Jurisprudence—the Next Step." *Columbia Law Review* 30 (1930): 431–65.

Mann, Patricia, and Edgar K. Lee. *Appearance and Reality in the Sunshine State: The Talented 20 Program in Florida*. Cambridge, Mass.: Harvard University, Civil Rights Project, 2003.

Merritt, Deborah Jones. "Constitutional Fact and Theory: A Response to Chief Judge Posner." *Michigan Law Review* 97 (1999): 1287–95.

Miller, Arthur Selwyn, and Jerome A. Barron. "The Supreme Court, the Adversary System, and the Flow of Information to the Justices: A Preliminary Inquiry." *Virginia Law Review* 61 (1975): 1187–1245.

Mody, Sanjay. "*Brown* Footnote Eleven in Historical Context: Social Science and the Supreme Court's Quest for Legitimacy." *Stanford Law Review* 54 (2002): 793–829.

Monahan, John, and Laurens Walker. "Social Authority: Obtaining, Evaluating, and Establishing Social Science in Law." *University of Pennsylvania Law Review* 134 (1986): 477–517.

———. *Social Science in Law: Cases and Materials*. 5th ed. New York: Foundation Press, 2002.

Myrdal, Gunnar. *An American Dilemma: The Negro Problem and Modern Democracy*. New York: Harper, 1944.

Orfield, Gary, with Michal Kurlaender, eds. *Diversity Challenged: Evidence on the Impact of Affirmative Action*. Cambridge, Mass.: Harvard Educational Publishing Group, 2001.

Orfield, Gary, and Edward Miller, eds. *Chilling Admissions: The Affirmative Action Crisis and the Search for Alternatives*. Cambridge, Mass.: Harvard Educational Publishing Group, 1998.

Paetzold, Ramona L., and Steven Willborn. *The Statistics of Discrimination: Using Statistical Evidence in Discrimination Cases*. St. Paul, Minn.: West Group, 2002.

Pildes, Richard H. "Is Voting-Rights Law Now at War with Itself? Social Science and Voting Rights in the 2000s." *North Carolina Law Review* 80 (2002): 1517–73.

Pildes, Richard H., and Richard G. Niemi. "Expressive Harms, 'Bizarre Districts,' and Voting Rights: Evaluating Election-District Appearances after *Shaw v. Reno*." *Michigan Law Review* 92 (1993): 483–587.

Porter, Theodore M. *Trust in Numbers: The Pursuit of Objectivity in Science and Public Life*. Princeton, N.J.: Princeton University Press, 1995.

Posner, Richard A. "Against Constitutional Theory." *New York University Law Review* 73 (1998): 1–22.

Pound, Roscoe. "Law in Books and Law in Action." *American Law Review* 44 (1910): 12–36.

Purcell, Edward A., Jr. *The Crisis of Democratic Theory: Scientific Naturalism and the Problem of Value*. Lexington: University Press of Kentucky, 1973.

Rosen, Paul L. *The Supreme Court and Social Science*. Urbana: University of Illinois Press, 1972.

Rothman, Stanley, Seymour Martin Lipset, and Neil Nevitte. "Does Enrollment Diversity Improve University Education?" *International Journal of Public Opinion Research* 15 (2003): 8–26.

Rustad, Michael, and Thomas Koenig. "The Supreme Court and Junk Social Science: Selective Distortion in Amicus Briefs." *North Carolina Law Review* 72 (1993): 91–162.

Ryan, James E. "The Limited Influence of Social Science Evidence in Modern Desegregation Cases." *North Carolina Law Review* 81 (2003): 1659–702.

Saks, Michael J., and Charles H. Baron, eds. *The Use/Nonuse/Misuse of Applied Social Research in the Courts.* Cambridge, Mass.: Abt, 1980.

Segal, Jeffrey A., and Harold J. Spaeth. *The Supreme Court and the Attitudinal Model.* New York: Oxford University Press, 1993.

Spann, Girardeau A. *The Law of Affirmative Action: Twenty-Five Years of Supreme Court Decisions on Race and Remedies.* New York: New York University Press, 2000.

Spencer, Herbert. *The Man versus the State.* New York: Appleton, 1892.

Sperlich, Peter W. "Trial by Jury: It May Have a Future." *Supreme Court Review* (1978): 191.

Sullivan, Kathleen M. and Gerald Gunther. *Constitutional Law.* 2d ed. New York: Foundation Press, 2004.

Tienda, Marta, et al. "Closing the Gap? Admissions and Enrollments at the Texas Public Flagships before and after Affirmative Action," 2003. Available at *http://www. texastop10. princeton.edu.*

Tribe, Laurence H. *American Constitutional Law.* 2d ed. Mineola, N.Y.: Foundation Press, Inc., 1988.

———. *American Constitutional Law.* 3d ed., vol. 1. New York: Foundation Press, 2000.

Wald, Patricia M. "Scholars in the Arena: Some Thoughts on Better Bridge Building." *Perspectives on Politics* 1, no. 2 (2003): 355–62.

Warren, Earl. "Science and the Law: Change and the Constitution." *Journal of Public Law* 12, no. 1 (1963): 3–8.

Wasby, Stephen L., Anthony A. D'Amato, and Rosemary Metrailer. *Desegregation from "Brown" to "Alexander": An Exploration of Supreme Court Strategies.* Carbondale: Southern Illinois University Press, 1977.

Yamamoto, Eric, Margaret Chon, Carol L. Izumi, Jerry Kang, and Frank H. Wu. *Race, Rights and Reparation: Law and the Japanese American Internment.* Gaithersburg, Md.: Aspen Law and Business, 2001.

Zack, Naomi. *Philosophy of Science and Race.* New York: Routledge, 2002.

Zick, Timothy. "Constitutional Empiricism: Quasi-Neutral Principles and Constitutional Truths." *North Carolina Law Review* 82 (2003): 115–221.

# INDEX

# ABOUT THE AUTHOR

ANGELO N. ANCHETA is an Assistant Professor of Law at the Santa Clara University School of Law, and directs the university's Katharine & George Alexander Community Law Center. He has practiced civil rights law and immigration law in California and previously taught at Harvard Law School, New York University School of Law, and UCLA School of Law. He holds degrees from UCLA and Harvard University and is the author of *Race, Rights, and the Asian American Experience.*